Tiberius Rata has provided the church with a clearly written, insightful synthesis of the often-neglected books of Ezra and Nehemiah. The author's style is concise and readable; he stays on track and refuses to deviate from his primary goal of illuminating the meaning and significance of the biblical text. One of the most useful features of this volume is its attention to contemporary relevance. Without violating the meaning of the ancient text in its context, the author derives helpful practical insights that are consistent with its original intention.

Robert B. Chisholm, Jr.,
Chair and Professor of Old Testament Studies,
Dallas Theological Seminary, Dallas, Texas

Tiberius Rata's work on Ezra–Nehemiah should be warmly received by pastors and teachers. His commentary is clear and to the point, yet he discusses some problems at length, furnishing thoughtfulness and insight for solutions. His viewpoint is solidly orthodox and reverent. His high view of Scripture and of the God of Scripture is reflected throughout the work. His work demonstrates competent scholarship and conveys a pastor's heart—the work of a pastor scholar. His outlines and comments are helpful for understanding the flow of the historical narrative and are suggestive for sermon preparation. He provides useful summaries—for example, summaries for the chronology of the book—for understanding the book within the Old Testament canon and timeframe. His use of Ancient Near Eastern sources and documents also give historical context for the books of Ezra–Nehemiah. I recommend this work for teachers in colleges and seminaries and also for teachers and pastors in the local church.

Russell Fuller,
Professor of Old Testament Interpretation,
Southern Baptist Theological Seminary, Louisville, Kentucky

This commentary on Ezra–Nehemiah is superbly written, beautifully illustrated and carefully documented. Dr. Rata has provided the student of Scripture with a thoughtful commentary on Ezra and Nehemiah that is wholistic in approach. He skillfully weaves together matters of the Hebrew text, historical backgrounds, theology and archaeological discoveries. Also not forgotten are the practical needs of the contemporary Christian.

This is a book suitable for the classroom, pastor's office, or the scholar's study.

John J. Davis,
President/Professor Emeritus,
Grace College and Grace Theological Seminary, Winona Lake, Indiana

Reasoned, researched, and concise, Rata's commentary on Ezra and Nehemiah opens a window on the historical setting for these significant books of the Old Testament. Carefully selected photographs, illustrations, and charts punctuate its pages and illuminate the text's background, literary context, and interpretation. This volume ably addresses the interests of laymen and pastors alike as they study the biblical text of the two books.

William D. Barrick,
Professor of Old Testament,
The Master's Seminary, Sun Valley, California

The strength of Rata's work is his synthesis of historical data, past research, and clear exposition of the text. His blending of careful attention to the details of Ezra–Nehemiah with pastoral sensitivity to its contemporary relevance will be of great help to those teaching and preaching an often-neglected part of the Old Testament canon.

Gary E. Yates,
Associate Professor of Biblical Studies,
Liberty Baptist Theological Seminary, Lynchburg, Virginia

Tiberius Rata combines exegetical skill, knowledge of the ancient world, and a pastor's heart in this volume. His explanations of the text are clear, forceful, yet concise. This work will assist the church in understanding its call to godly service to Christ and will motivate its readers to re-consecrate their lives and possessions to the work of the Kingdom.

Kenneth A. Mathews,
Professor of Divinity,
Beeson Divinity School, Birmingham, Alabama

Ezra–Nehemiah

A Mentor Commentary

Tiberius Rata

I dedicate this commentary to my parents
George and Maria Rata
who encourage continually
and
love unconditionally

Copyright © Tiberius Rata 2010

ISBN 978-1-84550-571-4

Published in 2010
in the
Mentor Imprint
by
Christian Focus Publications,
Geanies House, Fearn,
Ross-shire, IV20 1TW, Scotland.
www.christianfocus.com

Cover design by Daniel van Straaten

Printed and bound by MPG

Contents

Detailed Contents

Nehemiah

Acknowledgments

I would like to say a heartfelt "Thank you" to my teaching assistants and students Josh Topel, Kevin Becker, Kurt Kenyon, Darren Kloepper, Pat Park, Faith Olson and Jeremy Maurer for their help with the research for this project.

I would also like to express my deep gratitude to Diane Jasper, Jan Prewitt, and Sue Rowland of Calvary Bible Church, Kalamazoo, Michigan for their help in proofreading this document and for their invaluable input regarding language and style.

Introduction

The World of Ezra and Nehemiah

1.1 The Fall of the Babylonian Empire and the Rise of the Persian Empire

Because of their persistent idolatry and apostasy, God allowed Israel to be taken into exile by the Babylonians under the command of the despot Nebuchadnezzar (604-562 BC). The Babylonian army took Jewish captives in three waves, in 605, 597, and 587 BC. During the final invasion in 587 BC, the Babylonians not only destroyed the city gates and walls of Jerusalem, but also Israel's religious center, Solomon's temple; thus, the loss the Jews experienced was emotional, national, and spiritual, simultaneously. In addition to asserting his power over the Jews, Nebuchadnezzar also directed massive building projects during his reign: bridges, ziggurats, and a temple to the city-god Marduk. His successors could not come close to the achievements of their predecessor who reigned for forty-two years.

A second key figure in this historical period was Cyrus the Great, the founder of the Persian Empire, who became king of Elam around 559 BC. After Cyrus defeated the king of the Lydian empire in 546 BC, he turned his attention towards Babylonia. Cyrus overtook the capital city of Babylon on October 12, 539 BC after a bloody battle at Opis. Just nine years later (530 BC), he died in battle while pursuing more land for his already mammoth empire.

Table 1: Achaemenid Dynasty (559-330 BC)[1]

Emperor	Period of Reign
Cyrus II	c 559-530
Cambyses II	530-523
Bardiya	522
Darius I	522-486
Xerxes I	486-465
Artaxerxes I	465-424/3
Xerxes II	424/3
Darius II	423-405/4
Artaxerxes II	405/4-359
Artaxerxes III	359-338
Artaxerxes IV (Arses)	338-336
Darius III	336-331
Artaxerxes V	331

1.2 The Religion of the Persians

Persia was a land of religious tolerance. While Persia's kings themselves worshipped many pagan gods, they allowed and even aided the institution of the priesthood of various other religious groups.[2] Darius I (522-486) was greatly influenced by Zoroastrianism, the teachings of Zarathustra. It is possibly that by 480 BC Zoroastrianism became the official Persian religion.[3]

Zarathustra was born in eastern Iran around 628 BC, although some scholars date his life between 1700 and 1500 BC.[4] He was trained for service as a priest in a pagan cult, and at the age of thirty Zarathustra went down to a river to get some water for a pagan festival and allegedly received a heavenly vision.[5] The heavenly visitor named Ahura Mazda

---

1. Lindsay Allen, *The Persian Empire* (Chicago: UCP, 2005), 4.
2. Jon L. Berquist, *Judaism In Persia's Shadow* (Minneapolis: Fortress, 1995), 24.
3. See Edwin M. Yamauchi, *Persia and the Bible* (Grand Rapids: Baker, 1996), 411-433.
4. Ibid., 96.
5. Mary Boyce, *Zoroastrians* (London: Routledge & Kegan Paul, 1979), 18-19.

(which means "Wise Lord")[6] revealed "truth" to Zarathustra and commissioned him to teach others; however, people of his day did not commonly consider Zarathustra divine and he was venerated only much later after his death.[7] He preached monotheism, which may be the reason many refused to listen, for his teachings were a radical departure from the polytheistic thought of his day. The prophet's instructions also included a strict code of purity laws,[8] and correct conduct involved a strictly ethical life that honored mankind and the duty of man to care for the world and the animals within it.[9] Truth-telling was expected, water revered, and cleanliness encouraged. Ritual washings included passage through nine pits containing cattle urine, sand, and water.[10] Priests were responsible for daily sacrifices that normally involved the burning of a bull.

Not only did the Zoroastrians refuse to build temples, but they also erected no statues or altars: Herodotus reported that the Persians carved no images of their gods because it was considered folly to visualize them in human form.[11] The Persians revered fire and were encouraged to pray five times daily in the presence of fire. Zarathustra's teachings were recorded in a sacred book called *The Avesta*, which was divided into three parts. The first section, called the Yasna, included the main liturgy and the Gathas. The second part, called the Yashts, were hymns directed to various deities, and finally, the Videvdat contained the moral law code.[12] The Gathas contained seventeen poetic hymns addressed to Ahura Mazda [13]and were thought to be the original teachings of Zarathustra. The rest of *The Avesta* came much later as priests and scribes interpreted and wrote commentary on the Gathas. Although contemporaneous priests experienced

---

6. Winfried Corduan, *Neighboring Faiths* (Downers Grove: IVP, 1998), 119.
7. Boyce, 42.
8. Ibid., 77.
9. Siegfried J. Schwantes, *A Short History of the Ancient Near East* (Grand Rapids: Baker, 1965), 151.
10. Boyce, 45.
11. John M. Cook, *The Persian Empire* (New York: Schocken, 1983), 149.
12. Brian Dicks, *The Ancient Persians: How They Lived and Worked* (North Pomfret, Vt.,: David & Charles, 1979), 123.
13. Boyce, 17.

little difficulty in interpretation, some scholars believe the Gathas are "the most obscure and ambiguous compositions of all oriental religious literature."[14]

According to tradition, Zarathustra was stabbed to death by a pagan priest at the age of seventy-seven.[15] There is no evidence that commoners widely embraced Zarathustra's teachings, so it would be fair to conclude that the majority of the Persian culture remained essentially pluralistic.

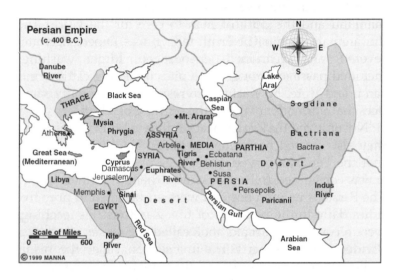

Map 1: The Persian Empire
Copyright 1999 MANNA All Rights Reserved. Used with permission.

1.3 The theology of Ezra

After being in Babylonian exile for seventy years, the Israelites were allowed to return to their homeland by edict of Cyrus the Great, founder of the Persian Empire. His edict not only allowed Israelites to return to their own land, but also to rebuild their temple in Jerusalem, the center of their religious life. Nehemiah was one of the leaders under whose leadership some of the Israelites returned home. The book of Ezra is divided into two main sections; Chapters 1–6 which concern God's restoring His people to the land, and

---

14. Edwin M. Yamauchi, *Persia and the Bible*, 403-404.
15. Boyce, 35.

Chapters 7–13 which chronicle God's reformation of His restored people.

A. What does the book of Ezra teach us about God?

Ezra introduces God as faithful to His word and a Keeper of His promises. He is the sovereign God who controls history, including Cyrus' conquests and edict. The Jews are able to return to their homeland and rebuild Jerusalem and their religious center not because of the goodness of Cyrus' heart, but rather at God's initiative in stirring Cyrus' spirit (1:1). The designation "God of heaven" is Cyrus' acknowledgement of God as the Creator God who commanded Cyrus to initiate the work of reconstruction in Jerusalem (1:2). Cyrus recognizes that God is with His chosen people, the Israelites, that He has a house ("The House of the LORD") in Jerusalem (1:3-4), and that He knows people's hearts and will stir them up to do the work of reconstruction (1:5).

God's faithfulness is clearly demonstrated when He enables His people to lay the temple's foundation in Chapter 3, and the people understand that their accomplishment is the result of God's blessing and His working through those who make themselves available for service. Yahweh, who reveals Himself and His will through His prophets (5:1), makes His presence (lit. "eye") felt by His people, which encourages them to continue the work despite fierce opposition (5:5). When God directs King Darius' heart to allow the rebuilding to continue and also to be funded with royal finances and resources (6:1-11) the Israelites are assured that God is on their side. They also recognize that Yahweh's decree preceded Cyrus' decree (6:14, 22). Ezra reveals Yahweh as the One who protects and provides for His people no matter who is on the throne in Susa (7:6). Even Artaxerxes indicates awareness that whatever God decrees from heaven will be accomplished on earth (7:23). As the work progresses, God's sovereignty is revealed in the big and little things as He directs the hearts and hands of the workers (8:18), and His kindness is demonstrated by His hearing and accepting the prayers and fasting of the faithful

(8:23). God protects the Israelites from the diabolical enemy as well as from day-to-day dangers along the way (8:31).

After the people are found guilty of breaking God's Law, several key characteristics of God are revealed: He is the just God who punishes sin, the compassionate God who shows grace and covenantal love to the remnant, and the merciful Father God who does not abandon His people (9:5-9). Although Ezra recognizes God's right to mete out justice, he pleads for the divine love and mercy that would spare the people's lives (9:13-15).

B. What does the book of Ezra teach us about God's people and the faithless?

Led by the priests and Levites, God's people respond to God's prompting and rise up to do the work of temple reconstruction (1:3-5). They are aided financially and materially by their Persian neighbors, an obvious parallel to the Egyptians helping God's people when they fled Egypt (Exod. 11-12). Cyrus appears to be a God-fearing man who obeys Yahweh's voice, even desiring to return what Nebuchadnezzar stole in 587 BC during the destruction of Jerusalem and its temple (1:7-8). The Jewish leaders are spiritually sensitive in discerning that the altar for sacrifices should be erected first. Together they accomplish the work, acknowledging that unity is imperative in God's kingdom (3:2-3). The people of God obey the Law given through Moses by keeping the Feast of Booths and the other festivals enumerated in the Torah (3:4-5).[16] The Israelites see the need for reconstruction, and they meet the need by providing finances and hiring workers to carry out the work (3:7-9). They rejoice at the completion of the foundation of the temple by following David's blueprint

---

16. Leviticus 23 states that the Festival of Booths or Tabernacles began on Tishri 15 and it was primarily a thanksgiving festival showing gratitude for God's provision (Exod. 34:22). It also commemorated the wilderness wandering, the booths (Succoth) being a reminder that the Israelites lived in tents during the 40-year commute from Egypt to the Promised Land (Lev. 23:42-43). It was at Succoth that the Israelites first came after leaving Rameses (Exod. 12:7). The Feast of Booths was observed during the post-exilic period (2 Chron. 8:13; Ezra 3:4; Zech. 14:16, 18, 19) and during the early church period.

as laid out in the Psalms: they praise and thank God responsively with singing and shouting (3:10-11),[17] although some members of the older generation are driven to tears of disappointment as they see a lesser version of Solomon's temple now in the process of reconstruction (3:12-13).

The book of Ezra also teaches us that God's people are frequently called to do His work in the face of strong opposition, often from unfaithful religious pretenders. Ezra presents the faithless as deceitful people who claim to worship Yahweh, but God's people discern untruth in them (4:1-3). The wicked then try to discourage God's people by resorting to bribes and lies, and in a letter to King Artaxerxes the faithless accuse the Jews of open rebellion (4:4-16). As a result, the work is temporarily stopped until Darius takes the throne (4:17-24). Encouraged by Yahweh's prophets, the people rise up to resume the work of rebuilding (5:1-2), and they continue working amid severe opposition (5:3-4). They recognize themselves as God's servants (5:11) and they accept the consequences of their sinful history (5:12). King Darius seems to have some belief in Yahweh, at least recognizing Him as the Creator God, the One who answers prayer, and the One who defeats His enemies (6:11-12). Worship is the Israelites' natural response to God's provision as the work is successfully completed (6:16-17; 21). Obedience to the Law of Moses follows joyful celebration and worship, because worship apart from obedience is worthless (6:19-21). In response to God's accomplishing great things on their behalf, the Israelites are grateful and they bless the One who extended His covenantal love to His people.

Ezra himself embodies the man of God who excels in the knowledge of God's Law (7:6) because he is wholly committed to studying and teaching it (7:10-11). He realizes that he must know *"What* says the LORD" before he rises to declare, *"Thus* says the LORD." He is also careful to maintain a good testimony. The Persian king Artaxerxes recognizes that Ezra is a servant of the Creator God and that he possesses God-given wisdom (7:12, 25). However, even

---

17. Ezra 1:10-11 gives us solid indication that at least part of the book of Psalms existed during this time, and that King David was closely associated with it.

though Artaxerxes shows reverence for Yahweh, he was likely not a follower of the true God since he refers to Ezra's God as "your God" (7:17) as opposed to "my God." Ezra is portrayed as a leader who inspires and gathers others to join him in the good work that God put on his heart (7:28). His focus on fasting, humility, and seeking God's guidance points to his spiritual depth and sensitivity (8:21-23). Ezra teaches the Israelites that they are holy to the LORD, a quality which includes both behavioral holiness—how they are to act; and also positional holiness—separation unto God in order to do His will and accomplish His purposes (8:28). Once again the people respond to God's Law, goodness, provision, and protection by worshipping Him, lived out here through sacrifices (8:35).

The Jewish officials have enough knowledge of and sensitivity to the Torah to realize that law-breaking has occurred among the Jews: the sanctified (the Hebrew people) has been mingled with the profane (the local pagans) in the practice of mixed marriages (9:1-2). These mixed marriages were not evangelistic in intent or accomplishment—the sacred people did not make the profane holy, but rather the profane defiled the holy. What grieves God also grieves the man of God, and Ezra's outward reaction (torn garments and pulled hair) is a window into his heart which is filled with pain and mourning at the death of conscience among God's people (9:3). The fact that "all who trembled at the words of the God of Israel gathered around their leader" shows that many were willing to be obedient to God. Ezra inspires the people to sit in silence as an expression of grief and mourning (9:4; 10:6) as he prays to God. In his prayer he identifies with the people that have sinned and confesses corporate sin (9:5-8), thereby displaying his humility, which is a key character trait for a man of God. Acknowledging God's sovereignty and holiness, he does not excuse the people's sin, but rather he confesses collective disobedience (9:9-12). Ezra does the only wise thing to do in this instance, he seeks divine grace by throwing himself on the mercy of the divine judge (9:13-15).

The faithful have hope of restoration based on correcting their wrong. First, they recognize their sin by admitting that they "have broken faith with (our) God and have married foreign women from the peoples of the land" (10:2). Second, they are willing to make right the wrong they have done by covenanting with God to "put[ting] away all these wives and children, according to the counsel of my lord and of those who tremble at the commandment of our God." The people are willing to do things "according to the Law" (10:3, 12). As a morally upright leader, Ezra is direct in pronouncing the judgment against the unfaithfulness of the people (10:10); and because genuine repentance is always followed by obedience, the people receive and obey the seemingly harsh command, "Separate yourselves from the peoples of the land and from the foreign wives" (10:11). The correction of the communal sin must start with the leaders, and so the first mentioned in the long list of people who have broken the law is the family of Jeshua, one of the leaders who worked with Zerubbabel in the time of Zechariah (10:18). In all, seventeen priests, ten Levites, and eighty-four lay Israelites were guilty. Most of the assembly agreed to repent and change, but Ezra still had opposition from a small minority (10:15).

1.4 The theology of Nehemiah

While the book of Nehemiah primarily reveals God as the One who restores His people to Himself and to their land, this book also portrays the complexity of God's nature and works. Nehemiah also juxtaposes the struggles and obedience of God's people with the evil actions and intents of those who rebel against God and try to derail the plans of His people.

A. What does the book of Nehemiah teach us about God?

In the book of Nehemiah, God's first revelation of Himself is as Creator (1:5). In his opening prayer Nehemiah prays to "the God of heaven,"[18] an expression which occurs

---

18. Genesis 24:3, 24:7, 2 Chronicles 36:23, Ezra 1:2, Nehemiah 1:2, 1:4, 1:5, 2:4, 2:20, and Jonah 1:9.

nine times in the Old Testament, all referring to Yahweh. Breneman suggests that "the phrase 'God of heaven' was commonly used in the Persian Empire, even by the Persians in speaking of their god."[19] The expression as used by Nehemiah points to God's creative power as well as to His awe-inspiring character. He is also the Covenant God, making and preserving covenants with His people. God hears the prayers of His people (1:6, 1:11, 2:4), forgives their sin (1:7),[20] gives laws, and provides instruction (1:7-8). Although God is loving and merciful, He is also holy, righteous, and just; therefore, He must judge and punish those who do not keep his laws and commandments (1: 8b).[21] Nehemiah is confident that God will redeem and restore his people (1:9-10).[22] He is fully committed to the rebuilding of Jerusalem; subsequently, he concludes his prayer by appealing to God's mercy and compassion as he prepares for a risky audience with King Artaxerxes. According to Ezra 4:21, Artaxerxes has commanded the ceasing of work in Jerusalem; so humanly speaking, Nehemiah knows his chances of success are slight. In appealing for God's mercy and compassion, he rightly recalls Yahweh's compassion to the patriarchs (2 Kings 13:23) and to His people in liberating them from Egypt (Exod. 33:19).

In Chapter 2, the phrase "the good hand of my God was upon me," points to a God who blesses, protects, and provides (2:8; 2:18).[23] "If this expression is derived from the secular sphere in the sense of royal bounty (1 Kings 10:13; Esther 1:7; 2:18), then its use here will be of particular significance: what appears at one level to be the bountiful grant of the Persian king turns out to be merely a channel

---

19. Mervin Breneman, *Ezra, Nehemiah, Esther*. NAC, vol. 10 (Nashville: Broadman and Holman, 1993), 171.

20. See Solomon's prayer in 2 Chronicles 6:40. Both Solomon and Nehemiah appeal to a God who sees and hears.

21. Nehemiah's prayer is rooted in God's Torah. Nehemiah 1:8-9 is a paraphrase of Deuteronomy 30:1-5.

22. This idea is not new or unique to Nehemiah. The tripartite sin-judgment-restoration motif is found throughout the prophetic material, especially the Minor Prophets.

23. The phrase "the hand of the Lord his God was on him" also occurs in Ezra 7:6, 9, 28; 8:18, 22, 31; Nehemiah 2:8, 18.

through which the bounty of the King of kings reaches his people."[24] Because it is God who sets men apart for ministry, Nehemiah is confident that Yahweh has called him to lead His people (2:12). "Nehemiah's spiritual need was direction from God. Even the valued few men he had as colleagues were not told everything: he did not chatter irresponsibly even to people who shared his ideals."[25] Nehemiah knows that God will give His people success (2:20); therefore, he does not retaliate when encountering opposition, but rather he expresses confidence in Yahweh's ability to make them prosper. Opposition does not paralyze Nehemiah, rather it causes him to get organized. "We will arise, and we will build," is Nehemiah's resolve (2:20). "The mention of the king's authority would be far more impressive to Sanballat than the mention of God,"[26] but Nehemiah appeals to God's sovereignty rather than the king's scepter.

After Chapter 3 describes the inspired teamwork approach under Nehemiah's leadership, the beginning of Chapter 4 focuses on the ongoing opposition led by Sanballat and Tobiah—creating the perfect backdrop against which God is presented as the One who hears the prayers of His faithful ones who are mocked and despised by men (4:4). "The whole prayer is reminiscent of such Psalms as 44, 74, and 79, and in particular of the situation which Hezekiah faced when threatened by Sennacherib."[27] Nehemiah encourages the people by exalting God's character and past acts in history (2:14), assuring them that this harassment is not the first time God's honor has been at stake, and He has always emerged victorious. "The language of Nehemiah ("Don't be afraid") is reminiscent of words of reassurance and victory from other leaders in Scripture (cf. Exod. 14:13;

---

24. H. G. M. Williamson, *Ezra, Nehemiah,* WBC., vol. 16 (Waco, Texas: Word, 1985), 93.
25. Raymond Brown, *The Message of Nehemiah,* BST (Downers Grove, Illinois: IVP, 1998), 54.
26. Loring W. Batten, *A Critical and Exegetical Commentary on The Books of Ezra and Nehemiah,* ICC (Edinburgh: T & T Clark, 1961), 204.
27. Williamson, 217. Also, see 2 Kings 19:14-19. It is important to note here that Nehemiah's prayer in light of the teachings of Jesus is not prescriptive but descriptive.

Num. 14:9; Deut. 20:3; 31:6; Josh. 10:25)."[28] The sovereign God causes the failure of the enemy's plan, a fact recognized by both God's people and their enemies (4:15). Nehemiah ascribes the credit "to God, who had 'frustrated their plan' – a parallel to the confusion and despair into which God had often cast His people's enemies of old (Exod. 15:14-16; 23:27-28; Deut. 2:25; 11:25, etc.)."[29]

Throughout the enemies' continued efforts to discourage the faithful from doing the work of reconstruction, Nehemiah remembers that God is the One who calls/sends one to do His work (6:12). For Nehemiah to run would have shown a lack of trust in the God who called him. If he had entered the temple to save his life, he would have broken the Mosaic Law.[30] He does neither of those things, showing his strength of character and purity of heart. Nehemiah appeals to God's faithfulness and asks Him to "remember" His enemies and their work (6:14). Knowing that God rewards both the righteous and the wicked, he leaves vengeance to God.[31] Nehemiah 6:15 doesn't merely sound a note of victory; it also gives us historical information. The reconstruction of the wall was done in only fifty-two days, reaching completion on the 25th day of Elul.[32] Subsequent verses are quick to point out that the work was done "with the help of our God", and that God's enemies and the surrounding nations recognized this fact (6:16). Blenkinsopp suggests that perhaps "the writer draws on the theme (familiar from hymns and prophetic sermons) of the nations being forced to acknowledge the hand of God in the fortunes of Israel (e.g. Ps. 118:23; 126:2)."[33]

Even though Chapters 7-13 focus on the reformation of the people, God still plays the major role, being the Source

28. Breneman, 198.
29. Williamson, 227.
30. See Breneman, 212.
31. Deut. 32:35; Ps. 94:1; Rom. 12:19.
32. While most scholars agree that Elul corresponds to August–September, some suggest that an October date is more likely. For an in-depth discussion regarding chronology, see R.A. Parker and W.H. Dubberstein, *Babylonian Chronology 626 Bc-A.D. 75* (Providence, Rhode Island: BUP, 1956).
33. Joseph Blenkinsopp, *Ezra–Nehemiah: A Commentary*, OTL (Philadelphia: Westminster, 1988), 273.

of both restoration and reformation. In Chapters 7-13 the spiritual reformation of the people is examined, with Nehemiah acknowledging once again (as in 2:11) that God inspired him ("My God put it into my heart") to lead the people into both a physical reconstruction and a spiritual reformation (7:5). "Doubtless he had earnestly pondered the grave problem of this great empty space enclosed with walls; then the solution comes to him, as to many earnest souls in ancient times and modern, by inspiration."[34] This census, unlike the one in 1 Chronicles 21, is initiated and approved by God.

The Law of God is central in the reformation of God's people, and their reaction to the reading of the Law is worship.[35] As Ezra concludes the reading of the Law, he blesses the Lord, "the great God" (8:6). This title given to God is unusual, appearing nowhere else in the Old Testament.[36] This great God must be worshipped, and following the revelation of God through His Law, the people "worshipped the Lord with their faces to the ground." After the reading of the Law and worship, the Levites helped the people understand the Law (8:8), and the Israelites mourned and wept as they realized their failure to keep it. The people knew the Law as the Law of Moses, but Nehemiah now makes it clear that God is the author of the Law (8:14). Moses was merely God's humble instrument through which He revealed Himself.[37]

The people's understanding of God as He reveals Himself and their ensuing worship of this great God are only part of the reformation process. The confession of sin is a most crucial element in the people's reformation (9:1-3). After the people confess their sins, they are exhorted by the Levites to

---

34. Batten, 264.
35. See Leslie Allen, "For He is Good…": Worship in Ezra–Nehemiah," in M.P. Graham, R.R. Marrs, and S.L. McKenzie (eds), *Worship and the Hebrew Bible* (Sheffield: Sheffield Academic, 1999), 15-34.
36. The title *hā'ĕlōhim haggāḏôl* (the great God) does not appear anywhere else in the Old Testament. However, the form *hā'ēl haggāḏôl* (an abbreviated form of the great God) can be found in Nehemiah 1:5; 9:32; Jeremiah 32:18; Daniel 9:4.
37. Nehemiah 9:3 mentions the Book of the Law of the Lord, again pointing to the divine provenance of the Law.

"Stand up and bless the LORD" (9:5).[38] Verse 5 begins a prayer rich in theology, which is organized as follows: (1) 9:6, God as Creator, (2) 9:7-8, God as Covenant-maker, (3) 9:9-11, God as Deliverer, (4) 9:12-21, God as Sustainer, and (5) 9:22-31, God as Land-giver. In contrast with the false idols which are time-bound, God is "from everlasting to everlasting" (9:5).[39] While the idols' names are meaningless, God's name is glorious and exalted (9:5b). God is the One who created heaven and earth, with the "heaven and earth" of Genesis 1 present here to point to His creation of everything.[40] God did not start a theistic evolutionary process and has now become a powerless bystander. He created then and is still actively involved in sustaining his creation (9:6). The verb employed here and translated "preserve" is the Hebrew verb *hāyāh* which means to live, to sustain life, to preserve life. Verse 6 concludes by affirming that the creation's proper response to its Creator and Sustainer is worship.[41]

Nehemiah affirms God's greatness in choosing and leading Abraham, but Abraham is not the main character on the cosmic and redemptive stage of history. God is the One who is great: He chose Abraham, brought him to the Promised Land and changed not just Abraham's name, but also his life (9:7). This Covenant God set the terms and conditions of the covenant made with Abraham. The end of verse eight emphasizes once again God's faithfulness. He is the Covenant-Maker and Covenant-Sustainer. Why? Because that is His character and very nature; He is right-eous altogether.

Nehemiah revisits the Exodus event as he continues his exaltation of the God who sees the affliction of the oppressed (9:9), and doesn't walk away. He remains close to His people,

---

38. See L.J. Liebreich, "The Impact of Nehemiah 9:5-37 on the Liturgy of the Synagogue," *HUCA* 32 (1961): 227-237.
39. See F.C. Fensham, "Neh 9 and Pss 105, 106, and 136: Post-Exilic Historical Traditions in Poetic Form," *JNSL* 9 (1981): 35-51.
40. For an in-depth look on the use of merism in the Hebrew Bible, see Joze Krasovec, "Merism: Polar Experssion in Biblical Hebrew, *Biblica*, 64/2 (1983): 231-239.
41. See Frederick C. Holmgren, "Faithful Abraham and the 'amānâ Covenant: Nehemiah 9,6-10,1" in *ZAW* 104/2 (1992): 249-254.

sees their plight, and hears their cry. In order to free His people from slavery, God "performs signs and wonders,"[42] and as a result God's name is exalted and His reputation magnified (9:10).[43] God's miracles did not end at the shore of the Red Sea (9:11), but continued through the wilderness period. After delivering His people from Egypt, He guided them through the wilderness by providing pillars of cloud and fire to lead them (9:12). Yet, God's guidance is best seen in the Law He has given through his servant Moses, not in the pillars of cloud and fire (9:13). The pillars will disappear, but God's Word will stand forever as our pillars in life and ministry. God also called His people to rest and sanctification by observing God's "holy Sabbath" (9:14). Nehemiah shows God as the One who provided bread and water for His people during their wilderness wandering (9:15). The expression "bread from heaven" occurs twice in the Old Testament, the first time in Exodus 16:4 where God promises the people that He will feed them in the wilderness. Nehemiah 9:15 is the only other place this expression occurs, now in the context of a historical look at God's fulfillment of His promise.

Even though the Israelites often responded to God's guidance and providence by rebelling against Him and His servants (9:16), God forgave them (9:17). Nehemiah contrasts God's graciousness and compassion with the unfaithfulness of the people. Furthermore, he presents God as being slow to anger and abounding in covenantal love.[44] Not only did God *not* forsake his people (9:17), He continued providing guidance for them through the pillars of cloud and fire (9:19)[45]

---

42. The expression "signs and wonders" appears frequently in Deuteronomy in Moses' homilies that focus on God's delivering his people from Egypt. Deuteronomy 4:34; 6:22; 7:19; 26:8; 29:3; 34:11. For an excellent treatment of the Exodus, see John J. Davis, *Moses and the gods of Egypt* (Winona Lake, Indiana: BMH, 1986).

43. In the Ancient Near East someone's name was equivalent to his/her reputation.

44. The chain of attributes "gracious and compassionate, slow to anger and abounding in lovingkindness" also appears in Exodus 34:6; Psalm 103:8; Joel 2:13; Jonah 4:2.

45. God's promise of not forsaking his people is also mentioned in Deuteronomy 31:6, 8, and 1 Kings 6:13.

because of His great compassion (9:19).[46] Besides the physical supply of bread and water, God also provided spiritually for His people (9:20) as they received and understood God's instruction through his Spirit.[47] God is the One who gave them victory in battle (9:22), prosperity in numbers and inheritance of the Promised Land (9:23-24). The expression "numerous as the stars of heaven" is a direct reference to the Abrahamic covenant (Gen. 12:2; 15:5). "This entire scene has the design and look of a covenant renewal ceremony (Exod. 34)."[48]

While God is loving and merciful, He is also holy, righteous, and just, and He must punish sin. He is the God who judges (9:27). Like delinquent tenants, the Israelites were evicted from their land by God, the righteous landlord. Even so, because He is a God of great compassion (9:27, 28, 31), He rescued them from the hand of their oppressors (9:28), patiently instructing and guiding them (9:29).

The expression *now therefore* in 9:32 presents a transition in Nehemiah's prayer. Up to this point, Nehemiah's prayer has been a historical reminder of God's goodness displayed from the covenant made with Abraham to the exilic period. At this point Nehemiah includes himself in the prayer by using the adverb "now," thus pointing to the present restoration period to which he belongs. The God to whom Nehemiah is praying is the same "great, mighty and awesome" God who is faithful to the covenant and who loves His people with a covenantal love. The fact that Nehemiah can call God "our God" points to the intimacy God shares with those who love and obey Him (9:32). Nehemiah recognizes God's fairness and confesses that God has acted justly in His judgment of a rebellious people (9:33).[49] After Nehemiah institutes radical reforms among the people (12-13), the book ends with Nehemiah praying that God will remember the defilement of the unfaithful and the good work He has done in the process of restoration (13:14,

---

46. Three times in the book of Nehemiah the noun "compassion" is modified by the adjective "great." The same expression "great compassion" is used to describe God in Isa. 54:7 and Dan. 9:18.

47. Some Greek versions have "holy spirit."

48. Breneman, 240.

49. Nehemiah confesses the fact that God is just both at the beginning (9:8) and the end of the prayer (9:33).

22, 29, 31). Brenemen affirms that "the book of Nehemiah begins with prayer and closes with prayer. For lasting results, ministry can never be separated from prayer."[50]

B. What does the book of Nehemiah teach us about God's people and the faithless?

While the book of Nehemiah is first and foremost about God, the book also gives us insight about God's people and their enemies.[51] The first verse of the book tells us the crucial part Nehemiah plays in this book.[52] In the first person he tells of his pain and mourning when he learned about the state of affairs in Jerusalem. While working for the Persian king Artaxerxes, Nehemiah has been made aware of the grave state of the exiles in Jerusalem (1:2-3), and in deep sadness he combines his tears with prayer and fasting, showing from the beginning of the book that Nehemiah is a man of prayer and fasting.[53] The man of God not only *sees* the need for reconstruction; he *feels* its spiritual significance because he is sensitive and spiritually astute (1:4). This first recorded prayer in the book of Nehemiah begins with a confession of sin (1:4-7). Nehemiah knows who God is, addressing Him accordingly as the Creator God (1:5). He also knows that God's judgment was brought about by the people's disobedience to the covenant God made with Moses. Nehemiah shows the mark of a true leader by including himself and his father's house among those who have sinned and brought about the Babylonian exile (1:6-7). After confessing personal and corporate sin, he pleads for God's help (1:8-11). Verse 8 shows that Nehemiah

---

50. Breneman, 275-6.
51. In this article Nehemiah and those who are doing the reconstruction are presented as God's people, while Sanballat, Tobiah, and those who oppose the reconstruction will be presented as the unfaithful. See David C. Kraemer, "On the Relationship of the Books of Ezra and Nehemiah," in *JSOT* 59 (1993): 73-92.
52. In the Hebrew Bible the book of Ezra–Nehemiah appears as a single book. The fact that both books have first person narratives in them suggests that both Ezra and Nehemiah have written the books that bear their names, with some editor/compiler putting the two together in a single book.
53. All great men and women of the Bible and of church history were men and women of prayer and fasting.

knows "what says the Lord"[54] through the Law given to his
servant Moses. His knowledge does not make Nehemiah
puffed up, rather his spirit of humility acknowledges that he
and his compatriots are merely servants of the Lord (1:10).
We learn in Chapter 1 that Nehemiah's position in the Persian
court was "the cupbearer to the king" (1:11). Williamson
states "royal cupbearers in antiquity, in addition to their skill
in selecting and serving wine and their duty in tasting it as
proof against poison, were also expected to be convivial and
tactful companions to the king."[55] Thus, Chapter 1 shows us
that Nehemiah leaves a highly respected, lucrative position
in order to follow God's call to rebuild Jerusalem and reform
its people.

Nehemiah's life is bathed in prayer (2:4). Brown states
that Nehemiah's prayer emphasizes the necessity of prayer,
describes the immediacy of prayer, reveals the intimacy of
prayer, demonstrates the confidence of prayer, and proves
the effectiveness of prayer.[56] Nehemiah shows respect for
his ancestors when he refers to Jerusalem as "the place
of my fathers' tombs" (2:5). His prayer shows that he is a
man of vision, seeing Jerusalem not as it is now, but what it
can become (2:6). And even though Nehemiah respects the
king's authority and generosity, he realizes God's provision
and protection are what will give him success (2:8).

Opposition persists even though God is with Nehemiah,
but in the midst of it Nehemiah's motivation surfaces. He
starts the work of reconstruction because he is seeking
"the welfare of the sons of Israel" (2:10). Sanballat the
Horonite and Tobiah the Ammonite stand in stark contrast
to Nehemiah: they are displeased that someone cares
for God's people (2:10).[57] Like a good leader, Nehemiah
assesses the damage (2:11-17a), initiates the rebuilding of
the wall of Jerusalem and encourages his Jewish brothers

---

54. Dr. Robert Smith, preaching professor at Beeson Divinity School, affirms
    that before one stands up and declares "Thus says the Lord," one must
    know *what* the Lord says.
55. Williamson, 174.
56. Brown, 47-48.
57. See W. C. Van Wyk and A.P.B. Breytenbach, "The Nature of Conflict in
    Ezra–Nehemiah," in *Hervormde Teologiese Studies* 57/3-4 (2001): 1254-1263.

to join him in the reconstruction project (2:17b-18a). The people are persuaded by Nehemiah's testimony, and they join the work (2:18b). Even though God's enemies mock and despise God's people (2:19), Nehemiah is confident in God's providence and assured that the God who called him will also give him success. Furthermore, Nehemiah refuses to compromise, denying his opponents a share of the land and legacy (2:20). Blenkinsopp clarifies that "the denial of a 'share' corresponds to a traditional formula denoting polit- ical dissociation (cf. 2 Sam. 20:1; 1 Kings 12:16), while 'claim' stands for the legal right to exercise jurisdiction."[58]

Chapter 3 is an example of ingenious teamwork by which God's people pursue the reconstruction of the walls. "The list of those engaged in the rebuilding of the walls of Jerusalem moves section by section round the wall in a counter-clockwise direction, making a full circuit from and to the Sheep Gate (3:1-32)."[59] This chapter also shows the remarkable leadership skills of Nehemiah who organizes the reconstruction of forty- five sections of Jerusalem's wall.[60] The high priest, Eliashib, leads by example and is mentioned first (3:1).[61] Fensham suggests that "Nehemiah wanted to show that he received the cooperation of the high priest and consequently also that of the other priests."[62] The Sheep Gate receives priority probably because "sheep destined for sacrifice usually were brought in there to the market."[63] The fact that the men from Jericho joined the work of reconstruction (3:2) indicates that these men viewed no distance too far to travel to be a part of this work. In addition to Jericho, Tekoa (3:5, 27), Gibeon, Mizpah (3:7), Zanoah (3:13), Beth-haccherem (3:14), Beth-zur (3:16), and Keilah (3:17) are also mentioned. People differed not just in their geographical provenance, but also in their professions and trades. Thus, goldsmiths (3:8, 31), perfumers (3:8), high

---

58. Blenkinsopp, 226.
59. Williamson, 198.
60. Ten gates are included in the reconstruction project (Neh. 3:1, 3, 6, 13-15, 26, 28-29, 31).
61. Ezra 10:6; Nehemiah 3:20-21.
62. F. Charles Fensham, *The Books of Ezra and Nehemiah* (Grand Rapids: Eerd- mans, 1982) , 173.
63. Breneman, 186.

ranking officials (3:9, 12, 14, 15, 16, 17), Levites (3:17), priests (3:22), temple servants (3:26), and merchants (3:32) submitted under Nehemiah's leadership to doing manual labor in order for the reconstruction to take place. In contrast to all these who exemplify humility and teamwork stand the "nobles of Tekoa" who "did not support the work" of the reconstruction.[64] Williamson states that the unwillingness of the leaders of the Tekoites to serve should not be surprising. "The return of the exiles from Babylon at any time is bound to have caused tensions with those who had remained in the land."[65]

The reconstruction continued to be opposed by Sanballat, Tobiah, and their supporters (4:1ff). For the second time in the book we are told that Nehemiah and the faithful are mocked by their enemies. Sanballat is singled out as one who gets very angry when hearing the good news of reconstruction progress. The principle that good progress will always cause someone to be displeased is good to remember when doing God's work. The anger of Sanballat's heart is expressed in mocking words which question the strength of the people ("What are these feeble Jews doing?"),[66] their resolve to rebuild the wall ("Are they going to restore it for themselves?"), and their religious zeal ("Can they offer sacrifices?") (4:2). As Tobiah joins the tirade of mocking and discouraging words, Nehemiah appeals for retribution to the God who called him to do the work (4:4-5). His prayer is not prescriptive but descriptive (4:4-5), and New Testament Christians should not hold up this prayer as a model to pray against those who oppose them. Rather, Jesus' principles laid out in Matthew 5:38-48 should be used as our guidelines for dealing with our enemies.

Despite overt opposition and insults, the work of the faithful continues and is rewarded because "the people had a heart to work" (4:6). The anger of the faithless (4:7) leads to them to conspire/plot against Jerusalem and to cause a

---

64. The Hebrew reads "their nobles did not bring their necks in the service of the Lord."

65. Williamson, 204.

66. The word "Jews" here might be used as an ethnic slur aimed at insulting the people's national heritage.

disturbance (to create confusion) in it (4:8).[67] And because piety does not replace hard work, the faithful react both by praying and by planning (4:9). However, even their faith, prayers, and planning cannot prevent weariness and discouragement (4:10).[68] "We can imagine the people singing this lament as they worked on the wall."[69] McConville believes that the lament in 4:10 was "a kind of chorus chanted during the work. Despite its somewhat negative tone, it may actually have had the function of keeping the men going – not unlike the 'spirituals' that encouraged enslaved laborers of more recent times."[70] Discouraging words lead into threatening words from the enemies (4:11); but instead of becoming paralyzed, the faithful become even more organized (4:12-13). Nehemiah's leadership skills surface again as he encourages the people by pointing not to their self-esteem, the post-modern response, but by reminding them of Yahweh's greatness and majesty (4:14).[71] While the workers return to the task, the faithless realize that God is against them (4:15-19). The faithful understand that the cause they're fighting is God's cause and they recognize His principal part in the war of words or swords.[72] Nehemiah leads by example in every way. The reconstruction continues (4:21) as Nehemiah perseveres in encouraging the people, planning and working side by side with his brothers (4:22-23).

Chapter 5 points to internal problems stemming from injustice, oppression, and economic hardship.[73] While his enemies

---

67. The number of enemies increase and now includes the Ashdodites.
68. Verse 10 contains a lament "indicative of the despair of melancholy." Williamson, 226.
69. Breneman, 196.
70. J. Gordon McConville, *Ezra, Nehemiah and Esther,* DST (Edinburgh: SAP, 1985), 91.
71. Nehemiah's leadership skills are also seen in the fact that he correctly assesses the situation ("When I saw their fear"), thus seeing the need for encouragement ("Do not be afraid").
72. The idea that God will fight for them is also present in Exod. 14:14; Deut. 1:30; 3:22; 20:4; Josh. 10:14, 42; 23:10.
73. There seems to be no support in this chapter for today's "prosperity gospel" euphoria created by those who only preach and teach the Bible selectively.

were angry in the face of good things, Nehemiah becomes angry in the face of injustice (5:6). Nehemiah confronts the sin of the nobles and rulers who are victimizing their brothers (5:7-8) and outlines steps for correction (5:9-11). The wrongdoers obey Nehemiah and move to make proper restitution (5:12-13a). Only after obedience and restitution take place can the people praise the Lord (5:13b). Unlike his predecessors, Nehemiah continues to lead by example, and even though he has been appointed governor, he does not operate with the "that's not in my job description" mentality. Rather, with humility, Nehemiah himself works on the wall (5:14-16). Yamauchi observes that "Nehemiah's behavior as governor was guided by principles of service rather than by opportunism."[74]

After facing the internal problems of injustice and oppression in Chapter 5, Nehemiah encounters external dangers in Chapter 6. Those who oppose the work of reconstruction continue their resistance by conspiring to harm Nehemiah, but God's hand is still upon him causing him to discern that the enemy's call to a meeting is a trap (6:1-2). Fensham observes, "Nehemiah suspected foul play. It is possible that he had received certain information which uncovered their plot; perhaps both sides made use of informers."[75] And while the enemy sends four requests for a meeting, Nehemiah turns down their invitation each time because his priorities are in order (6:3-4), and his main priority is the reconstruction of the wall. In this episode Nehemiah displays wisdom in discerning and replying as well as persistence in doing the work. His enemies resort to lying (6:5), but even though Nehemiah is accused of trying to overturn the Persian monarchy (6:6-7), he again discerns the enemy's lies (6:8). Knowing he might become weakened by all the external threats, Nehemiah prays that God will strengthen him (6:9). The enemy's plan to defeat Nehemiah continues with Tobiah and Sanballat bribing a priest by the name of Shemaiah, son of Delaiah,[76]

---

74. Edwin Yamauchi, *Ezra–Nehemiah* EBC4 (Grand Rapids: Zondervan, 1992), 710.

75. Fensham, *Ezra and Nehemiah*, 200. While Fensham may be correct, it is also possible that God helped Nehemiah discern the imminent danger.

76. 1 Chronicles mentions that Delaiah was a priest, thus Shemaiah was also a priest who had access to the temple where he suggests that Nehemiah seek refuge.

but Nehemiah realizes that Shemaiah was hired to scare him into sinning by entering the temple (6:12-13). "The strategy to discredit the leader is a subtle one and is common today."[77] Nehemiah prays a short imprecatory prayer which leaves the vengeance to God (6:14).

Until now Nehemiah has been a leader who sees the need, feels the need, prays to God about the need, and organizes people to accomplish the need. Now that task has been completed. Nehemiah 6:15 says that the wall was completed in 52 days. The speed with which the walls were rebuilt points to God's guidance and grace, and to Nehemiah's leadership skills. Even the faithless see that God's hand has been at work (6:16), although they do not repent of their rebellion but continue their work of intimidation (6:17-19).

Chapter 7 begins the second part of the book, which focuses on the reformation of God's people.[78] Nehemiah's wise leadership skills come to the forefront again as he appoints people to do the different tasks around Jerusalem (7:1). Hanani (1:2) is singled out as a faithful and God-fearing man (7:2).[79] Nehemiah proves again to be a superb organizer, delegating work at the temple (7:1), at the city gates (7:2-3), and planning the repopulation of Jerusalem (7:4). No task is too menial for Nehemiah if God is the One inspiring him. To accomplish the task of city repopulation, God guides Nehemiah to gather the leadership of the city and to take a census (7:5-72). Williamson affirms that "the purpose of the gathering was to draw up a census of the population, on the basis of which an equitable decision could be taken as to who should be moved into the city."[80]

In Chapter 8, the faithful gather in unity and ask Ezra, the great priest and teacher of the Law, to read from the Law of God given to the people through His servant Moses. Even though the reading takes about six hours, the people are attentive because their reformation can only be attained as they respond with

---

77. Breneman, 212.
78. Chapters 1-6 focus on the reconstruction of the wall while chapters 7-13 focus on the reformation of the people.
79. Hanani (7:2) is a shortened form of Hananiah (1:2).
80. Williamson, 271.

obedience to God's revelation (8:1-5). After Ezra blesses the LORD, the people respond by worshipping God (8:6).[81] Thirteen Levites interpret the Law, one of the many tasks of the Levites outlined in the Mosaic Law and practiced at the temple (Deut. 33:10; 2 Chron. 17:7-9; 35:3; Neh. 8:7-8). The people respond to the hearing and understanding of God's word by weeping. "The reading of the law and its explanation to the people had its effect. They became aware of their sins and wept."[82] Both Nehemiah and Ezra encourage the people to rejoice and to remember those who are too poor to feast (8:9-10). The people's understanding of the Law leads them first to repentance, and then to celebration: the tears turn into joy as they celebrate the full understanding of God's words to them (8:11-12).

The people's reformation continues with a time of prayer and fasting (9:1). The sackcloth and dirt represent the general signs for mourning, and subsequent verses indicate that their prayer was one of confession of sin and repentance. The community enters into a covenant renewal with Yahweh stressing purity, which separates them from those outside of the community of faith.[83] This covenant renewal takes place only after the Israelites have confessed and repented of their sins (9:2). The covenant renewal ceremonies continue for days, involving the reading of the Law, confession of sin, and worship of Yahweh (9:3). The prayer that follows (9:6-37) is introduced by the exhortation, "Arise, bless the LORD your God forever and ever" (9:5b), and continues by exalting God for His past redemptive acts in history.[84] The prayer also expresses the people's faith in the God who made a covenant with their father Abraham, the One who redeemed them from the Egyptian slavery, and also the One who justly punished them for their rebellion (9:6-21). Nehemiah 9:38 describes a covenant renewal between the Israelites and Yahweh. "The force of the agreement is attested by the fact of its being set in writing and sealed as a guarantee of its

---

81. The verbs "to worship" and "to bow down" are sometimes used together (Gen. 24:26, 28; Exod. 4:31; 12:27; 2 Chron. 29:29).

82. Fensham, *Ezra and Nehemiah*, 218.

83. See Saul Olyan, "Purity Ideology in Ezra–Nehemiah as a Tool to Reconstitute the Community," in *Journal for the Study of Judaism in the Persian, Hellenistic and Roman Period*, 35:1 (2004), 1-16.

84. See Part 1 "What does the book of Nehemiah teach us about God?"

authenticity and to preserve against subsequent tampering."[85] The people continue their resolve to be true to God's Law and to stop the practice of intermarrying with gentiles (10:28-39).[86]

The faithful gather for a special ceremony for the dedication of the temple (12:27-30) that involves the ritual of purification. Williamson suggests that this ritual "may have involved washing of self and of clothes, ritual sprinkling, the sacrifice of sin-offering, fasting, and abstinence from sexual intercourse; cf. Exodus 19:10, 14-15; Leviticus 16:28; Numbers 8:5-8, 19."[87] As a remarkable leader, Nehemiah leads in the organization of the processions and dedication service and the delegation of responsibilities at the temple (12:31-47).

The reading of God's Law continues to produce change in the life of the people, and they continue to separate themselves from those outside the Israelite community of faith (13:1-3). After being absent from Jerusalem to return to the Persian court for a time, Nehemiah returns to Jerusalem and immediately takes a firm stand against Tobiah who has defiled the temple by his presence there. Nehemiah orders that the rooms be cleansed (13:4-9). Fensham agrees that it was "an act of desecration to bring into a sacred chamber a profane person such as Tobiah."[88] Nehemiah reorganizes the Levites and reinstitutes the tithes that seem to have been forgotten during his absence (13:10-14).

The book of Nehemiah ends by emphasizing the godly leadership skills of Nehemiah. A godly leader confronts sin. Nehemiah confronts those who have forsaken the fourth commandment that set aside the Sabbath for rest and worship, and he demands that the Levites purify themselves and "sanctify the Sabbath day" (13:15-22). Lastly, Nehemiah confronts those who have married pagan women (13:23-31), reminding them that Solomon's downfall was brought about by the foreign wives who turned his heart away from the LORD (1 Kings 11:1-9).[89]

---

85. Williamson, 332.

86. Nehemiah 10:30-39 outlines the stipulations/obligations of the covenant. For more on the issue of "Intermarriage," see John Goldingay, *Old Testament Theology: Israel's Gospel,* vol. 1 (Downers Grove, IL: IVP, 2003), 747-751.

87. Williamson, 373.

88. Fensham, *Ezra and Nehemiah,* 261.

89. Fensham suggests that Nehemiah received permission from the Persian

Conclusion

The book of Nehemiah shows us the beauty and greatness of the God who creates, sustains that which He creates, makes covenants with humans, and restores His people to a genuine relationship with him. In God's economy there are servant-leaders like Nehemiah who accept God's call and work in His "vineyard," and there are those who oppose the work. Just as in the time of Nehemiah, God still calls people to do the work of ministry in the midst of opposition and ridicule.

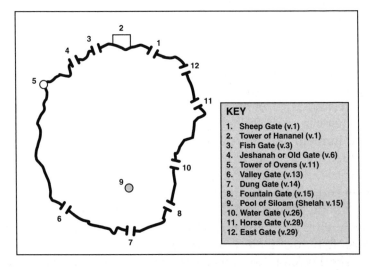

KEY
1. Sheep Gate (v.1)
2. Tower of Hananel (v.1)
3. Fish Gate (v.3)
4. Jeshanah or Old Gate (v.6)
5. Tower of Ovens (v.11)
6. Valley Gate (v.13)
7. Dung Gate (v.14)
8. Fountain Gate (v.15)
9. Pool of Siloam (Shelah v.15)
10. Water Gate (v.26)
11. Horse Gate (v.28)
12. East Gate (v.29)

1.5 Date and Authorship

Even though rabbinic tradition regarded the books of Ezra and Nehemiah as a unit written by Ezra, internal evidence suggests that the book of Ezra was primarily written by Ezra himself, while the book of Nehemiah was primarily written by Nehemiah.[90] The books appeared as two separate works

---

court and that is why he was able to strike some of the men and pull out their hair. Fensham, *Ezra and Nehemiah*, 267. Williamson is probably correct when he suggests that this incident was "localized and restricted," Nehemiah being "provoked by the children's language into a sudden and violent outburst." Williamson, 398-399.

90. The Babylonian Talmud (Bab. Bath. 15a) states the Ezra is the author of Chronicles and Ezra–Nehemiah. The rabbis also affirm that while Ezra began the work, Nehemiah completed it. Some editorial work was probably done, but this is minor in both form and scope. Because of

during the time of Origen (185-253 AD). Young suggests that the books were treated as one due to the "desire to make the total number of canonical books agree with the number of letters in the Hebrew alphabet." I concur with Harrison that it is best to view Ezra and Nehemiah as being "primarily responsible for the writings attributed to them; that they were contemporaries, with Ezra arriving in Jerusalem initially several years before Nehemiah; that their writings were in substantially their present form by about 440 and 430 BC respectively, and that the Chronicler compiled his work independently about 400 BC or slightly later."[91]

Table 2: Ezra–Nehemiah authorship views

Authors	Chronological implications	Scholars preferring view
Ezra and Nehemiah[1]	The names and dates in the biblical text are accurate	R.K. Harrison; Gleason Archer
Ezra[2]	Ezra started his work in 428 BC in the 37th year of Artaxerxes I (not the 7th year as the MT states)	W.F. Albright
The Chronicler[3]	2 Chronicles 36:22-23 presupposes Ezra 1	H.H. Grosheide, J.M. Myers, C.C. Torrey

Table 2 Notes:

1. Some final editing done by an unnamed editor/Chronicler is assumed.

2. This view also suggests that Ezra was the author of 1-2 Chronicles.

3. The proponents of this view do not agree on the extent of alterations made by the Chronicler, or how ethical the Chronicler was in his writing.

---

the similarity in language with 2 Chronicles 36:22-23, it is also possible that Ezra wrote Chronicles as well. The view that the Chronicler wrote both Ezra–Nehemiah and Chronicles was advanced by Torrey, Pfeiffer, Grosheide, and Myers. While Torrey and Pfeiffer take a more radical view that "Ezra is a forgery of the Chronicler," Grosheide and Myers suggest that "the Chronicler compiled Ezra–Nehemiah while using some reliable sources." See Fensham, *The Books of Ezra and Nehemiah,* 2-3.

91. Roland K. Harrison, *Introduction to the Old Testament* (Peabody, Massachusetts: Prince, 1999), 1135.

The fact that Ezra and Nehemiah were written by separate authors can be supported by the following internal evidence:[92]

- *Stylistic differences*. While Ezra's memoir is the first person, Nehemiah's memoir is recounted in the third person.
- *Language*. While Ezra uses both Hebrew and Aramaic, Nehemiah uses Hebrew alone.
- *Lists*. The lists in Ezra 2 and Nehemiah 7 would be redundant if part of one book and the work of one author.

---

92. For a more detailed discussion, see David Kraemer, "On the Relationship of the Books of Ezra and Nehemiah," in *JSOT* 59 (1993):73-92.

Ezra

Ezra 1

Outline
1:1-4 God moves the heart of Cyrus
1:5-11 God moves the heart of His people

I. God moves the heart of Cyrus (1:1-4)

> 1:1 In the first year of Cyrus king of Persia, that the word of the LORD by the mouth of Jeremiah might be fulfilled, the LORD stirred up the spirit of Cyrus king of Persia, so that he made a proclamation throughout all his kingdom and also put it in writing:[1]

Cyrus the Great was the dominant king of the Achaemenid dynasty and is credited with being the founder of the Persian Empire. He reigned from 559 to 530 BC, and under his rule Persia enjoyed great military expansion through dominance of Media, Lydia, Ionia, and even Babylonia.[2] The *first year* here refers "to the first year of the conquering of Babylon when he became king of Mesopotamia."[3] Through the eighth century prophet Isaiah, God calls Cyrus "my shepherd" (Isa. 44:28) and "the LORD's anointed" (Isa. 45:1), pointing to God's sovereign control of both history and

---

1. All Bible references are from the ESV translation.
2. E.M. Yamauchi, "Ezra–Nehemiah," in *Dictionary of the Old Testament Historical Books* (Downers Grove, Il., IVP, 2005), 286. The earliest mention of "Cyrus the king of Persia" occurs in the Nabonidus Chronicle (ANET, 306).
3. F. Charles Fensham, *The Books of Ezra and Nehemiah*, NICOT (Grand Rapids: Eerdmans, 1982), 42.

Cyrus' heart. Williamson correctly points out that "the biblical writer, however, is concerned not merely with the external facts of history, which he may have derived from the heading or other note of identification on the copy of the decree itself...; rather he is concerned with their divine ordering and purpose."[4] Through the prophet Jeremiah God revealed that the exile would last 70 years. Jeremiah 25:11 says, "This whole land shall become a ruin and a waste, and these nations shall serve the king of Babylon seventy years." The 70 years can refer to the period between the destruction of the temple (586 BC) and the time it was rebuilt (516 BC)[5], or it can describe the time lapsed from the destruction of Assyria (609 BC) to the edict of Cyrus (539 BC).[6] The Hebrew text is clear that the proclamation was put "in writing," an expression that "occurs only seven times in the Old Testament and is a technical term meaning "inscription" or "official document."[7]

> 1:2 Thus says Cyrus king of Persia: "The LORD,
> the God of heaven, has given me all the kingdoms
> of the earth, and he has charged me to build
> him a house at Jerusalem, which is in Judah.

The fact that Cyrus recognizes God as Yahweh is consistent with Achaemenid policy, that of using "the title of the god or gods recognized by the local population, but that this does not imply that they themselves were 'converted' to these religions from their own worship of Ahura Mazda."[8] The expression "God of heaven" occurs nine times in the Old Testament and each reference refers to Yahweh. Breneman suggests that "the phrase 'God of heaven' was commonly used in the Persian Empire even by the Persians in speaking

---

4. H.G.M. Williamson, *Ezra, Nehemiah*, WBC vol. 16 (Waco, Texas: Word, 1985), 9.

5. Jacob Myers, *Ezra–Nehemiah*, AB (Garden City, New York: Doubleday, 1965), 6.

6. Frolov suggests that God overruled the chronological part of Jeremiah's prophecy. See Serge Frolov, "The Prophecy of Jeremiah in Esr 1,1" in *ZAW* 116 (4:2004): 595-601.

7. Ibid., 4.

8. Williamson, 12.

of their god."[9] However, this God is not only the Creator
God, but also the God who directs Cyrus to rebuild the
temple in Jerusalem. Through the prophet Isaiah God "says
of Cyrus, 'He is my shepherd, and he shall fulfill all my
purpose'; saying of Jerusalem, 'She shall be built,' and of the
temple, 'Your foundation shall be laid'" (Isa. 44:28).

Cyrus cylinder – Inscribed in Babylonian cuneiform with
an account by Cyrus of his conquest of Babylon in 539 BC
and capture of Nabonidus, the last Babylonian king.

> 1:3 Whoever is among you of all his people, may his
> God be with him, and let him go up to Jerusalem,
> which is in Judah, and rebuild the house of the LORD,
> the God of Israel—he is the God who is in Jerusalem.

The word "all" used here points to a total repatriation
wherein all Jews from both the Assyrian and Babylonian
exile are invited to return to their homeland. The permissive
"let him go up" indicates that Cyrus does not command the
Jews to return, but rather he allows them to return. While
the Babylonians ruled with an iron fist, forcing their subjects
to worship their gods, Cyrus allowed those whom he
conquered to worship their own gods. The expression "the
God who is in Jerusalem" appears ten other times in Ezra,[10]
and points to Cyrus' practice of viewing deities in relation
to a place. Cyrus was "an Iranian polytheist"[11] whose view
of Yahweh is limited even though he knows Him by the
divine name (1:1).

> 1:4 And let each survivor, in whatever place
> he sojourns, be assisted by the men of his
> place with silver and gold, with goods and
> with beasts, besides freewill offerings for
> the house of God that is in Jerusalem.

Although not all those who were free to return wanted to
return, they were to assist those who wanted to do so. It is

9. Mervin Breneman, *Ezra, Nehemiah, Esther*. NAC, vol. 10 (Nashville: Broadman
   and Holman, 1993), 171. The expression also occurs in Genesis 24:3; 24:7;
   2 Chron. 36:23; Ezr. 1:2; Neh. 1:4; 1:5; 2:4; 2:20; Jonah 1:9.
10. Ezra 4:24; 5:2, 16, 17; 6:3, 12, 18; 7:16, 17, 19.
11. Edwin Yamauchi, "Archaeological Backgrounds of the Exilic and Postexilic
    Era, part 3: The Archaeological Background of Ezra," *BSac*137/547 (1980), 200.

also very plausible that, just as the Egyptians gave the Jews material possessions when they left Egypt in the time of Moses,[12] so did the Persians during this return. The parallels between Cyrus and Moses as deliverers were meant to encourage the people of God. Freewill offerings were also brought by the Israelites during the building of the tabernacle in the wilderness.[13] This time the freewill offerings were meant to finance the rebuilding of the temple in Jerusalem which had been destroyed by Nebuchadnezzar's army in 587/6 BC. This "second Exodus" represents the rebirth of the nation of Israel after the exile. The freewill offerings identify the Jewish community as a worshipping community that is meant to have Jerusalem and the temple[14] as its focus.

II. God moves the hearts of His people (1:5-11)

> 1:5-6 Then rose up the heads of the fathers' houses of Judah and Benjamin, and the priests and the Levites, everyone whose spirit God had stirred to go up to rebuild the house of the LORD that is in Jerusalem. [6]And all who were about them aided them with vessels of silver, with gold, with goods, with beasts, and with costly wares, besides all that was freely offered.

The writer is clear that God is in control of both history and people's hearts. It is He who stirs up the spirit of the people to take action. Judah and Benjamin are singled out because the Southern Kingdom was mainly made up of those two tribes, along with the tribe of Simeon which had been assimilated into the tribe of Judah.[15] The term "Judah and Benjamin" appears frequently in Chronicles, as well as Ezra–Nehemiah, and it does not imply a denial of the descendants

---

12. Exodus 12:35-36.
13. Exodus 35-36; Leviticus 7:16 and 22:23 also mention freewill offerings as part of God's instruction.
14. The term "house of God" is commonly used for the temple in Jerusalem, appearing more than 50 times in the Old Testament. See Melody D. Knowles, "Pilgrimage Imagery in the Returns in Ezra," in JBL 123/1 (2005):57-74.
15. In Judges, Judah and Simeon make a pact to act as one in the face of common enemies (Judg. 1:3, 17).

of the other ten tribes.[16] The remnant returning is divided
into three classes: priests, Levites, and laity. Verse 6 suggests
a reversal of fortunes for the Jews who were in exile. Now,
the people of God who are returning to their homeland do
so enhanced not only by golden and silver vessels, but also
by animals to help with transportation.

> 1:7 Cyrus the king also brought out the vessels
> of the house of the LORD that Nebuchadnezzar
> had carried away from Jerusalem and
> placed in the house of his gods.

The Chronicler depicts Nebuchadnezzar[17] as the one who
destroyed Jerusalem, burned the temple, and stole goods
from it (2 Chron. 36:18). Yamauchi explains that "conquerors
customarily carried off the statues of the gods of conquered
cities. The Hittites took the statue of Marduk when they conquered the city of Babylon. The Philistines took the ark of the
Jews and placed it in the temple of Dagon (1 Sam. 5:2). As
the Jews did not have a statue of the Lord, Nebuchadnezzar
carried off the temple goods instead."[18]

> 1:8 Cyrus king of Persia brought these out in
> charge of Mithredath the treasurer, who counted
> them out to Sheshbazzar the prince of Judah.

The name "Sheshbazzar" occurs four times in Ezra,[19] later
revealing that he was made governor by Cyrus (5:14) and
that he laid the foundation of the temple (5:16). While
some try to identify Sheshbazzar with Zerubbabel, that "is
an improbable hypothesis."[20] Some rabbis suggested that
"Sheshbazzar is identical with Daniel...because he endured

---

16. 1 Chronicles 12:16; 2 Chronicles 11:1, 3, 10, 12, 23; 15:2, 8, 9; 25:5; 31:1; 34:9;
    Ezra 4:1; 12:34; Nehemiah 11:4; 12:34.
17. Nebuchadnezzar's original Akkadian name was Nabû-kudduri-usur and
    it means "May God protect the crown prince." See *Ezra and Nehemiah,*
    BHQ 20 (Stuttgart: Deutsche Bibelgesellschaft, 2006), 39.
18. Edwin Yamauchi, *Ezra–Nehemiah*, EBC, 4:604.
19. Ezra 1:8, 11; 5:14, 16
20. Williamson, 17-18. "There is no direct evidence for regarding Sheshbazzar
    as a member of the Judean royal family." Josephus makes that correlation
    (*Ant.* 11.13-14).

six troubles."[21] The title "prince" is the Hebrew word *hannasi* which can be translated "prince," or "chief." Here it is probably just a synonym for "governor".

> 1:9-11 And this was the number of them: 30 basins of gold, 1,000 basins of silver, 29 censers, [10]30 bowls of gold, 410 bowls of silver, and 1,000 other vessels; all the vessels of gold and of silver were 5,400. [11]All these did Sheshbazzar bring up, when the exiles were brought up from Babylonia to Jerusalem.

The numbers do not add up: 30 + 1000 + 29 + 30 + 410 + 1,000 equals 2,499, and verse 11 mentions 5,400. Fensham suggests that "The transmission from Aramaic to Hebrew might have caused many of the problems in these verses."[22] Rabbi Rashi proposes that only important vessels were counted,[23] while Segal suggests that the list was compiled using symbols, accounting for the discrepancy in numbers. Segal cites Allrik who proposed that the numbers found in Ezra "were composed using symbols to represent the numbers, and not words... Such a system helps to explain the discrepancies between those two lists."

---

21. In Hebrew, Sheshbazzar sounds like "six troubles." Rabbi A. J. Rosenberg, *Daniel, Ezra, Nehemiah* (New York: Judaica, 2000), 117.
22. Fensham, 46-47.
23. Rosenberg, 118.

Table 3: The Chronology of Ezra[24]

Date	Events	Chapter Reference
538	The first return under Cyrus	1–2
538-536	The rebuilding of the altar and foundation of the temple	3
Post 538	The refused offer of help and ensuing opposition	4:1-5
520-515	Temple reconstruction hindered until Darius's second year, work revived under Haggai and Zechariah, Tattenai's investigation, Darius's support, and rebuilding of the temple	4:24–6:22
486	Opposition during the reign of Xerxes	4:6
465	Opposition during the reign of Artaxerxes	4:7
458	Return of Ezra with imperial grant	7–8
458	Problem of mixed marriages exposed and resolved	9–10
Post 458	Successful opposition to rebuilding of Jerusalem and its walls during the reign of Artaxerxes	4:8-23

Today's Christian leader can rest secure in the thought that the same God who directed history during the time of Ezra is the same God who directs our history. Despite economic uncertainties or corrupt government leadership at the local, nation, or global level, God is the One who is in charge of history. God can overcome any human obstacles to accomplish His will and plan, but just like in time of Ezra, He uses godly and committed men and women who are ready to submit to His Word and will.

---

24. A. Philip Brown II, "Chronological Anomalies in the Book of Ezra," in *BSac* 162/2 (2005), 37.

Ezra 2

Outline

I. The leaders of the restoration (2:1-2a)

> 2:1 Now these were the people of the province who came up out of the captivity of those exiles whom Nebuchadnezzar the king of Babylon had carried captive to Babylonia. They returned to Jerusalem and Judah, each to his own town.

The list of returnees is very well ordered: heading (vv.1-2), lists of people (vv. 3-35), list of priests (vv. 36-39), list of Levites (vv. 40), list of singers (vv. 41), list of gatekeepers (vv. 42), list of various temple servants (vv. 43-58), list of those with unknown genealogy (vv. 59-63), list of totals (vv. 64-67), list of temple gifts (vv. 68-69), and conclusion (vv. 70).

Verse 1 implies that some Jews never did return to their homeland, and we are not given their motives. The references to Nebuchadnezzar, Babylon, Jerusalem, and Judah could emphasize the absence of returnees from the Northern Kingdom. The geography of their return moves from specific (Jerusalem), to general (Judah, and back to specific (each to his own town).

> 2:2a They came with Zerubbabel, Jeshua,
> Nehemiah, Seraiah, Reelaiah, Mordecai, Bilshan,
> Mispar, Bigvai, Rehum, and Baanah.

The lists of names present in Ezra and Nehemiah are neither accidental nor coincidental, but rather they give "the feeling of national unity in response to Cyrus' decree, ascribes importance to each individual," and "gives the people a more central role than their leaders or the Temple."[1] Zerubbabel is mentioned first because he was the governor of Judah after Sheshbazzar (Hag. 1:1), and God calls him "my servant" (Hag. 2:23). He is listed among the descendants of David (1 Chron. 3:19), and most importantly, he appears in Jesus' genealogy (Matt. 1:12-13; Luke 3:27). Although not given the title of governor in Ezra or Nehemiah, he could be identified with either one of the unnamed governors mentioned in Ezra 2:63 or 6:7.

Jeshua the son of Jozadak "was the grandson of the last officiating high priest before the exile."[2] He is the Joshua of Haggai and Zechariah who was given the high priesthood after the return (Zech. 3:1-10). Seraiah is Ezra's father (7:1) and he appears with Nehemiah's list of priests (Neh. 12:1). Reelaiah appears as Raamiah in Nehemiah 7:7 and as Resaiah in the apocryphal book of Esdras (1 Esd. 5:8). Mordecai is a name associated with the Babylonian god Marduk, but he is not the Mordecai associated with the book of Esther. Nothing is known about Bilshan, Mispar (Mispereth in Nehemiah's list), Bigvai, Rehum (Nahum in Nehemiah's list), and Baanah. Zerubbabel, Bilshan, and Mordecai are Babylonian names, while Bigvai is of Persian provenance.[3]

---

1. Hayyim Angel, "The Literary Significance of the Name List in Ezra–Nehemiah," in *JBQ* 35/3 (2007), 146.
2. Williamson, 33.
3. Myers, 12.

II. Returnees identified by their name
or geographical location (2:2b-35)

2:2b-35 The number of the men of the people of Israel: [3]the sons of Parosh,[4] 2,172. [4]The sons of Shephatiah, 372. [5]The sons of Arah, 775. [6]The sons of Pahath-moab, namely the sons of Jeshua and Joab, 2,812. [7]The sons of Elam, 1,254. [8]The sons of Zattu, 945. [9]The sons of Zaccai,[5] 760. [10]The sons of Bani, 642. [11]The sons of Bebai, 623. [12]The sons of Azgad, 1,222. [13]The sons of Adonikam,[6] 666. [14]The sons of Bigvai, 2,056. [15]The sons of Adin, 454. [16]The sons of Ater,[7] namely of Hezekiah, 98. [17]The sons of Bezai, 323. [18]The sons of Jorah, 112. [19]The sons of Hashum, 223. [20]The sons of Gibbar, 95. [21]The sons of Bethlehem, 123. [22]The men of Netophah, 56. [23]The men of Anathoth, 128. [24]The sons of Azmaveth, 42. [25]The sons of Kiriath-arim,[8] Chephirah, and Beeroth, 743. [26]The sons of Ramah and Geba, 621. [27]The men of Michmas, 122. [28]The men of Bethel and Ai, 223. [29]The sons of Nebo, 52. [30]The sons of Magbish, 156. [31]The sons of the other Elam, 1,254. [32]The sons of Harim, 320. [33]The sons of Lod, Hadid, and Ono, 725. [34]The sons of Jericho, 345. [35]The sons of Senaah,[9] 3,630.

The people listed here appear with the formulas "sons of X" and "men of Y." In these verses, the sons of X are clearly identified by their family name. Some scholars actually translate *bᵉnê* as "the family of."[10] Pahath-Moab (v. 6) means the governor of Moab and it reflects a state of affairs developed during the united monarchy when Moab was

---

4. Parosh means "flea," and it might be a nickname.
5. Zaccai is an abbreviated form of Zechariah, and it means "Yahweh has remembered."
6. Adonikam means "The lord has risen up."
7. Ater means "left-handed," and it might be a nickname.
8. Since there is no town named Kiriath-arim in the vicinity of Gibeon, it seems that this is a scribal error where the actual town was Kiritah-jearim (as in Neh. 7:29). If not a scribal error, this could be an archaic way of writing the town name.
9. Mishna Taanith IV 5 (Tosephta Taanith 82) affirms that Senaah was an important clan belonging to the tribe of Benjamin. See, R. Zadok, "A Note on SN'H," in *VT* 38/4 (1988):483-486.
10. See Williamson, 21ff.

under Judean control. It is not clear why some people are identified by their personal name while others are identified by their geographical location. It is possible that those identified by their geographical location are the poor who did not own land or property.[11]

III. The priests (2:36-39)

> 2:36-39 The priests: the sons of Jedaiah, of the house of Jeshua, 973. [37]The sons of Immer, 1,052. [38]The sons of Pashhur, 1,247. [39]The sons of Harim, 1,017.

More priestly families returned from the exile than the four mentioned here; however, their number is significant because they make up about 10 percent of the total number of returnees. Williamson suggests that "in the postexilic period there is a steady development of the priestly hierarchy, a development attested to in various lists in the OT which culminated in the emergence of the system of twenty-four priestly courses."[12] Jedaiah, Pashhur, and Immer occur also in 1 Chronicles 9:10-13 and Nehemiah 11:10-14.

IV. The Levites (2:40-42)

> 2:40 The Levites: the sons of Jeshua and Kadmiel, of the sons of Hodaviah, 74.

The shortest list belongs to the Levites. Without the temple the Levites became a neglected group, forced to do other work. "Their disengagement is why a special appeal had to be made to them later to join in the task of rebuilding Jerusalem and its temple institutions (Ezra 8:15ff)."[13] It is notable that the Levites and the priests are recognized as being part of distinct classes.

> 2:41 The singers: the sons of Asaph, 128.

Since the singers have not yet attained Levitical status, they are also treated separately from the Levites. It could be that "they were appointed by the king for service in the

---

11. Williamson, 34.
12. Williamson, 35.
13. Myers, 18.

temple," and they "played by their own accompaniment (1 Chron. 15:16)."[14] Asaph was David's contemporary and he is credited with being the author of Psalms 50 and 73-83. While other musicians returned with Ezra later (7:7), only the Asaphites are mentioned here.

> 2:42 The sons of the gatekeepers: the sons
> of Shallum, the sons of Ater, the sons of
> Talmon, the sons of Akkub, the sons of
> Hatita, and the sons of Shobai, in all 139.

The initial group of gatekeepers is divided into six divisions, although more would come with Ezra (7:7). Blenkinsopp explains that "one of their principal functions was to protect the ritual purity of the temple precincts (2 Chron. 23:19), and some of them were in charge of the temple stores (1 Chron. 9:6-27)."[15] They play an important role in Nehemiah as they are frequently mentioned in the same context with the priests and Levites (Neh. 10:28; 12:47; 13:5).

V. The temple servants and the descandents of Solomon's servants (2:43-58)

> 2:43-58 The temple servants: the sons of Ziha, the
> sons of Hasupha, the sons of Tabbaoth, [44]the sons
> of Keros, the sons of Siaha, the sons of Padon, [45]the
> sons of Lebanah, the sons of Hagabah, the sons of
> Akkub, [46]the sons of Hagab,[16] the sons of Shamlai,
> the sons of Hanan, [47]the sons of Giddel,[17] the sons
> of Gahar, the sons of Reaiah, [48]the sons of Rezin, the
> sons of Nekoda, the sons of Gazzam, [49]the sons of
> Uzza, the sons of Paseah, the sons of Besai, [50]the sons
> of Asnah, the sons of Meunim, the sons of Nephisim,
> [51]the sons of Bakbuk,[18] the sons of Hakupha, the sons
> of Harhur, [52]the sons of Bazluth, the sons of Mehida,

---

14. Loring Batten, *A Critical and Exegetical Commentary on the Books of Ezra and Nehemiah*, ICC (Edinburgh: T & T Clark, 1961), 85.

15. Blenkinsopp, 89.

16. Hagab means "locust," or "grasshopper," and it might be a nickname.

17. Giddel is an abbreviated form of Giddeliah, and it means "Yahweh has made great."

18. Bakbuk means "flask," and it might be a nickname.

the sons of Harsha, [53]the sons of Barkos, the sons
of Sisera, the sons of Temah, [54]the sons of Neziah,
and the sons of Hatipha. [55]The sons of Solomon's
servants: the sons of Sotai, the sons of Hassophereth,
the sons of Peruda, [56]the sons of Jaalah, the sons of
Darkon, the sons of Giddel, [57]the sons of Shephatiah,
the sons of Hattil, the sons of Pochereth-hazzebaim,
and the sons of Ami. [58]All the temple servants
and the sons of Solomon's servants were 392.

While the temple servants were not slaves, many of them were
of non-Israelite background. Blenkinsopp proposes that some
of the names are of Egyptian, Arabian, Babylonian, Edomite,
and Ugaritic descent.[19] Batten suggests that these servants
"were subordinate temple officers, performing the humblest
functions at the sanctuary."[20] It could be that many of them
"have come to Israel initially as prisoners of war, since these
are the names of tribes whom we know were defeated during
the period of the monarchy."[21] Their inclusion together with
the sons of Solomon's servants, however, further reveals that
they were not slaves, but rather servants.

VI. Returnees without a family record (2:59-63)

2:59-63 The following were those who came up from
Tel-melah, Tel-harsha, Cherub, Addan, and Immer,
though they could not prove their fathers' houses or
their descent, whether they belonged to Israel: [60]the
sons of Delaiah, the sons of Tobiah, and the sons
of Nekoda, 652. [61]Also, of the sons of the priests:
the sons of Habaiah, the sons of Hakkoz,[22] and the
sons of Barzillai[23] (who had taken a wife from the
daughters of Barzillai the Gileadite, and was called by
their name). [62]These sought their registration among
those enrolled in the genealogies, but they were not
found there, and so they were excluded from the

---

19. Blenkinsopp, 91.
20. Batten, 87.
21. Williamson, 36.
22. Hakkoz means "the thorn," and it could be a nickname.
23. Barzillai means "man of iron," and it could be a nickname.

priesthood as unclean. [63]The governor told them they were not to partake of the most holy food until there should be a priest to consult Urim and Thummim.

While most Jews kept their family records intact, some did not. Some of these were proselytes since they could not even prove that "they belonged to Israel" (2:29b). These are only identified with their Babylonian towns from which they came, although the location of those towns is unknown. The concern for purity was dominant, which is why verse 62 explains that these "unclean" ones were excluded from the priesthood. Olyan affirms that "lineage defilement is passed on from generation to generation, apparently disqualifying all males in the polluted line from priestly service."[24] The title "governor" is a translation of the Persian word *hattiršāṭā* used for Nehemiah (Neh. 7:65, 69; 8:9; 10:2). Here, the governor is not named, although some assume that it could be Sheshbazzar or Zerubbabel.[25] Williamson explains that,

> Urim and Thummim were sacred lots from which answers to direct questions could be received. They could have been two small objects, such as pebbles or sticks, which were marked in some way and which were drawn out of the Ephod to give, according to the combinations, a "yes," "no" or "no answer" response.[26]

VII. Statistics and settlement (2:64-67)

2:64-67 The whole assembly together was 42,360, [65]besides their male and female servants, of whom there were 7,337, and they had 200 male and female singers. [66]Their horses were 736, their mules were 245, [67]their camels were 435, and their donkeys were 6,720.

The total given in verse 64 is about 11,000 higher than the sum of the preceding numbers. The discrepancy could be explained by the fact that their women were included in the total number. While this seems like a small number

---

24. Saul M. Olyan, "Purity Ideology in Ezra–Nehemiah as a Tool to Reconstitute the Community," in JSJ 35/1 (2004):9.
25. 1 Esdras 9:49 names Nehemiah as the governor; Myers identifies him as Zerubbabel (20); Williamson suggests that both Sheshbazzar and Zerubbabel are likely candidates (37).
26. Williamson, 37.

compared with the total, it is feasible that the majority of the returnees were young, unmarried men. The animals listed here were used both for travel and burden.

> 2:68-70 Some of the heads of families, when they came to the house of the LORD that is in Jerusalem, made freewill offerings for the house of God, to erect it on its site. [69]According to their ability they gave to the treasury of the work 61,000 darics of gold, 5,000 minas of silver, and 100 priests' garments. [70]Now the priests, the Levites, some of the people, the singers, the gatekeepers, and the temple servants lived in their towns, and all the rest of Israel in their towns.

Verse 68 reveals that the temple was not yet rebuilt, thus the need for the freewill offerings. Their giving "according to their ability," reminds us of Jesus' words to the woman who poured out the ointment of pure nard upon His head, "She has done what she could" (Mark 14:8). God never asks us to do more than we can, but what we can do, we should do. Even though the repatriated community was poor, the amount of money they raised is estimated at around $238,000.[27]

Table 4: Comparison between the Ezra 2 and Nehemiah 7 lists of returnees

Name	Ezra 2	Nehemiah 7
Zerubbabel	x	x
Jeshua	x	x
Nehemiah	x	x
Seraiah[1]	x	-
Reelaiah[2]	x	-
Mordecai	x	x
Bilshan	x	x
Mispar	x	x
Bigvai	x	x
Rehum[3]	x	-
Baanah	x	x
Parosh	x	x
Shephatiah	x	x
Arah	x	x
Pahath-moab	x	x

27. Myers, 21.

Name	Ezra 2	Nehemiah 7
Jeshua	x	x
Joab	x	x
Elam	x	x
Zattu	x	x
Zaccai	x	x
Bani	x	x
Bebai	x	x
Azgad	x	x
Adonikam	x	x
Bigvai	x	x
Adin	x	x
Ater	x	x
Bezai	x	x
Jorah	x	-
Hashum	x	x
Gibbar[4]	x	-
Azmaveth[5]	x	-
Kiriath-arim	x	-
Chephirah	x	x
Beeroth	x	x
Ramah	x	x
Geba	x	x
Michmas	x	x
Nebo	x	x
Magbish	x	-
(the other) Elam	x	x
Harim	x	x
Lod	x	x
Hadid	x	x
Ono	x	x
Jericho	x	x
Senaah	x	x
Priests		
Jedaiah	x	x
Jeshua	x	x
Immer	x	x
Pashhur	x	x
Harim	x	x
Levites		
Jeshua	x	x
Kadmiel	x	x
Hodaviah[6]	x	-

Name	Ezra 2	Nehemiah 7
Singers		
Asaph	x	x
Shallum	x	x
Ater	x	x
Talmon	x	x
Akkub	x	x
Hatita	x	x
Shobai	x	x
Temple Servants		
Ziha	x	x
Hasupha	x	x
Tabbaoth	x	x
Keros	x	x
Siaha[7]	x	-
Padon	x	x
Lebanah	x	-
Hagabah	x	-
Akkub	x	x
Hagab	x	-
Shamlai[8]	x	-
Hanan	x	x
Giddel	x	x
Gahar	x	x
Reaiah	x	x
Rezin	x	x
Nekoda	x	x
Gazzam	x	x
Uzza	x	x
Paseah	x	x
Besai	x	x
Asnah	x	-
Meunim	x	x
Nephisim[9]	x	-
Bakbuk	x	x
Hakupha	x	x
Harhur	x	x
Bazluth[10]	x	-
Mehida	x	x
Harsha	x	x
Barkos	x	x
Sisera	x	x

Name	Ezra 2	Nehemiah 7
Temah	x	x
Neziah	x	x
Hatipha	x	x
The Songs of Solomon's Servants		
Sotai	x	x
Hassophereth	x	-
Peruda[11]	x	-
Jaalah	x	-
Darkon	x	x
Giddel	x	x
Shephatiah	x	x
Hattil	x	x
Pochereth-hazzebaim	x	x
Ami[12]	x	-
Those Without Family Records		
Delaiah	x	x
Tobiah	x	x
Nekoda	x	x

Table 4 Notes:
1. Mentioned in Nehemiah 10:2 as one who signed the covenant.
2. Nehemiah 7:7 has Raamiah.
3. Mentioned in Nehemiah 10:25 as one who signed the covenant.
4. Nehemiah 7:25 has the place-name Gibeon. The text of Ezra is to be preferred because of the "sons of" formula.
5. Nehemiah 12:29 has Azmaveth as a geographical location.
6. Listed among the descendants of David and Solomon in 1 Chronicles 3:24 and among the returnees from exile in 1 Chronicles 9:7.
7. Nehemiah 7:47 has Sia.
8. Nehemiah 7:48 has Shalmai.
9. Nehemiah 7:52 has Nephushesim.
10. Nehemiah 7:54 has Bazlith.
11. Nehemiah 7:57 has Perida.
12. Nehemiah 7:59 has Amon.

The lists of returnees remind us of God's faithfulness in keeping His promises. Through Jeremiah God foretold that the exile would last 70 years. The return from the Babylonian exile is not an abstract concept, but can be seen in the faces of those who return. Just as there is a God behind the return promise, so there are people who are named and seen as the face of the return fulfillment. Today's Christian leader must always be mindful of God's faithfulness, but also that the people whom we serve have names and faces. We are not called to serve numbers but needy people. We are not called to minister to statistics but to saints.

Ezra 3

I. Sacrifices to God: the foundation of worship (3:1-6)

> 3:1 When the seventh month came, and the
> children of Israel were in the towns, the
> people gathered as one man to Jerusalem.

The seventh month in the Jewish calendar is the month of Tishri (September/October). This reference probably refers to the seventh month that the Jews have been returned from exile. Most scholars agree that the year is 537 BC.[1] It took the Jews about seven months to settle back into the land and now they are ready to reinstitute the sacrificial system. The fact that they come "as one man" points to their unity of heart and purpose.

---

1 Fensham, *Ezra and Nehemiah,* 59; Blenkinsopp, *Ezra–Nehemiah,* 74; Wilhelm Rudolph, *Esra und Nehemia,* HAT 20 (Tübingen: J.C.B. Mohr, 1949), 29.

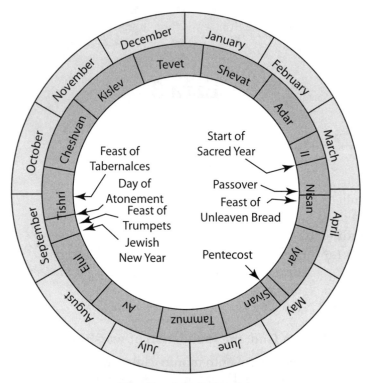

The Jewish Calendar

3:2 Then arose Jeshua the son of Jozadak, with his
fellow priests, and Zerubbabel the son of Shealtiel
with his kinsmen, and they built the altar of the
God of Israel, to offer burnt offerings on it, as it
is written in the Law of Moses the man of God.

Jeshua the son of Jozadak[2] is mentioned along with Zerubbabel
by the prophet Haggai (1:1), but by this time he has become high
priest.[3] Jeshua and Zerubbabel appear together throughout
Ezra and Nehemiah (Ezra 2:2; 3:2, 8; 4:3; 5:2; Neh. 7:7; 12:1) and
in the book of Haggai (1:1, 12, 14; 2:2, 4).[4]

---

2. Jozadak means "Yahweh has acted rightly."
3. In Haggai and Zechariah the high priest's name is spelled יְהוֹשֻׁעַ, while in
    Ezra–Nehemiah it is spelled יֵשׁוּעַ.
4. Zechariah 3 has Joshua as a key character while Zerubbabel plays an
    important role in Zechariah 4.

The returnees understand the importance of worship through sacrifices, and this leads them to build the altar as their first priority. Indeed, God spoke through Moses regarding the importance of bringing burnt offerings.[5] Bernhard W. Anderson notes that "one of the most important items in the baggage that Ezra brought from Babylonia was a copy of the book of the Law of Moses."[6] The fact that a written Law of Moses existed at this time contradicts Wellhausen's documentary hypothesis (JEDP) which suggests that a redactor combined all the sources together in the late fifth century.[7] It was the people's departure from the Law of Moses that resulted in their exile. Now, their desire to obey the Law to the smallest detail indicates their understanding of the correlation between disobedience and judgment, obedience and blessing.

> 3:3 They set the altar in its place, for fear was
> on them because of the peoples of the lands,
> and they offered burnt offerings on it to the
> Lord, burnt offerings morning and evening.

During the exilic period non-Jews settled in the land, and their presence now instills fear in the people of God. Later in Ezra and Nehemiah we see that these fears were justified because the Jews encounter much opposition from foreigners. These could include people from surrounding nations such as Ammon, Moab, Edom, Samaria, and Egypt.

---

5. In Leviticus 14:18-20 the Law was clear that the priest must bring a burnt offering in order to make atonement for the person healed of a skin disease. The verb "to atone for" can mean "to wipe away," "to purge," "to purify, or "to make atonement." As a result, he will be pronounced clean and thus forgiven, ready to confidently enter God's presence. The concept is important to the sacrificial theology of Leviticus because atonement will cleanse a person from all sins, known and unknown. The language employed affirms that physical impurity is purified while moral impurity must be forgiven. Sometimes, the expression burnt offering (Num. 15:3; Deut. 12:6; 1 Sam. 15:22; 2 Kings 5:17; Isa. 43:23) is a figure of speech called merism, and points to all sacrifices. The Law's intent was to ban all sacrifices offered to anyone else but Yahweh.
6. Quoted in H.L. Ellison, "The Importance of Ezra," in *EQ* 53/1 (1981), 49.
7. For some excellent arguments for an early date of the Pentateuch and against the JEDP hypothesis, see Kenneth A. Mathews, *Genesis 1-11:26*, NAC (Nashville: B & H, 2001), 71-81, and Allen P. Ross, *Creation and Blessing* (Grand Rapids: Baker, 1998), 24-36).

Ibn Ezra suggests that the people built the altar so that God "would aid them against their adversaries."[8] The altar is necessary for the people to bring burnt offerings both morning and evening. This daily morning and evening sacrifice consisted of a lamb prepared in flour and oil, with wine as the drink offering (Exod. 29:38-42; Num. 28:3-8).

> 3:4-6 And they kept the Feast of Booths, as it is written, and offered the daily burnt offerings by number according to the rule, as each day required, and [5]after that the regular burnt offerings, the offerings at the new moon and at all the appointed feasts of the LORD, and the offerings of everyone who made a freewill offering to the LORD. [6]From the first day of the seventh month they began to offer burnt offerings to the LORD. But the foundation of the temple of the LORD was not yet laid.

Along with the Passover and the Day of Atonement (Yom Kippur), the Feast of Booths or Tabernacles was one of the three most important religious celebrations for the Jews. The Festival of Booths began on Tishri 15 (September/October), and it was primarily a thanksgiving festival showing gratitude for God's provision (Exod. 34:22). It also commemorated the wilderness wandering, the booths (Succoth) being a reminder that the Israelites lived in tents during the forty-year commute from Egypt to the Promised Land (23:42-43). It was to Succoth that the Israelites first came after leaving Rameses (Exod. 12:7). The Feast of Booths was observed during the post-exilic period (2 Chron. 8:13; Ezra 3:4; Zech. 14:16, 18, 19) and during the early church period. This is the only festival wherein the Israelites were commanded to rejoice before the Lord (Lev. 23:40).

Ross explains that the freewill offering "was an offering that could be made any time. The soul of the worshipper might simply be overflowing with joy over God and his benefits. Such freewill offerings were (and are) the essence of a living faith."[9] It is easy to see how the returnees' feelings

---

8. Rosenberg, 126.
9. Allen P. Ross, *Holiness to the* LORD: *A Guide to the Exposition of the Book of Leviticus* (Grand Rapids: Baker, 2002), 182.

of gratitude translated into freewill offerings to the LORD. However, since the foundation of the Temple has not yet been laid, much more work remains to be done. After all, the temple had been central to Israel's worship and their understanding of God since Solomon first built it in 967 BC.

II. Bringing the very best: the materials for the temple (3:7)

> 3:7 So they gave money to the masons and
> the carpenters, and food, drink, and oil to the
> Sidonians and the Tyrians to bring cedar trees
> from Lebanon to the sea, to Joppa, according to the
> grant that they had from Cyrus king of Persia.

The preparation for rebuilding of the temple parallels the building of the original temple during the Solomonic era. Masons or stonecutters are employed (1 Chron. 22:2) along with carpenters (1 Chron. 22:15), and payment is made in quantities of food, drink, and oil (2 Chron. 2:10). Myers correctly points out that "no permission from Sidon and Tyre was required since it belonged to the king of Persia."[10] The wood from Lebanon has special meaning, always being used in special building projects and portrayed as superior in value.[11] Cyrus is credited not only with giving the edict which allowed the return of the Jews, but also with paying part of the expenses necessary for the temple's reconstruction.

III. Beginning to build (3:8-9)

> 3:8-9 Now in the second year after their coming
> to the house of God at Jerusalem, in the second
> month, Zerubbabel the son of Shealtiel and Jeshua
> the son of Jozadak made a beginning, together
> with the rest of their kinsmen, the priests and the
> Levites and all who had come to Jerusalem from
> the captivity. They appointed the Levites, from
> twenty years old and upward, to supervise the
> work of the house of the LORD. [9]And Jeshua with
> his sons and his brothers, and Kadmiel and his

---

10. Myers, *Ezra–Nehemiah*, 27.
11. 1 Kings 4:33; 5:6, 14; Psalm 92:12; Song of Songs 3:9; Isaiah 60:13; Ezekiel 31:16; Hosea 14:5.

sons, the sons of Judah, together supervised the
workmen in the house of God, along with the sons of
Henadad and the Levites, their sons and brothers.

The rebuilding of the temple starts in the second month
as did the building of Solomon's temple (1 Kings 6:1;
2 Chron. 3:2).[12] The leaders of the project are named here
as Zerubbabel and Jeshua. Sheshbazzar also played a role
(5:16), but either he played a lesser role because he was old,
or he died before the "second, successful attempt to build
the temple."[13] The Levites are appointed to supervise the
work, and the minimum qualifying age is set at twenty. In
the Pentateuch the minimum qualifying age is set at thirty
(Num. 4:3, 23, 30), but it seems that the age was lowered
here due to the smaller number of Levites that returned. It
could also be that the "range of functions associated with
the Levitical office increased."[14] The fact that both Yahweh
and Elohim were used for the divine name can be seen in
the fact that the "House of God (Elohim)" and "House of the
LORD (Yahweh)" are used interchangeably.

IV. Praising and giving thanks to the LORD (3:10-13)

3:10-11 And when the builders laid the foundation
of the temple of the LORD, the priests in their
vestments came forward with trumpets, and the
Levites, the sons of Asaph, with cymbals, to praise
the LORD, according to the directions of David king
of Israel. [11]And they sang responsively, praising
and giving thanks to the LORD, "For he is good,
for his steadfast love endures forever toward
Israel." And all the people shouted with a great
shout when they praised the LORD, because the
foundation of the house of the LORD was laid.

The focus here is not on the physical details of laying the
foundation, but rather on the joyous ceremony that accompanied it. The details closely parallel the dedication of

---

12. April–May was the beginning of the dry season, thus this would be the
proper time to start building.
13. Fensham, *Ezra and Nehemiah*, 63.
14. Blenkinsopp, *Ezra–Nehemiah*, 101.

Solomon's temple (2 Chron. 7:6). The trumpets used were not the ram's horns, but rather the long, straight, metal instruments used for the assembly call (Num. 10:2), alarm call (2 Chron. 13:12-14), and for celebrations (1 Chron. 16:6). The refrain "for His steadfast love endures forever" points to God's character and nature, and occurs several times in the Psalms, as well as in Chronicles (1 Chron. 16:34, 41; 2 Chron. 5:13; 7:3, 6; 20:21), and Jeremiah (33:11). The love of God (Hésed) is a reminder of God's covenantal love and now they are celebrating it through shouting and singing. God's covenantal love has been manifested not just in their return to the land, but now in the reestablishment of the temple worship.

Table 5: Parallels between 2 Chronicles 7 and Ezra 3

2 Chronicles 7:6	Ezra 3:10-11
The priests stood at their posts; **the Levites** also, with the *instruments* for music to the Lord that **King David** had made for giving thanks to the Lord — **for his steadfast love endures forever** — whenever David offered praises by their ministry; opposite them **the priests** sounded **trumpets**, and all Israel stood.	And when the builders laid the foundation of the temple of the Lord, **the priests** in their vestments came forward with **trumpets**, and **the Levites**, the sons of Asaph, with *cymbals*, to praise the Lord, according to the directions of **David king of Israel**. And they sang responsively, praising and giving thanks to the Lord, "For he is good, **for his steadfast love endures forever** toward Israel." And all the people shouted with a great shout when they praised the Lord, because the foundation of the house of the Lord was laid.

3:12-13 But many of the priests and Levites and heads of fathers' houses, old men who had seen the first house, wept with a loud voice when they saw the foundation of this house being laid, though many shouted aloud for joy, [13]so that the people could not distinguish the sound of the joyful shout from the sound of the people's weeping, for the people shouted with a great shout, and the sound was heard far away.

The prophet Haggai gives us insight into why some people were crying in the face of what seems to be good news. In Haggai 2:3 God is posing a series of questions, "Who is left among you who saw this house in its former glory? How do you see it now? Is it not as nothing in your eyes?" It seems that the older people who have seen the glory of Solomon's temple were bitterly disappointed even though the temple had not yet been rebuilt. The foundation alone told them that the rebuilt temple would not rise to the level of the original. It could be that the smaller stones used here did not compare with the huge blocks used in Solomon's temple.[15] The weeping of the older people clashed with the shouts of joy of those who saw the laying of the foundation not as a disappointment but as a great achievement.

The lessons of Ezra 3 are very important for today's Christian leader. Worship as our response to God's grace and mercy towards us needs to be expressed by bringing our best. While the returning community during the time of Ezra brought dead sacrifices (as the Law required), we are asked to bring ourselves as living sacrifices. According to the apostle Paul, this will be our spiritual worship which will be acceptable to God (Rom. 12:1-2). Besides bringing ourselves as living sacrifices, singing praises to God is also part of our response to God in worship. Music then, is not about us, is not about style, but it should always be about Him, the God whom we worship. To this end, contemporary composers and writers have correctly identified God as "our audience of One."

---

15. Fensham, *Ezra and Nehemiah*, 65.

Ezra 4

Outline

I. 4:1-3 The source of the opposition[1] (4:1-3)

> 4:1-2 Now when the adversaries of Judah and Benjamin heard that the returned exiles were building a temple to the Lord, the God of Israel, [2]they approached Zerubbabel and the heads of fathers' houses and said to them, "Let us build with you, for we worship your God as you do, and we have been sacrificing to him ever since the days of Esarhaddon king of Assyria who brought us here."

The adversaries identify themselves as those who were brought to Israel by Esarhaddon, king of Assyria, the youngest son of Sennacherib.[2] Esarhaddon ruled Assyria from 681-669 BC and repopulated the land after many were taken into exile. Such repopulations were not so unusual

---

1. There seems to be a repeated pattern in chapters 4 and 5: Encounter (4:1-5; 5:1-5), Request (4:6-16; 5:6-17), Decree (4:17-22; 5:1-12), and Enactment (4:23-24; 5:13-15). See Stefan C. Matzal, "The Structure of Ezra IV-VI," in *VT* 50/4 (2000): 566-568.
2. 2 Kings 19:37 and Isaiah 37:38 recount the assassination of Sennacherib and the beginning of the reign of Esarhaddon.

since other Assyrian kings such as Sargon II (722-705 BC) and Ashurbanipal (669-633 BC) did it during their respective reigns. The request of the adversaries seems innocent, "Let us build with you," and seems to have the right motivation, "for we worship your God as you do." The adversaries suggest that they are converts to Judaism since they have been worshipping Yahweh since arriving in the land. However, the Chronicler clarifies that these adversaries were not monotheistic, but rather syncretistic in their worship, "So they feared the LORD but also served their own gods, after the manner of the nations from among whom they had been carried away" (2 Kings 17:33). Batten suggests that the adversaries are Samaritans,[3] although many scholars reject that hypothesis, calling it anachronistic.[4]

> 4:3 But Zerubbabel, Jeshua, and the rest of the heads of fathers' houses in Israel said to them, "You have nothing to do with us in building a house to our God; but we alone will build to the LORD, the God of Israel, as King Cyrus the king of Persia has commanded us."

In today's world, the leaders would certainly be called exclusivists, and probably culturally insensitive as well. However, it is important to note that they were concerned with the purity of the people and not concerned about their popularity index. The leaders were expected "to maintain the integrity of the Jewish community" and thus continue God's "plan of redemption."[5] They also make reference to Cyrus' edict (1:2-4), thus giving their adversaries both a spiritual and a political reason for not accepting their help.

II. The persistence of the opposition (4:4-5)

> 4:4-5 Then the people of the land discouraged the people of Judah and made them afraid to build [5]and bribed counselors against them to frustrate their purpose, all the days of Cyrus king of Persia, even until the reign of Darius king of Persia.

---

3. Batten, *Ezra and Nehemiah*, 127.
4. See Williamson, *Ezra/Nehemiah*, 49; Blenkisopp, *Ezra–Nehemiah*, 107.
5. Brenemen, *Ezra, Nehemiah, Esther*, 97.

The opposition's first weapon is discouragement, which then led to fear. This fear was supposed to paralyze the people of God, and in some respects it did, but only for a while (4:24). Corruption was alive and well even then, and the opposition found corrupt counselors to carry out their plan. Blenkinsopp suggests that these counselors were "officials in the imperial bureaucracy."[6] The people of God had a divinely appointed purpose which the opposition tried to frustrate. We are reminded that opposition is not necessarily a sign that we're doing something wrong, but it can be a sign that we're doing something right. The Chronicler shows the opposition as being constant and continuing throughout Cyrus' reign (559-530 BC), until the reign of Darius (522-486 BC).

III. The many faces of opposition (4:6-22)

> 4:6 And in the reign of Ahasuerus, in the beginning
> of his reign, they wrote an accusation against
> the inhabitants of Judah and Jerusalem.

While verses 5 and 24 relate information from the reign of Darius, verses 6-23 are from later times, namely, the reigns of Xerxes (486-465 BC) and Artaxerxes I (465-424 BC). It is clear that the main concern of the author is not to give us a chronological line of events, but rather he wants to stress the theme of persistent opposition that spanned more than a century. The adversaries take the political route of addressing their grievance to the king himself. Ahasuerus is identified with Xerxes, although we are not told the content of the letter addressed to the king. Rabbinic tradition asserts that the adversaries ask the king to stop the work of rebuilding the temple.[7]

> 4:7 In the days of Artaxerxes, Bishlam and
> Mithredath and Tabeel and the rest of their
> associates wrote to Artaxerxes king of Persia. The
> letter was written in Aramaic and translated.

---

6. Blenkinsopp, *Ezra–Nehemiah*, 108.
7. Rosenberg, *Daniel, Ezra, Nehemiah*, 131.

Ezra 4:8-6:18 is written in Aramaic, the "diplomatic lingua franca of the Persian empire, and translated into Persian."[8] The Hebrew employed suggests that Bishlam "was the leader of the group – the group of archivists whose report is the source of the Aramaic letters in Ezra 4:8-6:12."[9]

4:8-16 Rehum the commander and Shimshai the scribe wrote a letter against Jerusalem to Artaxerxes the king as follows: [9]Rehum the commander, Shimshai the scribe, and the rest of their associates, the judges, the governors, the officials, the Persians, the men of Erech, the Babylonians, the men of Susa, that is, the Elamites, [10]and the rest of the nations whom the great and noble Osnappar deported and settled in the cities of Samaria and in the rest of the province Beyond the River. [11](This is a copy of the letter that they sent.) "To Artaxerxes the king: Your servants, the men of the province Beyond the River, send greeting. And now [12]be it known to the king that the Jews who came up from you to us have gone to Jerusalem. They are rebuilding that rebellious and wicked city. They are finishing the walls and repairing the foundations. [13]Now be it known to the king that if this city is rebuilt and the walls finished, they will not pay tribute, custom, or toll, and the royal revenue will be impaired. [14]Now because we eat the salt of the palace and it is not fitting for us to witness the king's dishonor, therefore we send and inform the king, [15]in order that search may be made in the book of the records of your fathers. You will find in the book of the records and learn that this city is a rebellious city, hurtful to kings and provinces, and that sedition was stirred up in it from of old. That was why this city was laid waste. [16]We make known to the king that if this city is rebuilt and its walls finished, you will then have no possession in the province Beyond the River."

---

8. Blenkinsopp, *Ezra–Nehemiah*, 112.
9. Richard C. Steiner, "Why Bishlam (Ezra 4:7) Cannot Rest 'In Peace': On the Aramaic and Hebrew Sound Changes that Conspired to Blot Out the Remembrance of Bel-Shalam the Archivist," in *JBL* 126/2 (2007), 401.

Those who address Artaxerxes are identified not as lower class citizens, but rather scribes, commanders, judges, governors, and officials who were foreigners deported to Judah by Osnappar, who is probably Asshurbanipal (668-627 BC). The opposition's hatred is evident in their referral to Jerusalem as "that rebellious and wicked city." The adversaries suggest that the future looks bleak for the Persian court if Jerusalem is rebuilt. They imply that the Jews will then stop paying their taxes and the royal bank of Persia will thus be depleted of funds. Yamauchi indicates that the tax "has been estimated that between \$20 million and \$35 million in taxes were collected annually by the Persian king."[10]

King of Assyria Esarhaddon
(681-669 BC)

Artaxerxes I (465-424 BC)

4:17-22 The king sent an answer: "To Rehum the commander and Shimshai the scribe and the rest of their associates who live in Samaria and in the rest of the province Beyond the River, greeting. And now [18]the letter that you sent to us has been plainly read before me. [19]And I made a decree, and search has been made, and it has been found that this city from of old has risen against kings, and that rebellion and sedition have been made in it. [20]And mighty kings have been over Jerusalem, who ruled

---

10. Edwin Yamauchi, "Archaeological Backgrounds of the Exilic and Postexilic Era, part 3: The Archaeological Background of Ezra," *BSac*137/547 (1980), 201.

over the whole province Beyond the River, to whom
tribute, custom, and toll were paid. [21]Therefore make
a decree that these men be made to cease, and that
this city be not rebuilt, until a decree is made by me.
[22]And take care not to be slack in this matter. Why
should damage grow to the hurt of the king?"

The king's research revealed that indeed Judah's kings had
a history of revolt. It could be that Hezekiah's revolt against
the Assyrian king Sennacherib was chronicled (2 Kings 18:7).
However, there had also been other kings who rebelled against
their oppressors. Both Jehoiakim and Zedekiah rebelled against
Nebuchadnezzar (2 Kings 24:1, 20), and both suffered the
consequences. The adversaries' letter was deemed credible and
the king's decree—motivated by personal reasons—was clear;
the work was to stop and it had to stop immediately.

IV. The consequences of opposition (4:23-24)

4:23-24 Then, when the copy of King Artaxerxes'
letter was read before Rehum and Shimshai the
scribe and their associates, they went in haste to the
Jews at Jerusalem and by force and power made
them cease. [24]Then the work on the house of God
that is in Jerusalem stopped, and it ceased until the
second year of the reign of Darius king of Persia.

The narrative switches from the time of Artaxerxes (465-
424/3) back to the time of Darius (522-486). This is "the first
chronological anomaly that occurs in the book of Ezra…To
this point the narrative has followed a strictly chronological
line despite the numerous gaps left in the history."[11] Ezra
tells the story out of order to remind the reader that, in
spite of opposition, King Darius supported the work of
reconstruction. Indeed, under Darius "the Persian Empire
reached its greatest power and splendor."[12]

Israel's enemies carried out King Artaxerxes' ruling "in
haste" and used force to bring to a standstill their work of
reconstruction. Verse 24 goes with verse 5, with verses 6-23 as

---

11. A. Philip Brown II, "Chronological Anomalies in the Book of Ezra," in
    BSac 162/645 (2005), 38.
12. Brenemen, Ezra, Nehemiah, Esther, 106.

parenthetical. Fensham concurs that Chapter 4 "is not meant to be in chronological sequence; rather, it supplies us with a logical thought pattern wherein the most important actions of the Samaritans against the Jews are enumerated." Darius I ruled Persia from 522 until 486 BC and under his rule "the Persian Empire reached its greatest power and splendor." The condition of the city wall at this stage is the condition of which Nehemiah hears (Neh. 1:3). Even though the adversaries won this battle, they will eventually lose the war since the wall will be reconstructed in spite of persistent, malevolent opposition.

Opposition to God's work did not originate, nor did it cease with Ezra and Nehemiah. While this opposition was accompanied by lies, pressures, and persecutions, God's work succeeded because it was of God and not of man. This truth should be a great comfort and encouragement to Christians in all times and all places when confronted with opposition to God's work. Even so, today's Christian leaders should always be on guard, being ready to deal with opposition, being mindful that the Christian does not spend his/her life on a playground, but rather on a battlefield.

The tomb of Darius I at Persepolis

Ezra 5

Outline

I. The rebuilding of the temple starts again (5:1-2)

5:1-2 Now the prophets, Haggai and Zechariah
the son of Iddo, prophesied to the Jews who
were in Judah and Jerusalem, in the name of
the God of Israel who was over them. ²Then
Zerubbabel the son of Shealtiel and Jeshua the son
of Jozadak arose and began to rebuild the house
of God that is in Jerusalem, and the prophets
of God were with them, supporting them.

After sixteen years of the reconstruction work being at a
standstill, it is the Word of the Lord that jumpstarts the
process anew. The prophetic office did not die during the
Babylonian exile and God's prophets did not become extinct.
A prophet was an intermediary who communicated God's
message to His people, and during this time of crisis God
uses Haggai and Zechariah to reinvigorate His people. The
book of Haggai focuses on the necessity of rebuilding the
temple while Zechariah focuses on God's sovereignty and
human responsibility. Both Haggai and Zechariah speak "in
the name of the God of Israel" who was "over them." God
was over both the prophets and the people, and believing

that He is sovereignly in control gives the leaders incentive to resume the work of rebuilding. Zerubbabel is identified as "governor of Judah" by Haggai, and he plays an important role both in Ezra and Nehemiah. Jeshua (Joshua) is identified by Haggai as a high priest, so Zerubbabel and Jeshua served both as civic and spiritual leaders.[1] The prophets continue to offer support to the leaders and the people as the rebuilding continues – both spiritual and material help – illustrating the concept of teamwork being characteristic of doing God's work.

II. The rebuilding of the temple is challenged again (5:3-5)

> 5:3-5 At the same time Tattenai the governor of the province Beyond the River and Shethar-bozenai and their associates came to them and spoke to them thus, "Who gave you a decree to build this house and to finish this structure?" [4]They also asked them this: "What are the names of the men who are building this building?" [5]But the eye of their God was on the elders of the Jews, and they did not stop them until the report should reach Darius and then an answer be returned by letter concerning it.

Tattenai appears as "governor of across the river" in a Babylonian document dating back to June 5, 502 BC[2] As representative of the Persian Empire he wanted to make sure that the Jews are not revolting against the establishment. Furthermore, he asks a most logical question, "Who is in charge here?" Unlike previous times, the work is not stopped, the clear reason being that "the eye of their God was on the elders of the Jews." When something is "under the eye of God" in the Old Testament, it is under His watch.[3] Thus, what gives the people of God success is not their skill but God's protection and providence.

---

1. Haggai 1:1. Some people assume that Zerubbabel is not mentioned again because he was removed from office due to seditious activity, but that *argumentum e silentio* is pure conjecture.
2. Myers, *Ezra/Nehemiah*, 44.
3. Judges 18:6; Psalm 33:18; Zechariah 9:1.

III. The rebuilding of the temple is
reported to Darius (5:6-17)

> 5:6-10 This is a copy of the letter that Tattenai the
> governor of the province Beyond the River and
> Shethar-bozenai and his associates the governors
> who were in the province Beyond the River sent to
> Darius the king. [7]They sent him a report, in which
> was written as follows: "To Darius the king, all
> peace. [8]Be it known to the king that we went to the
> province of Judah, to the house of the great God. It
> is being built with huge stones, and timber is laid in
> the walls. This work goes on diligently and prospers
> in their hands. [9]Then we asked those elders and
> spoke to them thus, 'Who gave you a decree to build
> this house and to finish this structure?' [10]We also
> asked them their names, for your information, that
> we might write down the names of their leaders.

Tattenai and the other officials were "imperial trouble-
shooters, armed with powers of punishment."[4] They were
considered the king's eyes and ears and were part of the
king's elaborate spying system. The region "Beyond the
River" is the Trans-Euphrates region, west of the Euphrates
River that included Israel.[5] The report includes (1) an evalu-
ation of the construction, (2) a conversation with the Jewish
leaders regarding the construction, and (3) a request of
inquiry into the historical archives regarding the decree of
Cyrus the Great. It is fascinating that these officials refer to
the Jerusalem temple as "the house of the great God."[6] Have
they concluded that Yahweh is indeed a great God, or are
they just offering "a token of reverence for the God of this
territory?"[7] It is certain though that these officials recognize
that the Jews are diligent in their work, and moreover, that

---

4. David J.A. Clines, *Ezra, Nehemiah, Esther*, NCB (Grand Rapids: Eerdmans, 1984), 85-86.

5. Outside of Ezra–Nehemiah, the expression "Beyond the River" also occurs in Joshua 24:3, 14-15 and Isaiah 7:20.

6. The phrase can also be translated "the great house of God" but it would be unlikely that these Persians would be monotheists worshipping the One True God, Yahweh.

7. Fensham, *Ezra and Nehemiah*, 82.

the work is prospering. Even so, Tattenai and the other officials want to know whether the Jews have the proverbial work permit, and also the names of their leaders. It could be that Tattenai was impressed with the massive structure and thought it looked "more like a fortress than a sanctuary!"[8]

> 5:11-12 And this was their reply to us: 'We are the servants of the God of heaven and earth, and we are rebuilding the house that was built many years ago, which a great king of Israel built and finished. [12]But because our fathers had angered the God of heaven, he gave them into the hand of Nebuchadnezzar king of Babylon, the Chaldean, who destroyed this house and carried away the people to Babylonia.

The Jews introduce themselves as "the servants of the God of heaven and earth," thus exalting God as the Creator God, a notion that was novel to the Persians who worshipped Zarathustra. The Jews give Tattenai a compressed history lesson dating back to Solomon, who is declared "a great king of Israel." Their historical account is complete in the sense that it does not omit the sins of the people which caused their loss of country and temple. Breneman correctly points out that "the Jews, understanding the theological reasons for their calamity, did not hesitate to tell their neighbors why they had suffered that exile."[9]

> 5:13-17 However, in the first year of Cyrus king of Babylon, Cyrus the king made a decree that this house of God should be rebuilt. [14]And the gold and silver vessels of the house of God, which Nebuchadnezzar had taken out of the temple that was in Jerusalem and brought into the temple of Babylon, these Cyrus the king took out of the temple of Babylon, and they were delivered to one whose name was Sheshbazzar, whom he had made governor; [15]and he said to him, "Take these vessels, go and put them in the temple that is in Jerusalem, and let the house of God be rebuilt on its site." [16]Then this Sheshbazzar

---

8. Warren Wiersbe, *The Bible Exposition Commentary: History* (Colorado Springs: Victor, 2003), 614.
9. Breneman, *Ezra, Nehemiah*, Esther, 111.

came and laid the foundations of the house of God
that is in Jerusalem, and from that time until now
it has been in building, and it is not yet finished.'
[17]Therefore, if it seems good to the king, let search
be made in the royal archives there in Babylon, to
see whether a decree was issued by Cyrus the king
for the rebuilding of this house of God in Jerusalem.
And let the king send us his pleasure in this matter."

Ten times in the Old Testament Cyrus is called "king of
Persia," yet here he is presented as "king of Babylon."
Indeed, on the Cyrus cylinder are the following words, "I am
Cyrus, king of the world, great king, legitimate king, king
of Babylon, king of Sumer and Akkad."[10] Since the Persians
have defeated the Babylonians, Cyrus became also the king
of Babylon when it became a part of the Persian Empire.

Tattenai's letter to Darius relates the Jews' account of Cyrus'
edict (1:1-4), the return of the vessels taken from the temple,
and the appointment of Sheshbazzar as governor (1:8, 11) (an
appointment which affirms that during this time "governing
authority was separated from religious authority").[11]
However, even though Sheshbazzar started the work on the
foundation of the temple, it was Zerubbabel who completed
it (3:10). A period of sixteen years has passed between the
original attempt to rebuild in 536 BC and the resumption of the
work under Darius in 520 BC Since a regime change has taken
place, Tattenai advises Darius to check the historical records
and verify the authenticity of Cyrus' decree. Williamson
suggests that "the formula 'if it pleases X' is another standard
feature in official Aramaic epistolography."[12]

Since the temple was the symbol of God's presence with
His people, it had to play a crucial role in the life of the
Israelites. Even though the church building has not replaced
the temple, the principle of the importance of God's presence
remains. While human obstacles are ever present, Christ's
followers need always to seek and rely on God's presence,
which is one's source of strength and solace.

---

10. *ANET*, 316.
11. Sean E. McEvenue, "The Political Structure in Judah from Cyrus to
    Nehemiah," in CBQ 43 (1981): 353.
12. Williamson, *Ezra, Nehemiah*, 80.

Ezra 6

Outline

I. God moves the heart of the King (6:1-12)

6:1-12 Then Darius the king made a decree, and search was made in Babylonia, in the house of the archives where the documents were stored. ²And in Ecbatana, the capital that is in the province of Media, a scroll was found on which this was written: "A record. ³In the first year of Cyrus the king, Cyrus the king issued a decree: Concerning the house of God at Jerusalem, let the house be rebuilt, the place where sacrifices were offered, and let its foundations be retained. Its height shall be sixty cubits and its breadth sixty cubits, ⁴with three layers of great stones and one layer of timber. Let the cost be paid from the royal treasury. ⁵And also let the gold and silver vessels of the house of God, which Nebuchadnezzar took out of the temple that is in Jerusalem and brought to Babylon, be restored and brought back to the temple that is in Jerusalem, each to its place. You shall put them in the house of God." ⁶"Now therefore, Tattenai, governor of the province Beyond the River, Shethar-bozenai, and your associates the

governors who are in the province Beyond the River,
keep away. [7]Let the work on this house of God alone.
Let the governor of the Jews and the elders of the
Jews rebuild this house of God on its site. [8]Moreover,
I make a decree regarding what you shall do for
these elders of the Jews for the rebuilding of this
house of God. The cost is to be paid to these men
in full and without delay from the royal revenue,
the tribute of the province from Beyond the River.
[9]And whatever is needed—bulls, rams, or sheep for
burnt offerings to the God of heaven, wheat, salt,
wine, or oil, as the priests at Jerusalem require—
let that be given to them day by day without fail,
[10]that they may offer pleasing sacrifices to the God
of heaven and pray for the life of the king and his
sons. [11]Also I make a decree that if anyone alters
this edict, a beam shall be pulled out of his house,
and he shall be impaled on it, and his house shall be
made a dunghill. [12]May the God who has caused his
name to dwell there overthrow any king or people
who shall put out a hand to alter this, or to destroy
this house of God that is in Jerusalem. I Darius
make a decree; let it be done with all diligence."

Towering at 1,800 meters, Ecbatana (Hegmataneh) was a key
city during the Achaemenid dynasty and served as summer
residence for the Persian court.[1] Persian kings would
usually reside in Babylon during the winter, in Susa during
the spring, and in Ecbatana during the summer. The fact
that Cyrus' edict was found on a scroll suggests that Persian
records were kept on royal parchments.[2] Indeed, the less
oppressive climate of Ecbatana would be more conducive to
the preservation of parchments. The written record agrees
with Cyrus' edict found in Ezra 1, and it also gives the
details regarding the size of the temple. If this temple had
been built according to this edict (60 mult 60), it would have

---

1. Lindsay Allen, *The Persian Empire* (Chicago: UCP, 2005), 62.
2. Roland de Vaux, *The Bible and the Ancient Near East* (Garden City:
   Doubleday, 1971), 90.

been larger than Solomon's temple (60 mult 20 mult 30),[3] but we know that, in reality, the rebuilt temple was smaller than Solomon's temple.[4] Cyrus' allotment of funds for the reconstruction surely points to God's providence in caring for His people. After all, "The earth is the LORD's and the fullness thereof, the world and those who dwell therein."[5]

Darius' instructions are directed to Tattenai, the very governor who initiated the correspondence with the king. "Keep away," is short, clear, and to the point, but it is much more than that. Rundgren suggests that it is a technical, legal term that basically means "accusation rejected."[6] Not only is Tattenai to allow the reconstruction of the temple, but this must be done "on its site." Fensham clarifies that this was not unusual since the Ancient Near East civilizations practiced the rebuilding of their sanctuaries precisely on the site where the previous buildings stood.[7] The Persians' recognition of Zerubbabel as governor shows that the Jews were allowed some degree of self-governance.

Darius' reply includes two further decrees which facilitate the rebuilding process. The first decree portrays Darius as a generous king who is concerned with the welfare of the Jewish leadership. Darius also wants to ensure the correct practice of the cult, thus he orders that the Jews be provided animals and food necessary for "pleasing sacrifices."[8] Bulls, rams, and sheep were necessary for burnt offerings, while wheat, salt, wine, and oil were needed for different types of meal offerings. Although Darius was probably not worshipping Yahweh, he was hoping that these decrees would prompt the Jews to pray to Yahweh on behalf of himself and his family.

Darius' determination to see that his edict is taken seriously and carried out fully is seen in the severity of punishment for those who so much as alter his edict. The

---

3. 1 Kings 6:2.
4. Haggai 2:3.
5. Psalm 24:1.
6. F. Rundgren, "Über einen juristichen Terminus bei Esra 6:6," *ZAW* 70 (1958): 213.
7. Fensham, *Ezra and Nehemiah*, 89.
8. Darius' generosity and concern with the Jewish cult is not unique. Previous kings such as Cyrus and Cambyses also showed concern for their subjects.

punishment will affect both the person and his family since "his house shall be made a dunghill." The punishment of impaling might seem too harsh or even fictitious; however, many ancient covenants carried curses or punishments that were intended as a deterrent. Blenkinsopp states that "impaling was a Persian practice inherited from the Assyrians, generally reserved for the most serious crimes, especially sedition and the violation of treaty oaths."[9] The curse in verse 12 invoked against any king or people who would alter this edict or destroy the temple is the literary seal with which Darius concludes his decrees. The Deuteronomic expression, "The God who has caused his name to dwell there" (Deut. 12:5) is a good indication that a Jewish scribe influenced Darius' wording of his edict.[10]

II. God's House is completed (6:13-15)

> 6:13-15 Then, according to the word sent by Darius the king, Tattenai, the governor of the province Beyond the River, Shethar-bozenai, and their associates did with all diligence what Darius the king had ordered. [14]And the elders of the Jews built and prospered through the prophesying of Haggai the prophet and Zechariah the son of Iddo. They finished their building by decree of the God of Israel and by decree of Cyrus and Darius and Artaxerxes king of Persia; [15]and this house was finished on the third day of the month of Adar, in the sixth year of the reign of Darius the king.

The sovereignty and providence of God are clearly displayed as His plan is fulfilled with the help of pagan, syncretistic people. Man's efforts are successful because of God's divine intervention and communication of His message through His prophets Haggai and Zechariah. The absence of any mention of Zerubbabel leads some to believe that he died before the completion of the temple.[11] Even though Artaxerxes reigned much later (465-424/3 BC), he is mentioned to reinforce the

9.   Blenkinsopp, *Ezra–Nehemiah*, 127-128.
10. Breneman, 117-118; Myers, 52; Williamson, 83.
11. Fensham, *Ezra and Nehemiah*, 92.

argument that the reconstruction was accomplished due to divine providence which goes beyond one king's reign. Cyrus, Darius, and Artaxerxes each played a role in the rebuilding of the temple and of Jerusalem. Cyrus gave the edict which began the reconstruction, the temple was completed during Darius' reign, and the city walls were completed during the reign of Artaxerxes.

The rebuilding of the temple was complete on the third day of the month of Adar, which is the twelfth month of the Babylonian calendar and corresponds to our months of February/March. The sixth year of the reign of Darius is 516/515 BC.

III. God's House is dedicated (6:16-18)

> 6:16-18 And the people of Israel, the priests and the Levites, and the rest of the returned exiles, celebrated the dedication of this house of God with joy. [17]They offered at the dedication of this house of God 100 bulls, 200 rams, 400 lambs, and as a sin offering for all Israel 12 male goats, according to the number of the tribes of Israel. [18]And they set the priests in their divisions and the Levites in their divisions, for the service of God at Jerusalem, as it is written in the Book of Moses.

The expression "the people of Israel" conveys the idea that the temple belongs to all the Israelites, not only to the tribes of Judah and Benjamin. The Aramaic word for dedication is *ḥănukkah*, "the name of the Jewish holiday that celebrates a similar rededication of the temple after its defilement by the Seleucid King Antiochus IV."[12] The dedication ceremony is very similar to that of Solomon's temple, but the number of the sacrifices is small by comparison. That is understandable when one considers that the returnees belonged to an impoverished community that cannot compare to Solomon's golden age.[13] The twelve male goats brought as a sin offering for all Israel, not just Judah and Benjamin, symbolize the post-exilic community's understanding that the blessed

---

12. Breneman, *Ezra, Nehemiah, Esther*, 119.
13. At the dedication of Solomon's temple the people sacrificed 22,100 cattle and 20,000 sheep and goats (1 Kings 8:63).

stage they are in is a complete, not a partial, restoration. It has been decades since the priests and the Levites have carried out their duties, and now they are again ready for "service of God at Jerusalem." The rabbis dictated that "the priests were divided into twenty-four watches, representing the twenty-four priestly clans" with each watch serving for one week.[14] The fact that they are following the instruction found in the book of Moses[15] points again to the people's desire to return to God and His commandments given through His servant Moses.[16] Indeed, the Pentateuch mentions the use of male goats for sin offering during the Day of Atonement (Lev. 16:5) as well as the Passover feast (Exod. 12:5).

IV. God's people celebrate the Passover (6:19-22)

6:19-22 On the fourteenth day of the first month, the returned exiles kept the Passover. [20]For the priests and the Levites had purified themselves together; all of them were clean. So they slaughtered the Passover lamb for all the returned exiles, for their fellow priests, and for themselves. [21]It was eaten by the people of Israel who had returned from exile, and also by everyone who had joined them and separated himself from the uncleanness of the peoples of the land to worship the LORD, the God of Israel. [22]And they kept the Feast of Unleavened Bread seven days with joy, for the LORD had made them joyful and had turned the heart of the king of Assyria to them, so that he aided them in the work of the house of God, the God of Israel.

It is only fitting that they celebrate the Passover since that celebration reminds them of their greatest deliverance, the

---

14. Rosenberg, *Daniel, Ezra, Nehemiah,* 147.
15. The Book of Moses probably refers to the Pentateuch since it is there that legal prescriptions abound.
16. Those who suggest that the Pentateuch is the work of a historian who put all the documents together after the exile, falls short again. It is clear that by this time the Pentateuch was in existence and, most importantly, in use. Also, this clarifies that the author of Ezra is not the same as the author of Chronicles, since the Chronicler clearly states that the organization of the priests and Levites is to be done according to David's directives.

one from under the Egyptian yoke. Moses instructed the people who would enter the Promised Land to keep the Passover (Num. 9:4). After entering the Promised Land, the Israelites, under the leadership of Joshua, celebrated the Passover at Gilgal (Josh. 5:10). During the monarchy period, the Passover seems to have been neglected, because the people celebrated it after Josiah's reform around the year 627 BC (2 Kings 23:21). The community of the Jews who returned from the exile keeps the Passover, as God commanded through Moses, on the fourteenth day of the first month, the month of Nissan (Lev. 23:5). The Israelites' commitment to obeying the Law of Moses is evident in their inviting non-Jews to their celebration and worship. These outsiders followed the purification rites as instructed in the Law (Num. 9:14).[17] Some rabbis affirm that these "are proselytes, who were separated from the defilement of the nations to cleave to Israel."[18] The Feast of Unleavened Bread was celebrated in conjunction with the Passover (Exod. 12:15-17) as in the time of Moses and Hezekiah (2 Chron. 30:21).

Just as God directed the heart of Cyrus, God also moved the heart of Darius, who is called here the king of Assyria. Fensham explains that "because Darius was also the sovereign of Assyria, he could easily have been called king of Assyria."[19] In any event, God is in control; it is His will that is carried out despite who is on the earthly throne. Williamson astutely points out that the author "invites us to interpret his historical account in theological terms, which implies that from it his readers may also learn lessons and draw conclusions of a less time-bound nature."[20] The celebration of God's people is crowned with joy because God brought them back, God allowed them to rebuild the temple, and God allowed them to worship Him in His house. The Israelites and the Gentiles are secondary characters in this great drama whose main Player is also the Director.

---

17. Fensham suggests that "the Samaritans would definitely have been excluded." Fensham, *Ezra and Nehemiah*, 96.
18. Rosenberg, *Daniel, Ezra, Nehemiah*,148.
19. Ibid.
20. Williamson, *Ezra, Nehemiah*, 85.

Ezra 7

Outline

I. God sends His man (7:1-6)

7:1-6 Now after this, in the reign of Artaxerxes king of Persia, Ezra the son of Seraiah, son of Azariah, son of Hilkiah, [2]son of Shallum, son of Zadok, son of Ahitub,[1] [3]son of Amariah, son of Azariah, son of Meraioth, [4]son of Zerahiah, son of Uzzi, son of Bukki, [5]son of Abishua, son of Phinehas, son of Eleazar, son of Aaron the chief priest – [6]this Ezra went up from Babylonia. He was a scribe skilled in the Law of Moses that the Lord the God of Israel had given, and the king granted him all that he asked, for the hand of the Lord his God was on him.

In the beginning of Chapter 7, another chronological anomaly appears. Brown notes that "chapters 1-6 begin with Cyrus's first year and end with Darius's seventh year, a twenty-year span. The total time span covered in the first six chapters, however, stretches over eighty years – from Cyrus to an unspecified time during the reign of Artaxerxes (4:6-23)."[2] Chapter 7's

---

1. Ahitub is a descriptive name and it means "The brother is good."
2. A. Philip Brown II, "Chronological Anomalies in the Book of Ezra," in *BSac* 162/645 (2005), 43.

introductory expression "Now after this" refers to the preceding narrative detailed in chapters 5 and 6, namely, Tattenai's investigation, King Darius' support, and the successful rebuilding of the temple.

This is also the first time the name of Ezra appears in the book. Ezra is the Aramaic form of the Hebrew Azariah and means "Yahweh helps/has helped." His lineage traces back to Aaron, the brother of Moses, who is introduced here as "the chief priest." Ezra is not presented in the Bible as a high priest, although there are some who suggest that Ezra "came to Jerusalem as the real high priest of the family of Aaron."[3] His ancestor Seraiah was killed by Nebuchadnezzar about 130 years before (2 Kings 25:18-21), so the genealogy presented here skips a couple of generations.[4] Ezra is introduced as a "scribe skilled in the Law of Moses," but according to the genealogy given, it is certain that he was both priest and scribe. Schaeder postulates that "Ezra was secretary for Jewish affairs in the Persian government."[5] We cannot dispute the fact that he held an important position in the Persian Empire since the king entrusted him with an important mission. Ezra's status when he comes from Babylon suggests that the Jews prospered even in the Babylonian exile and that God even allowed them to be educated.[6] Again it is emphasized that Ezra's success was not due to his own strength, intelligence, or connections, but rather because "the hand of the LORD his God was on him."

II. God's man has a heart for God (7:7-10)

> 7:7-10 And there went up also to Jerusalem, in the seventh year of Artaxerxes the king, some of the people of Israel, and some of the priests and Levites, the singers and gatekeepers, and the temple servants. [8]And he came to Jerusalem in the fifth month, which was in the seventh year of the king.

3. Williamson, *Ezra, Nehemiah,* 91.
4. This could be due to intentional or unintentional scribal error or textual corruption.
5. Myers, *Ezra–Nehemiah,* 60.
6. This is indeed consistent with the Daniel narrative (Daniel 1-3).

> [9]For on the first day of the first month he began
> to go up from Babylonia, and on the first day of
> the fifth month he came to Jerusalem, for the good
> hand of his God was on him. [10]For Ezra had set
> his heart to study the Law of the LORD, and to do
> it and to teach his statutes and rules in Israel.

Ezra arrived in Jerusalem on the first day of Ab (August), 458 BC, the seventh year of the reign of Artaxerxes I. Being a leader, Ezra had a following; thus, religious leaders as well as common folk followed Ezra's leadership and returned with him to their native land. His journey was successful because God's good hand was upon him.[7]

What sets Ezra apart is his heart. His heart was set to *study* the Law of the LORD. His heart was set to *obey* the Law of the LORD. His heart was set to *teach* the Law of the LORD. Ezra loved God, God's Word, and God's people. Ezra serves as an example for godly leaders everywhere since before one gets up to say "Thus says the LORD," one must know *what* says the LORD. In order for Ezra to know what God says, he must study God's Word. The Law of the LORD referred to the Law given by God through Moses at Sinai, and it became synonymous with the first five books of the Bible we now know as the Pentateuch and the Jews knew as the Torah. But because knowing the Law of the LORD does not make one a godly leader, Ezra sets his heart to put into practice what the Law teaches.

In the gospels, Jesus is constantly provoked and opposed by Pharisees, Sadducees, and Scribes whom Jesus calls "hypocrites." Hypocrisy was one of the main obstacles for those who would follow Jesus; however, hypocrisy was not born in New Testament times. Rather, it was defined and refined during Old Testament times, and practiced with wicked diligence by many civil and religious leaders in Israel. Ezra stands at the other end of the spectrum as being one who not only knows the Law, but also as one who does what the Law says. But because Ezra loves God's people, he

---

7. Eight times in Ezra–Nehemiah we are told that God's hand was upon either Ezra, Nehemiah, or the faithful; six times in Ezra (7:6, 9, 28; 8:18, 22, 31), and twice in Nehemiah (2:8, 18).

also sets his heart to teach this Law to the people of Israel. Kidner affirms that Ezra "was a model reformer in that what he taught he had first lived, and what he lived he had first made sure of in the Scriptures. With study, conduct, and teaching put deliberately in this right order, each was able to function properly and at its best: study was preserved from unreality, conduct from uncertainty, and teaching from insincerity and shallowness."[8]

III. God directs the heart of the king (7:11-26)

7:11-16 This is a copy of the letter that King Artaxerxes gave to Ezra the priest, the scribe, a man learned in matters of the commandments of the LORD and his statutes for Israel: [12]"Artaxerxes, king of kings, to Ezra the priest, the scribe of the Law of the God of heaven. Peace. And now [13]I make a decree that anyone of the people of Israel or their priests or Levites in my kingdom, who freely offers to go to Jerusalem, may go with you. [14]For you are sent by the king and his seven counselors to make inquiries about Judah and Jerusalem according to the Law of your God, which is in your hand, [15]and also to carry the silver and gold that the king and his counselors have freely offered to the God of Israel, whose dwelling is in Jerusalem, [16]with all the silver and gold that you shall find in the whole province of Babylonia, and with the freewill offerings of the people and the priests, vowed willingly for the house of their God that is in Jerusalem.

The introductory verse 11 is written in Hebrew, with the rest of the letter being written in Aramaic (7:12-26). It is clear that this is no ordinary letter, but rather a diplomatic communication which introduces Ezra as being "learned in the commandments of the LORD." Fensham suggests that "the author of this verse combined the Persian office of secretary with that of a Jewish scholar of the law of God."[9] The letter follows the basic outline of a letter: address,

---

8. Derek Kidner, *Ezra and Nehemiah*, TOTC (Downers Grove, IVP, 1979), 62.
9. Fensham, *The Books of Ezra and Nehemiah*, 104.

greeting, transition, various clauses, and final warning.[10] Artaxerxes calls himself "king of kings," a title commonly found in Persian official documents.[11]

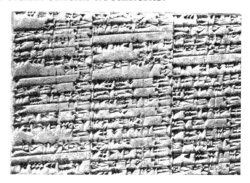

Fragment of Behistun cuneiform inscription[12]

In the letter, Artaxerxes recognizes Ezra as priest and scribe, and he further recognizes God as the Creator God by referring to Him as "the God of heaven."[13] In the same spirit as Cyrus' edict, Artaxerxes permits the Jews to return to their native land. The presence of the seven counselors is not unprecedented, since Cyrus also surrounded himself with seven counselors.[14] The book of Esther also mentions "seven princes of Persia and Media" who had special access to the king (Esth. 1:14). The letter indicates that the Israelites already possessed the written Law of Moses, so the Law of Moses could not have been written in the post-exilic period, as some scholars suggest. The letter of Artaxerxes sets up parallels to the Exodus event. Just as in the Exodus from Egypt, the Israelites now go to their land with silver and gold (Exod. 11:2; 12:35). The imagery not only points back to the Exodus from Egypt, but it also has pilgrimage

---

10. This outline is similar to the other royal letters found in Ezra 4:17-22 and 6:11-12.

11. Blenkinsopp, *Ezra–Nehemiah*, 147.

12. In the Behistun inscription, Darius calls himself "the great king, king of kings, king in Persia, king of the countries."

13. The expression "God of heaven" appears twenty-two times in the Old Testament, and thirteen of those times it appears in the books of Ezra and Nehemiah.

14. Myers, *Ezra–Nehemiah*, 58.

nuances in that this "second Exodus" ends with sacrifice. This Israelite community is a worshipping community that is prompted to return not because of the king's edict, but because of God's grace.[15]

> 7:17-20 With this money, then, you shall with all diligence buy bulls, rams, and lambs, with their grain offerings and their drink offerings, and you shall offer them on the altar of the house of your God that is in Jerusalem. [18]Whatever seems good to you and your brothers to do with the rest of the silver and gold, you may do, according to the will of your God. [19]The vessels that have been given you for the service of the house of your God, you shall deliver before the God of Jerusalem. [20]And whatever else is required for the house of your God, which it falls to you to provide, you may provide it out of the king's treasury.

We cannot know for certain how Artaxerxes knew about the requirements for sacrifices to Yahweh, but it may be that Ezra himself and other Jews were faithfully keeping the Law even in a foreign land. The king's request was not unprecedented since the Passover Papyrus discovered at Elephantine indicates that even Darius II authorized the keeping of the Festival of Unleavened Bread.[16] The vessels that are mentioned in verse 19 might be the same ones mentioned in 8:25-27, but the king's generosity extends to "whatever else is required for the house of your God." Artaxerxes' blank check to Ezra is a testament to a sovereign God who is in charge no matter who is on the throne in Susa.

---

15. See Melody D. Knowles, "Pilgrimage Imagery in the Returns in Ezra," in *JBL* 123/1 (2004), 73.
16. *ANET*, 491.

Fragment of the Passover Papyrus from Elephantine[17]

7:21-24 "And I, Artaxerxes the king, make a decree to all the treasurers in the province Beyond the River: Whatever Ezra the priest, the scribe of the Law of the God of heaven, requires of you, let it be done with all diligence, [22]up to 100 talents of silver, 100 cors of wheat, 100 baths of wine, 100 baths of oil, and salt without prescribing how much. [23]Whatever is decreed by the God of heaven, let it be done in full for the house of the God of heaven, lest his wrath be against the realm of the king and his sons. [24]We also notify you that it shall not be lawful to impose tribute, custom, or toll on anyone of the priests, the Levites, the singers, the doorkeepers, the temple servants, or other servants of this house of God.

The generosity of the king's offer is best understood in light of the fact that the annual tribute for the whole province Beyond the Rives was 350 silver talents.[18] Artaxerxes wants

---

17. Elephantine is an island in the Nile where "a garrison of Jewish mercenaries and their families lived," during the fifth century BC. See James K. Hoffmeier, *The Archaeology of the Bible* (Oxford: Lion Hudson, 2008), 118.
18. Breneman, *Ezra, Nehemiah, Esther,* 134-135.

God's will to be done in order to prevent God from pouring out His wrath upon him and his sons. His request is not unprecedented since Darius made a similar plea (6:10). Artaxerxes' command also prohibited the taxation of those directly associated with the work at the temple.

Even though many scholars reject the authenticity of this letter due to its favorable nature regarding the Jews, Fensham correctly points out that "It is most unlikely that the letter of Artaxerxes can be regarded as fictitious, because the author had an intimate knowledge of the temple personnel."[19] Indeed, archaeological evidence points to the fact that the Persians granted tax-exempt status to the clergy.[20]

> 7:25-26 "And you, Ezra, according to the wisdom of your God that is in your hand, appoint magistrates and judges who may judge all the people in the province Beyond the River, all such as know the laws of your God. And those who do not know them, you shall teach. [26]Whoever will not obey the law of your God and the law of the king, let judgment be strictly executed on him, whether for death or for banishment or for confiscation of his goods or for imprisonment."

The king now addresses Ezra directly, recognizing that the man of God possesses godly wisdom which will help him appoint magistrates and judges. The two legal positions point to the fact that two kinds of tribunals existed, one dealing with customary/religious law and one for state/civil law.[21] Ezra is not only to appoint judges, but he is also to teach those who do not know the law. Artaxerxes' decree ends with the king establishing punishments ranging from paying a fine (confiscation of goods) to the death penalty. The word translated "banishment" occurs also in the Elephantine Papyri and "it comes from the Persian word *srausya*, which can be translated "punishment," or

---

19. Fensham, *The Books of Ezra and Nehemiah*, 107.
20. David Janzen, "The 'Mission' of Ezra and the Persian-Period Temple Community," in *JBL* 119/4 (2000), 633-634.
21. Richard N. Frye, *The Heritage of Persia* (Cleveland/New York: World, 1963), 100.

"banishment."[22] The presence of the death penalty is not unusual here since this type of penalty was widely used in all Ancient Near Eastern empires.

IV. "Blessed be the Lord!" (7:27-28)

> 7:27-28 Blessed be the Lord, the God of our fathers, who put such a thing as this into the heart of the king, to beautify the house of the Lord that is in Jerusalem, [28]and who extended to me his steadfast love before the king and his counselors, and before all the king's mighty officers. I took courage, for the hand of the Lord my God was on me, and I gathered leading men from Israel to go up with me.

The credit for the things that are being accomplished does not go to Ezra or to the Persian king. Rather, the credit goes to the Lord, the God of the exiles, the God of those who lived during the monarchy, the God of those who lived in the time of the Judges, the God of those who conquered Jericho and settled the Promised Land, the God of those who wandered in the wilderness, and the God of the patriarchs. It is the Lord who directed the heart of the king to rule in favor of His people. The expression "Blessed be the Lord, the God of our fathers," appears only here in the Old Testament, although the expression "Blessed be the Lord," appears twenty-seven times. "Blessed be the Lord" introduces a prayer or doxology, which emphasizes the sovereignty of God along with His steadfast love (ḥesed). "I took courage" is better translated with the Hebrew passive "I was strengthened," because Ezra's strength came from God and it was not something that came from within himself. The strength that he received from the Lord led him to encourage and motivate others to go with him, thus proving himself to be a true leader. Verse 27 resumes the Hebrew portion of the book and here Ezra speaks in the first person, prompting some to suggest that this is the beginning of the so-called Ezra memoir.

---

22. See *Ezra and Nehemiah,* BHQ 20 (Stuttgart: Deutsche Bibelgesellschaft, 2006), 42-43.

This chapter presents Ezra as an example of godly leadership. Like Ezra, today's Christian leader needs to be "skilled" in handling God's Word. This skill is not inherited, thus, the leader needs to "set his heart to study" God's Word. Only then will he be able to teach it to others. There is nothing more disheartening than a lazy Bible teacher, and there is nothing more encouraging than an industrious and Spirit-filled Bible teacher who follows Ezra's example in diligently studying God's Word before getting up to say "Thus says the Lord." Like Ezra, today's Christian leader needs God's wisdom to teach and delegate. This godly wisdom proceeds from God and it stands in stark contrast with earthly, Godless wisdom (James 3:13-18).

Ezra 8

Outline

I. The list of the family heads who returned (8:1-14)

8:1-14 These are the heads of their fathers' houses, and this is the genealogy of those who went up with me from Babylonia, in the reign of Artaxerxes the king: ²Of the sons of Phinehas, Gershom. Of the sons of Ithamar, Daniel. Of the sons of David, Hattush. ³Of the sons of Shecaniah, who was of the sons of Parosh, Zechariah, with whom were registered 150 men. ⁴Of the sons of Pahath-moab, Eliehoenai[1] the son of Zerahiah, and with him 200 men. ⁵Of the sons of Zattu, Shecaniah the son of Jahaziel, and with him 300 men. ⁶Of the sons of Adin, Ebed the son of Jonathan, and with him 50 men. ⁷Of the sons of Elam, Jeshaiah the son of Athaliah, and with him 70 men. ⁸Of the sons of Shephatiah, Zebadiah the son of Michael,[2] and with him 80 men. ⁹Of the sons of Joab,

---

1. Eliehoenai means "To Yahweh are my eyes." Brockington notes that "the majority of Hebrew proper names were in origin short sentences which might be either verbal or nominal." See Brockington, *Ezra, Nehemiah, and Esther,* 41.
2. Michael means "Who is like God?"

Obadiah the son of Jehiel, and with him 218 men. [10]Of
the sons of Bani, Shelomith the son of Josiphiah, and
with him 160 men. [11]Of the sons of Bebai, Zechariah,
the son of Bebai, and with him 28 men. [12]Of the sons
of Azgad, Johanan the son of Hakkatan,[3] and with
him 110 men. [13]Of the sons of Adonikam, those who
came later, their names being Eliphelet, Jeuel, and
Shemaiah, and with them 60 men. [14]Of the sons of
Bigvai, Uthai and Zaccur, and with them 70 men.

Verse 1 is written in the first person and continues the so-
called Ezra memoirs that began in 7:28. Artaxerxes has
already been mentioned and gives credibility to the events
(4:7, 8, 11; 6:14; 7:1, 7, 11, 12, 21).[4] The authenticity of the
list can be verified through the fact that most of the names
appear elsewhere in Chronicles, Ezra, and Nehemiah. One
interesting feature of this list is that the house of David is
singled out.

II. "The servants for the temple of our God" (8:15-20)

8:15-20 I gathered them to the river that runs to
Ahava, and there we camped three days. As I
reviewed the people and the priests, I found there
none of the sons of Levi. [16]Then I sent for Eliezer,[5]
Ariel, Shemaiah, Elnathan, Jarib, Elnathan,[6] Nathan,
Zechariah, and Meshullam, leading men, and for
Joiarib and Elnathan, who were men of insight,
[17]and sent them to Iddo, the leading man at the
place Casiphia, telling them what to say to Iddo
and his brothers and the temple servants[7] at the
place Casiphia, namely, to send us ministers for the
house of our God. [18]And by the good hand of our
God on us, they brought us a man of discretion,

---

3. Hakkatan means "the little one," and it could be a nickname.
4. Artaxerxes' name also appears three times in Nehemiah (2:1; 5:14; 13:6).
5. Eliezer means "God is help."
6. Elnathan means "God has given."
7. The word hanneṭinim refers to a class of temple servants called the
   Nethinim (Ezra 2:43, 58, 70; 8:17, 20; Neh. 3:31; 7:46, 60, 72; 10:29; 11:21).
   See Ezra and Nehemiah, BHQ 20 (Stuttgart: Deutsche Bibelgesellschaft,
   2006), 43.

of the sons of Mahli the son of Levi, son of Israel,
namely Sherebiah with his sons and kinsmen, 18;
[19] also Hashabiah, and with him Jeshaiah of the
sons of Merari, with his kinsmen and their sons,
20; [20] besides 220 of the temple servants, whom
David and his officials had set apart to attend the
Levites. These were all mentioned by name.

As Ezra inspects the returnees close to Ahava—a place that
could be associated with one of the canals of the Euphrates
River, but whose exact location is uncertain—he realizes
that the Levites are missing. It could be that the Levites were
neither numerous nor useful in a temple-less Babylonian
captivity, but they will be very much needed in Jerusalem to
help with the priestly duties at the soon-to-be-rebuilt temple.
The names of Ariel and Elnathan[8] don't appear elsewhere
in Ezra, Nehemiah, or Chronicles, but the names of Eliezer,
Shemaiah, Jarib, Nathan, Zechariah, Meshullam, Joiarib,
do.[9] Iddo was the leader at Casiphia—another unknown
location that could have served as a cult center or sanctuary—and should not be confused with Zechariah's ancestor.[10] The word "brothers" means "kinsmen" and is not to
be taken literally. Ezra is asking that Iddo and his kinsmen
move from their present ministry position in an otherwise
unknown place to minister in Jerusalem, the God-ordained
center of Israelite worship. Both Ezra and Nehemiah refer
to the temple as "the house of our God" (Ezra 8:17, 25, 30,
33; 9:9; Neh. 10:32-34, 36-39; 13:4).[11] The expression "the
good hand of God" appears three times in Ezra–Nehemiah
(Ezra 7:9; 8:18; Neh. 2:8) and it points to God's goodness in
protecting and providing for His people.

---

8. The name "Elnathan" occurs three times in 8:16 referring to three different
   individuals.
9. This leads some scholars to doubt the authenticity of this list. See Arvid
   S. Kapelrud, *The Question of Authorship in the Ezra–Narrative: A Lexical
   Investigation* (Oslo: Jacob Dybwad, 1944), 45-46.
10. In Hebrew, the Iddo of Casiphia is spelled אִדּוֹ while the Iddo the ancestor
    of Zechariah is spelled עִדּוֹ.
11. Outside of Ezra–Nehemiah, the expression occurs only two other times: in
    Psalm 135:2 and Joel 1:16.

Ezra's request for ministers for the House of God is fulfilled by a Levite named Sherebiah, whose name appears eight times in Ezra–Nehemiah.[12] He is described as a leader among priests (Ezra 8:24), one who helped the people understand the Law (Neh. 8:7), one who led in the corporate confession of sin during the time of Nehemiah (Neh. 9:4-5), one who signed the covenant (Neh. 10:12), and as one who was in charge of the songs of thanksgiving (Neh 12:8). Sherebiah is described as a man of discretion, the word here translated as the Hebrew word *sekel*, meaning "insight," or "understanding." The word is elsewhere used to describe a discerning woman (1 Sam. 25:3), the wise King Solomon (2 Chron. 2:11), those who fear the LORD (Ps. 111:10), and people of good sense (Prov. 13:15; 16:22; 19:11). The term can also be translated "skill" (1 Chron. 26:14; 2 Chron. 30:22). The other two leaders mentioned among the 220 Levites who came at Ezra's appeal are Hashabiah and Jeshaiah.[13] A list of all 220 Levites is not provided.

III. The people of God humble themselves (8:21-23)

> 8:21-23 Then I proclaimed a fast there, at the river Ahava, that we might humble ourselves before our God, to seek from him a safe journey for ourselves, our children, and all our goods. [22]For I was ashamed to ask the king for a band of soldiers and horsemen to protect us against the enemy on our way, since we had told the king, "The hand of our God is for good on all who seek him, and the power of his wrath is against all who forsake him." [23]So we fasted and implored our God for this, and he listened to our entreaty.

Ezra's call to fasting is correlated with specific prayers for protection which are part of the farewell services. Here it is also correlated with an attitude of humility, which is actually one of the purposes of the fast.[14] The expression "to

---

12. Ezra 8:18, 24; Nehemiah 8:7; 9:4-5; 10:12; 12:8, 24.
13. Hashabiah is also mentioned in Nehemiah 12:24 as one of the chief of the Levites.
14. The infinitive construct employed (*lehiṯʿannôṯ*) is best classified an

seek from him" is synonymous with praying.[15] God's protection is sought since the road to Jerusalem is both long and
likely dangerous.

Fasting is almost nonexistent in the Christian life today,
even though all the great men and women of the Bible
and throughout church history were men and women of
prayer *and* fasting. However, it seems ludicrous to talk
about fasting in a time where there is a fast food place at
every corner. Between 1861 and 1954 no book was written in
English about fasting. Some see fasting as something people
did in the past and which is not relevant for today. John
Wesley, the founder of Methodism said, "Some lifted fasting
above the Bible and above reason, while others have totally
ignored it." John Chrysostom, one of the greatest preachers
of the fifth century said, "Fasting is, as much as lies in us,
an imitation of the angels, a condemning of things present,
a school of prayer, a nourishment of the soul, a bridle of
the mouth…it mollifies rage, it appeases anger, it calms the
tempests of nature, it excites reason, it clears the mind, it
disturbs the flesh, it chases away night-pollutions, it frees
from headache. By fasting, a man gets composed behavior,
free utterance of his tongue, right apprehensions of his
mind."[16] Fasting gained a bad reputation during the Middle
Ages when many abused it and practiced it just to be seen
by others. Some people have seen fasting as something
belonging only to the Jewish religion and saw no correlation
to Christianity.[17]

Verse 22 shows Ezra's tension between his understanding
of the providence of God and the responsibility of humans
within God's providence. Ezra is saying to himself, "Since
I told the king that God's good hand has protected us thus
far, how then can I now ask for a security detail?" So Ezra
does what is imbedded in his character—he prays and he

---

infinitive of purpose; "we fasted for the purpose of humbling ourselves."

15. This is different than the concept of seeking the Lᴏʀᴅ, which has more of
a concept of repentance, or turning back to God (2 Chron. 11:16; 20:4; Isa.
55:6; Jer. 50:4; Amos 5:6).

16. John Piper, *A Hunger for God* (Wheaton, IL: Good News, 1997), 125.

17. Richard Foster, *The Celebration of Discipline* (New York: Harper & Row,
1978), 41-42. This paragraph appears also in my treatment of Nehemiah 1:4.

fasts. Some scholars suggest that Ezra's decision against a royal military escort had to do with avoiding "attracting the attention of their future neighbors whose enmity might be further aroused."[18]

Other people of God besides Ezra who combined fasting with prayer were Nehemiah (Neh. 1:4), Daniel (Dan. 9:3), Anna (Luke 2:36-37), and many in the early church (Acts 13:3; 14:23). It seems that Jesus presents fasting as a Christian expectation when he answers a question posed by John's disciples by saying, "Can the wedding guests mourn as long as the bridegroom is with them? The days will come when the bridegroom is taken away from them, and then they will fast" (Matt. 9:15; Mark 2:20; Luke 5:35).

The expression "And [God] listened to our entreaty" is one of the Christian's greatest encouragements and comforts. Our God is not a deaf, granite-carved God who does not care about His children. Rather, our God is the only true God, and the One who hears our prayer (Gen. 30:17, 22; Exod. 2:24; Judg. 13:9; 1 Sam. 1:19; 1 Chron. 4:10; 2 Chron. 1:11). When Ezra and his compatriots prayed and fasted, they experienced the power of fasting and praying manifested in God answering their prayers.

IV. Keepers of God's silver and gold (8:24-30)

8:24-30 Then I set apart twelve of the leading priests: Sherebiah, Hashabiah, and ten of their kinsmen with them. [25]And I weighed out to them the silver and the gold and the vessels, the offering for the house of our God that the king and his counselors and his lords and all Israel there present had offered. [26]I weighed out into their hand 650 talents of silver, and silver vessels worth 200 talents, and 100 talents of gold, [27]20 bowls of gold worth 1,000 darics, and two vessels of fine bright bronze as precious as gold. [28]And I said to them, "You are holy to the LORD, and the vessels are holy, and the silver and the gold are a freewill offering to the LORD, the God of your fathers. [29]Guard them and keep them until

---

18. Myers, *Ezra, Nehemiah*, 71.

> you weigh them before the chief priests and the
> Levites and the heads of fathers' houses in Israel at
> Jerusalem, within the chambers of the house of the
> Lord." [30]So the priests and the Levites took over the
> weight of the silver and the gold and the vessels, to
> bring them to Jerusalem, to the house of our God.

The large amount of gold and silver in their possession leads Ezra to appoint the leading priests as the guardians of this great treasure. This is in accordance with Torah's teaching that the Levites were to guard the sacred objects associated with the tabernacle, while the priests had authority over the Levites (Lev. 3:8, 31; 4:7-15). Because the amount of gold and silver described here adds up to about 3¾ tons of gold and 24½ tons of silver, many scholars reject the authenticity of the list. Williamson suggests that the original list was "transmitted inaccurately, either out of a desire to magnify the glory of the temple by exaggerating the value of the offerings," or "by an error through misunderstanding of figures or weights."[19] However, since the people who contributed were connected to the very generous Persian court, and since the number of Jews cannot be underestimated, such a charitable outcome should not be denied.

Ezra reassures the people that they are "holy to the Lord," and this Lord is the same as "the God of your fathers." The expression "holy to the Lord" originates in the Pentateuch and it first appears in conjunction with God setting apart the priesthood for service at the tabernacle (Exod. 28:36).[20] The expression appears only one other time in Ezra–Nehemiah, and it refers to the sacred day when Ezra read the Law of the Lord to the people (Neh. 8:9). It could be that the Israelites needed to be reminded of their special status before the Lord since they had sojourned a long time among a profane people who worshipped other gods. The absence of the temple and subsequently the absence of atonement provision were conducive to the people falling into complacency. Through

---

19. Williamson, *Ezra, Nehemiah,* 119.
20. The expression "holy to the Lord" also refers to the Sabbath day (Exod. 31:15), the tithe (Lev. 27:30), and the children of Israel (Deut. 7:6; 14:2, 21; 26:19).

Ezra, God reminded the people that they were set apart for Him and for His purposes. Just like in the Pentateuch, not only are people holy but offerings and temple vessels are also set apart to be used for sacred purposes. It seems that some temporary quarters have been assigned to hold these sacred vessels and offerings. Williamson states that "the chambers of the temple were rooms around the edges of parts of the temple area used both for administration and storage and for the priest's personal convenience."[21]

V. The people of God reach Jerusalem (8:31-36)

> 8:31-36 Then we departed from the river Ahava on the twelfth day of the first month, to go to Jerusalem. The hand of our God was on us, and he delivered us from the hand of the enemy and from ambushes by the way. [32]We came to Jerusalem, and there we remained three days. [33]On the fourth day, within the house of our God, the silver and the gold and the vessels were weighed into the hands of Meremoth the priest, son of Uriah,[22] and with him was Eleazar the son of Phinehas, and with them were the Levites, Jozabad the son of Jeshua and Noadiah the son of Binnui. [34]The whole was counted and weighed, and the weight of everything was recorded. [35]At that time those who had come from captivity, the returned exiles, offered burnt offerings to the God of Israel, twelve bulls for all Israel, ninety-six rams, seventy-seven lambs, and as a sin offering twelve male goats. All this was a burnt offering to the LORD. [36]They also delivered the king's commissions to the king's satraps and to the governors of the province Beyond the River, and they aided the people and the house of God.

After twelve days spent around the region of the Ahava River, Ezra and his entourage leave for Jerusalem. God's hand of protection was on them, and it was God who delivered them from the unnamed enemy who ambushed them on the way.

---

21. Williamson, *Ezra, Nehemiah*, 120.
22. Uriah means "Yahweh is my light."

God's hand was on Ezra from the beginning (7:6, 9) and it was also evident as Ezra planned the trip to Jerusalem (7:28). Ezra recognized that God's hand also brought him Mahli, a wise Levite leader (8:18). The word translated "delivered" in verse 31 can also be translated "protected," thus it is not clear if the bandits actually attacked the caravan or not, but it is clear that it was God who protected or delivered Ezra and his followers. The distance between Ahava and Jerusalem has been estimated at around 900 miles, and it is estimated that a large caravan could travel at a speed of around nine miles per day. Thus, "the journey lasted some four months."[23] The three days of apparent inactivity can be explained by the need to find shelter for "some five thousand immigrants."[24]

Meremoth's name is first mentioned here, but he will be mentioned again, along with Eleazar and Jozabad, among the ones who separated themselves from foreign wives (10:36). In the book of Nehemiah, Meremoth has an active role in the reconstruction of Jerusalem (Neh. 3:4, 21), and he also appears among those who signed the covenant (Neh. 10:6). The presence of gold and silver is essential because of "a foundry where precious metals used to redeem tithes were collected, melted down and recast in standardized measures in order to be used as means of payment. These metals were then stored in the temple treasury."[25] Jozabad also appears among the Levites who explain the Law to the people after Ezra reads it to the returnees (Neh. 8:7).

Worship had been restored in Jerusalem after the altar had been rebuilt under the leadership of Jeshua and Zerubbabel (Ezra 3:2). The returnees finally have the opportunity to bring sacrifices, something that was impossible in a temple-less exile. The fact that they sacrificed "twelve bulls for all Israel" indicates that for those present, the concept of "the lost tribes of Israel" was nonexistent. Thus, they brought twelve bulls for the twelve tribes of Israel. The ninety-six

---

23. Ibid.
24. Blenkinsopp, *Ezra–Nehemiah*, 171.
25. Joachim Schaper, "The Temple Treasury Committee in the Times of Nehemiah and Ezra," in *VT* 47/2 (1997): 204.

rams are divisible by twelve as well, so the only number not divisible by twelve is seventy-seven.[26] The number seventy-seven might be used here as a "literary device to denote a fairly large number."[27] All the offerings were "a burnt offering to the LORD," indicating that even the sin offering, which was usually only partially burned with the rest being offered to the priests, was burned completely to the LORD.

The word translated "satrap" is a Persian loanword that refers to a high official. The word appears only once in Ezra–Nehemiah and twelve other times in post-exilic texts.[28] The satraps along with the governors followed the king's instructions and aided the people of God in their work of reconstruction.

Chapter 8 teaches two important leadership principles that need to be practiced by today's Christian leaders: humility (vv. 21-23) and integrity (vv. 24-30). In Ezra's case, this humility was seen in his dependence on the sovereign God who alone can provide safety for His people. Ezra's integrity can be seen in his delegating the care of the offering for the house of God, realizing that both the offering and those who handle it must be holy to the LORD. History has proven that when unholy people handle that which is holy to the LORD, corruption is bred, and oppression reigns.

---

26. 1 Esdras 8:66 has seventy two.
27. Fensham, *The Books of Ezra and Nehemiah*, 122.
28. Esther 3:12; 8:9; 9:3; Daniel 3:2, 3, 27; 6:2, 3, 4, 5, 7, 8.

Ezra 9

Outline

I. The sin of the people (9:1-4)

> 9:1-4 After these things had been done, the officials approached me and said, "The people of Israel and the priests and the Levites have not separated themselves from the peoples of the lands with their abominations, from the Canaanites, the Hittites, the Perizzites, the Jebusites, the Ammonites, the Moabites, the Egyptians, and the Amorites. [2]For they have taken some of their daughters to be wives for themselves and for their sons, so that the holy race has mixed itself with the peoples of the lands. And in this faithlessness the hand of the officials and chief men has been foremost." [3]As soon as I heard this, I tore my garment and my cloak and pulled hair from my head and beard and sat appalled. [4]Then all who trembled at the words of the God of Israel, because of the faithlessness of the returned exiles, gathered around me while I sat appalled until the evening sacrifice.

Some leaders (lit. "heads") report to Ezra regarding the sin of intermarrying with pagan nations. God's Law given through Moses was very clear concerning this very important issue, clearly prohibiting marriage between Israelites and foreigners. After God made the covenant with the Israelites on Sinai, after they defiled themselves by worshipping the golden calf made by Aaron, and after Moses interceded on the people's behalf, God renewed the covenant with them:

> "Observe what I command you this day. Behold, I will drive out before you the Amorites, the Canaanites, the Hittites, the Perizzites, the Hivites, and the Jebusites. Take care, lest you make a covenant with the inhabitants of the land to which you go, lest it become a snare in your midst. You shall tear down their altars and break their pillars and cut down their Asherim (for you shall worship no other god, for the LORD, whose name is Jealous, is a jealous God), lest you make a covenant with the inhabitants of the land, and when they whore after their gods and sacrifice to their gods and you are invited, you eat of his sacrifice, and you take of their daughters for your sons, and their daughters whore after their gods and make your sons whore after their gods." (Exod. 34:11-16)

A similar list was presented in Deuteronomy as well.

> "When the LORD your God brings you into the land that you are entering to take possession of it, and clears away many nations before you, the Hittites, the Girgashites, the Amorites, the Canaanites, the Perizzites, the Hivites, and the Jebusites, seven nations more numerous and mightier than yourselves, and when the LORD your God gives them over to you, and you defeat them, then you must devote them to complete destruction. You shall make no covenant with them and show no mercy to them. You shall not intermarry with them, giving your daughters to their sons or taking their daughters for your sons, for they would turn away your sons from following me, to serve other gods. Then the anger of the LORD would be kindled against you, and he would destroy you quickly." (Deut. 7:1-4)

The problem with these other nations was not their ethnicity, but their worship practices.[1] Fensham correctly points out that the reason for this attitude had nothing to do with racism, but with a concern for the purity of the religion of the Lord...The influence of a foreign mother, with her

---

1. Some scholars suggest that "concern with ethnic purity and objections to intermarriage are the products of the socio-economic issues of the era." See Tamara C. Eskenazi, "Out from the Shadows: Biblical Women in the Postexilic Era," in *JSOT* 54 (1992):35.

connection to another religion, on her children would ruin the pure religion of the Lord and would create a syncretistic religion running contrary to everything in the Jewish faith. In the end it was a question of the preservation of their identity, their religious identity.[2]

It was especially distressing that even the priests and the Levites compromised themselves by disobeying the very Law they were supposed to uphold and teach. Not only were these leaders compromised, but the text suggests that some took the lead role in this grave disobedience. The end of verse 2 clearly states that "in this faithlessness the hand of the officials and chief men has been foremost" (Ezra 9:2).

The news of the people's disobedience grieves Ezra so deeply that he exteriorizes his pain by tearing his clothes and pulling his hair. It was the custom of many Ancient Near Eastern people to tear their clothes and to dishevel their hair as a sign of mourning (2 Sam. 13:19; 2 Kings 22:1; Job 1:20; Isa. 22:12); the tearing of clothes being "a modified form of ritual nakedness," and the pulling of hair a modified form of hair shaving.[3] Ezra's actions reveal what is in his heart while drawing attention to his remonstration. The word "appalled" appears in this form only three times, twice in Ezra and once in Daniel (Ezra 9:3-4; Dan. 11:31), and translates "appalled, stupefied, or reduced to shuddering."[4] Other God-fearing men and women join Ezra, ministering to him with their presence until the time of the evening sacrifice. The faithful post-exilic community was often described as those who tremble at the Word of God (Ezra 10:3; Isa. 66:2, 5). The gravity of the situation and the pain in his heart leads Ezra to fall to his knees in prayer.

This passage can serve as an example for today's Christian leaders who need to identify with their people, mourn for both personal and corporate sins. Like Ezra, today's leaders

---

2. Fensham, The Books of Ezra and Nehemiah, 124.

3. Blenkinsopp, Ezra–Nehemiah, 177. See also, Morris Jastrow, "The Tearing of Garments as a Symbol of Mourning with Especial Reference to the Customs of the Ancient Hebrews," in JAOS 21 (1900): 23-39.

4. The Hebrew word is a masculine, singular participle in the rare polel stem from the root šmm.

need to spend a considerable amount of time in prayer, not as a last resort but as a first impulse.

II. The prayer of the righteous[5] (9:5-15)

> 9:5-15 And at the evening sacrifice I rose from my fasting, with my garment and my cloak torn, and fell upon my knees and spread out my hands to the Lord my God, [6]saying: "O my God, I am ashamed and blush to lift my face to you, my God, for our iniquities have risen higher than our heads, and our guilt has mounted up to the heavens. [7]From the days of our fathers to this day we have been in great guilt. And for our iniquities we, our kings, and our priests have been given into the hand of the kings of the lands, to the sword, to captivity, to plundering, and to utter shame, as it is today. [8]But now for a brief moment favor has been shown by the Lord our God, to leave us a remnant and to give us a secure hold within his holy place, that our God may brighten our eyes and grant us a little reviving in our slavery. [9]For we are slaves. Yet our God has not forsaken us in our slavery, but has extended to us his steadfast love before the kings of Persia, to grant us some reviving to set up the house of our God, to repair its ruins, and to give us protection in Judea and Jerusalem. [10]"And now, O our God, what shall we say after this? For we have forsaken your commandments, [11]which you commanded by your servants the prophets, saying, 'The land that you are entering, to take possession of it, is a land impure with the impurity of the peoples of the lands, with their abominations that have filled it from end to end with their uncleanness. [12]Therefore do not give your daughters to their sons, neither take their

---

5 McCarthy notes that "the genre of the speech is difficult to define. It is a sermon, a confession, a call for new resolution. Structurally, it is a 'covenantal formulation' on its way to becoming liturgical prayer, but the covenantal form still gives it a general context." See McCarthy, "Covenant and Law in Chronicles-Nehemiah," in CBQ 44 (1982): 33.

daughters for your sons, and never seek their peace or prosperity, that you may be strong and eat the good of the land and leave it for an inheritance to your children forever.' [13]And after all that has come upon us for our evil deeds and for our great guilt, seeing that you, our God, have punished us less than our iniquities deserved and have given us such a remnant as this, [14]shall we break your commandments again and intermarry with the peoples who practice these abominations? Would you not be angry with us until you consumed us, so that there should be no remnant, nor any to escape? [15]O Lord the God of Israel, you are just, for we are left a remnant that has escaped, as it is today. Behold, we are before you in our guilt, for none can stand before you because of this."

After a day spent in stunned silence, Ezra's first words are directed to the One who hears prayers. His kneeling position with arms extended to heaven was conventional for that day and age; however, Ezra's position is descriptive, not normative. One cannot legislate Ezra's position as being the only correct prayer position for today's Christian.[6] This is further clarified when we see that Ezra's cloak and garments are torn, a clear sign of pain and mourning. His actions would definitely attract attention to the seriousness of the offense and the gravity of the situation.

In prayer, Ezra confesses sin, identifying with the people and confessing corporate sin.[7] Although he refers to God as "my God," he confesses "our iniquities." The sin he confesses is that of disobeying God's commandments. Ezra acknowledges that the exile was a direct result of the people's sin, but that the return from exile was a direct result of God's steadfast love for His people (v. 9). "The citations in verses 11-12 are a conglomeration of expressions borrowed from various parts of Scripture."[8] Indeed, the echoes from Leviticus 18

---

6. Dean Merrill does make a compelling argument that kneeling in prayer reduces our temptation to make speeches to God, and it reminds us "who's who in the dialogue." See Dean Merrill, "Whatever Happened to Kneeling," *Christianity Today* 36 (1992): 24-25.
7. Ezra's reaction and prayer is very similar to Daniel's (Dan. 9:3-19).
8. Fensham suggests that the writer uses texts from Leviticus 18, 20,

and Ezekiel 37 classify the sin of intermarriage as an abomi-
nation and denote the guilty as morally impure.[9] In prayer,
Ezra confesses the sin of intermarriage with pagans. He
cannot believe that the people have once again gone against
God's Law, especially after they have experienced God's graciousness in allowing them to return from exile.[10] Verse 14
contains two rhetorical questions. The first one "Shall we
break your commandments again and intermarry with the
peoples who practice these abominations?" requires a "No"
answer. The second question, "Would you not be angry with
us until you consumed us?" requires a positive answer. In
prayer, Ezra exalts God and affirms God's justice and righteousness.[11] Only by confessing their sin and invoking God's
grace can the people hope to escape the penalty they have
brought upon themselves by disobeying God's Word.

Even though things are improving, the text is clear that the
reader should expect more. The people have not gotten their
entire land back, the temple is less glorious than Solomon's,
and there is still no Davidic king on the throne. These great
expectations will only be fulfilled through Christ's first and
second comings.

Ezra's prayer is a monument to the importance of prayer
for today's Christian leader. Programs, no matter how
elaborate or extravagant, can never substitute for a deep
prayer life. Like Ezra, we need to learn how to confess
personal and corporate sin. Like Ezra, we need to learn to
identify ourselves with the people to whom we minister.
The leader with a "holier-than-thou" attitude will not get far,
while the leader who humbles himself in order to identify
with the one who has wronged, will succeed in being like

Deuteronomy 4, 18, 2 Kings 16, 21, and Ezekiel 37. See Fensham, *The Books of Ezra and Nehemiah*, 131.

9. Jonathan Klawans, "Idolatry, Incest, and Impurity: Moral Defilement in Ancient Judaism," in *JSJ* 29/4 (1998), 399.

10. Dead Sea Scrolls discovered at Qumran affirm that the Essene community there also had legislation prohibiting intermarriage between Israelites and foreigners. See Christine Hayes, "Intermarriage and Impurity in Ancient Jewish Sources," in *HTR* 92/1(1999): 3-36.

11. The Hebrew word *ṣaddiq* can be translated both "just" or "righteous." However, in post-exilic times the word has become synonymous with "grace." Thus, when God is just, He imparts grace.

our Lord Jesus "who made himself nothing," took the form of a servant, and humbled himself for our sake (Phil 2:7-8).

Ezra 10[1]

Outline

I. The leaders' exhortation: holiness (10:1-4)

10:1-4 While Ezra prayed and made confession, weeping and casting himself down before the house of God, a very great assembly of men, women, and children, gathered to him out of Israel, for the people wept bitterly. [2]And Shecaniah the son of Jehiel, of the sons of Elam, addressed Ezra: "We have broken faith with our God and have married foreign women from the peoples of the land, but even now there is hope for Israel in spite of this. [3]Therefore let us make a covenant with our God to put away all these wives and their children, according to the counsel of my lord and of those who tremble at the commandment of our God, and let it be done according to the Law. [4]Arise, for it is your task, and we are with you; be strong and do it."

---

1. In Chapter 9 Ezra writes in the first person, while Chapter 10 is written in the third person. Eissfeldt suggests that Chapter 10 comes from a different source than Ezra's memoir, while Rudolph suggests that the Chronicler was using Ezra's memoir while writing this chapter. See O. Eissfeldt, *The Old Testament: An Introduction* (New York: Harper and Row, 1965), 544, and W. Rudolph, *Esra und Nehemia,* HAT 20 (Tübingen: J.C.B. Mohr, 1949), 93.

Ezra led by example. He prayed and wept over the sins of the people, and because he was a true leader, the people followed his example. Leader and followers weep together over the sin of intermarriage with foreign women. But since repentance means more than weeping over sins, Shecaniah[2] encourages Ezra to take action. Even though he is not listed among the guilty, Shecaniah is a lay leader who identifies with the people. He admits guilt: "We have broken faith with our God and have married foreign women." The phrase "foreign women" appears ten times in the Old Testament.[3] It first appears in conjunction with King Solomon who married foreign women who are identified as Moabite, Ammonite, Edomite, Sidonian, and Hittite. Both the Kings and the Ezra–Nehemiah contexts suggest that these women were "idolatrous, non-Jewish women." Thus, "it was not intermarriage with foreigners as such that caused Ezra such consternation, but with foreigners who, whether syncretistic or pagan, were idolaters."[4]

Shecaniah had knowledge of the law forbidding inter-marrying, and he admits guilt. He doesn't downplay it by saying that "everybody's doing it." More importantly, he does not lose hope that things can be rectified. "Even now there is hope for Israel in spite of this," are his relevant words of trust. Shecaniah also knows history. He knows that God wants to be in relationship with His people and He does so by means of covenants. Shecaniah could not have been a stranger to the covenants God made with Abraham, Moses, and David. The stipulations of the covenant are extreme. Those guilty of the sin of intermarriage with foreign women must commit to "put away" not only wives but also children. While the proposal seems harsh in view of contemporary Christian understanding, the proposal was aimed at keeping God's children from profaning the sacred institution of marriage. "To put away" is the expression used in conjunction with divorce in Deuteronomy 24:3.[5] Since

2. Shecaniah first appears on the list of returnees in Ezra 8:5.
3. 1 Kings 11:1; Ezra 10:2, 10-11, 14, 17-18; Nehemiah 13:26-27.
4. A. Philip Brown II, "The Problem of Mixed Marriages in Ezra–Nehemiah 9-10," in *BSac* 162/648 (2005), 449.
5. There is key difference between the Deuteronomy 24 and Ezra 10 contexts..

Jewish men married foreign women contrary to the Law of God, these marriages were considered illegal from the start. Shecaniah encourages Ezra to take action and assures him of populist support. The exhortation "be strong" could have reminded Ezra of Moses' encouraging words to Joshua (Deut. 31:7) and God's words to Joshua (Josh. 1:6, 9).

II. The people's response: repentance (10:5-17)

10:5-6 Then Ezra arose and made the leading priests and Levites and all Israel take oath that they would do as had been said. So they took the oath. [6]Then Ezra withdrew from before the house of God and went to the chamber of Jehohanan the son of Eliashib,[6] where he spent the night, neither eating bread nor drinking water, for he was mourning over the faithlessness of the exiles.

The Israelites follow godly leadership and they show that they will obey the stipulations of the covenant by sealing it with an oath. Oath-taking was very common in the Ancient Near East. In the absence of documentation, binding transaction depended on one's word as a means of legal enforcement. "The oath maintained the obligation to speak honestly."[7] Verse 6 continues to give us insight into Ezra's heart. His pain and distress constrain him to continue his absolute fast.[8]

10:7-8 And a proclamation was made throughout Judah and Jerusalem to all the returned exiles that they should assemble at Jerusalem, [8]and that if anyone did not come within three days, by order of the officials and the elders all his property should be forfeited, and he himself banned from the congregation of the exiles.

Deuteronomy 24 did not deal with situations in which foreign women were present, while Ezra 10 deals specifically with Law-breaking.

6. Eliashib means "May God restore," or "God will restore."

7. Brad Creed, "Oaths," in *Holman Bible Dictionary*, (Nashville: Holman, 1991), 1034.

8. An absolute fast is absent of food or water. For an excellent resource on fasting, see Kent D. Berghuis, "A Biblical Perspective on Fasting," *BibSac* 158 (Jan–March 2001): 86-103.

The punishment for not taking the oath included dire penalties. To be banned from the community of the faithful was to be on the same level with the unclean lepers. In this case, however, the leprosy would be spiritual in nature. Those who would continue in their disobedience of the Law would also become homeless. Thus, through their disobedience, these people would miss out on the promised blessings of restoration. It is God who is faithful in providing for them, but through lack of repentance, they fail to benefit from God's promises. The faithless would live in self-imposed exile due to disobedience and refusal to live in holiness.

> 10:9-11 Then all the men of Judah and Benjamin assembled at Jerusalem within the three days. It was the ninth month, on the twentieth day of the month. And all the people sat in the open square before the house of God, trembling because of this matter and because of the heavy rain. [10]And Ezra the priest stood up and said to them, "You have broken faith and married foreign women, and so increased the guilt of Israel. [11]Now then make confession to the LORD, the God of your fathers and do his will. Separate yourselves from the peoples of the land and from the foreign wives."

The ninth month of the Jewish calendar is the midwinter month of Kislev which brings to Israel the early winter rains. The people's trembling had both internal and external causes. The cold, heavy, midwinter rain made them miserable from a physical perspective, but their sin made them miserable from a spiritual perspective. It has been said that the truth will set you free, but first it will make you miserable.[9] Ezra doesn't hold back and he doesn't compromise the truth. Rather, he confronts the people directly, saying, "you have broken faith and married foreign women." The expression "make confession to the LORD" can also be translated "Thank the LORD." Thus, to make confession means to exalt God. Williamson correctly points out that "the penitent who

---

9. The quote is attributed to James A. Garfield, the twentieth president of the United States.

renounced his sin and threw himself upon the mercies of God rendered that true praise of trust and love, from which confession springs."[10]

Confession of sin must be followed by doing God's will and not one's own. "Separate yourselves" points to the heart of God's holiness. To be holy means to be set apart from the world and for the purposes of God. Ezra's exhortations "do His will," and "separate yourselves," point to the dual aspect of holiness. To be holy means to be set apart *from* the world, but it also means to be set apart *to* God—to do His will and work. One cannot do one without the other. One must separate from whatever causes one to be profane rather than holy. In the case of the returnees, this meant separation from their foreign wives and the local population who were worshipping foreign, dead gods. Holiness then, is not just more important than the closest human relationship, but it is the most important since it focuses on one's relationship with a holy God.

> 10:12-14 Then all the assembly answered with a loud voice, "It is so; we must do as you have said. [13]But the people are many, and it is a time of heavy rain; we cannot stand in the open. Nor is this a task for one day or for two, for we have greatly transgressed in this matter. [14]Let our officials stand for the whole assembly. Let all in our cities who have taken foreign wives come at appointed times, and with them the elders and judges of every city, until the fierce wrath of our God over this matter is turned away from us."

Admission of guilt is a very necessary and important part of the repentance process. The people agree with Ezra's indictment and respond, "It is so; we must do as you have said." The inclement weather as well as the gravity of the situation prohibit the people from meeting any longer, thus they suggest a sensible alternative which would have a delegation of leaders oversee the process of meeting with the individuals who have broken God's Law. The people have a good understanding of the theology of retribution, but they

---

10. Williamson, *Ezra, Nehemiah*, 155.

also understand that repentance brings about God's grace and mercy.

> 10:15-17 Only Jonathan the son of Asahel and Jahzeiah the son of Tikvah opposed this, and Meshullam and Shabbethai the Levite supported them. [16]Then the returned exiles did so. Ezra the priest selected men, heads of fathers' houses, according to their fathers' houses, each of them designated by name. On the first day of the tenth month they sat down to examine the matter; [17]and by the first day of the first month they had come to the end of all the men who had married foreign women.

The fact that some oppose God's work and the good initiatives of His people is a recurring theme in Ezra–Nehemiah. It is remarkable that even Meshullam, who is a leader (8:6), and Shabbethai, who is a Levite, are part of this small opposing movement. They do not appear in the list of offenders (10:18-33), and we are not told specifically what they were opposing. It could be they oppose Ezra's call to separate from foreign wives and the pagan people, or it could be that they "may have pressed for more immediate action."[11] Despite the opposition, Ezra takes into account the people's recommendation (10:14) and a commission of leaders is established to hear the matter at hand. Their task is "to examine the matter" of 110 cases, and their work lasts for three months.

III. The list of offenders (10:18-44)

> 10:18-19 Now there were found some of the sons of the priests who had married foreign women: Maaseiah, Eliezer, Jarib, and Gedaliah, some of the sons of Jeshua the son of Jozadak and his brothers. [19]They pledged themselves to put away their wives, and their guilt offering was a ram of the flock for their guilt.

---

11. Myers, *Ezra, Nehemiah*, 86.

The list has no title and includes seventeen priests, six Levites, three gatekeepers, one singer, and eighty-four laity. Just as in the days of Eli (1 Sam 1-3), even some sons of the priests have committed the sin of intermarriage. The fact that the list starts with the priests highlights the fact that religious leaders and their families are not exempt from sin. However, they obey Ezra's command and "pledge themselves to put away their wives." The guilt offering is described in Leviticus 5:14-26 and it generally suggests unintentional behavior. Fensham suggests that this would not be impossible in this case because even though the exiles knew the Law, "the finer distinctions and the interpretation of certain stipulations could have escaped them."[12]

> 10:20-24 Of the sons of Immer: Hanani and Zebadiah. [21]Of the sons of Harim: Maaseiah, Elijah, Shemaiah, Jehiel, and Uzziah. [22]Of the sons of Pashhur: Elioenai, Maaseiah, Ishmael, Nethanel, Jozabad, and Elasah. [23]Of the Levites: Jozabad, Shimei, Kelaiah (that is, Kelita), Pethahiah, Judah, and Eliezer. [24]Of the singers: Eliashib. Of the gatekeepers: Shallum, Telem, and Uri.

The remaining cultic officials include the Levites, the singers, and the gatekeepers. The lower social classes such as temple servants are not mentioned in this list, indicating that the list possibly is not comprehensive. Rudolph suggests that a complete list would be too embarrassing for the Chronicler.[13]

> 10:25-44 And of Israel: of the sons of Parosh: Ramiah, Izziah, Malchijah,[14] Mijamin, Eleazar, Hashabiah, and Benaiah.[15] [26]Of the sons of Elam: Mattaniah, Zechariah, Jehiel, Abdi, Jeremoth, and Elijah. [27]Of the sons of Zattu: Elioenai, Eliashib, Mattaniah, Jeremoth, Zabad, and Aziza. [28]Of the sons of Bebai were Jehohanan, Hananiah, Zabbai, and Athlai. [29]Of the sons of Bani were Meshullam, Malluch, Adaiah,

---

12. Fensham, *The Books of Ezra and Nehemiah*, 143.

13. Rudolph, *Esra und Nehemia*, 97. For Rudolph the larger the number of those who married foreign women, the more embarrassing it would be for the leaders of Israel.

14. Malchijah means "Yahweh is (my) king."

15. Benaiah means "Yahweh has built."

Jashub, Sheal, and Jeremoth. [30]Of the sons of Pahath-moab: Adna, Chelal, Benaiah, Maaseiah, Mattaniah, Bezalel, Binnui, and Manasseh. [31]Of the sons of Harim: Eliezer, Isshijah, Malchijah, Shemaiah,[16] Shimeon, [32]Benjamin, Malluch, and Shemariah. [33]Of the sons of Hashum: Mattenai, Mattattah, Zabad, Eliphelet, Jeremai, Manasseh, and Shimei. [34]Of the sons of Bani: Maadai, Amram, Uel, [35]Benaiah, Bedeiah, Cheluhi, [36]Vaniah, Meremoth, Eliashib, [37]Mattaniah, Mattenai, Jaasu. [38]Of the sons of Binnui: Shimei, [39]Shelemiah, Nathan, Adaiah, [40]Machnadebai, Shashai, Sharai, [41]Azarel, Shelemiah, Shemariah, [42]Shallum, Amariah, and Joseph. [43]Of the sons of Nebo: Jeiel, Mattithiah, Zabad, Zebina, Jaddai, Joel, and Benaiah. [44]All these had married foreign women, and some of the women had even borne children.

The list including the laity is set under the rubric of "Israel," (7:7; 9:1; Neh. 11:3) and it ends abruptly by indicating that "some of the women had even borne children." From a text-critical perspective, the Hebrew text is corrupt beyond repair. The apocryphal book 1 Esdras has "and they sent them and the children away." The LXX follows the MT. The book of Ezra in general, and Chapter 10 in particular, emphasize the gravity of sinning against the LORD by breaking His Law.

The book ends on a very practical note for today's Christian leader. After moments of prayer and fasting there comes a time for action. There needs to come a time when we get off of our knees and respond to the need(s) at hand. Ezra's prayer and fasting is followed by confession, repentance, and separation from sin. This was exactly how Jesus' ministry began, "Repent and believe in the gospel" (Mark 1:15). Jesus' message was not, "Work harder," "Get a degree," or "Think more positively." The message of repentance of and separation from sin was Ezra's message, was Jesus' message, and needs to be our message. Piety is no substitute for action, and action without prayer is

---

16. Both Shimeon and Shemaiah mean "Yahweh has heard."

dangerous. But when the two of them get the same place at the table, much is accomplished for the Kingdom of God.

Nehemiah 1

Outline

I. The man of God hears the bad news (1:1-3)

1:1-3 The words of Nehemiah the son of Hacaliah.
Now it happened in the month of Chislev, in the
twentieth year, as I was in Susa the capital, ²that
Hanani, one of my brothers, came with certain
men from Judah. And I asked them concerning
the Jews who escaped, who had survived the
exile, and concerning Jerusalem. ³And they
said to me, "The remnant there in the province
who had survived the exile is in great trouble
and shame. The wall of Jerusalem is broken
down, and its gates are destroyed by fire."

The fact that a good portion of the book is told in a first
person narrative suggests that Nehemiah is responsible for
most of the material present in the book. His name means
"Yahweh comforts" and was a common name in Israel.[1] His
father's name, Hacaliah, is of unknown meaning and origin.

---

1. Nahum is the shortened form of Nehemiah and is based on the same
    Hebrew root, *naham*, which can be rendered "to comfort." Two other
    men are named Nehemiah in the book of Ezra–Nehemiah (Ezra 2:2; Neh.
    3:16; 7:7). The name appears in extra-biblical literature such as Sirach 48:13

Nehemiah received the bad news about Jerusalem while in Susa during the twentieth year of the reign of Artaxerxes (Neh. 2:1)[2]. Darius made Susa the capital of the Persian Empire in 521 BC.[3] Located 150 miles north of the Persian Gulf, it was the winter residence of Persian kings, and it was here that Artaxerxes took up residence in 461 BC.[4]

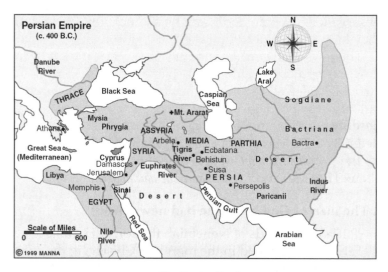

The Persian Empire

Copyright 1999 MANNA All Rights Reserved. Used with permission.

Although the exile lasted seventy years as the prophet Jeremiah prophesied (Jer. 25:11-12), some of the Jews who had escaped and survived the exile were still living in Judah. Hanani, who brought news of their dire condition, appears again in Chapter 7:2 when Nehemiah appoints him to a position of leadership. Nehemiah calls him "my brother"

---

and 2 Maccabees 1:18-36. Nehemiah's name appears as Neḥemyahu on a seventh century BC. Arad ostracon. See Edwin Yamauchi, "Archaeological Backgrounds of the Exilic and Postexilic Era, part 4: The Archaeological Background of Nehemiah," in *BSac* 137/548 (1980), 296.

2. Artaxerxes I ruled from 465 to 424/3 BC, thus his twentieth year would have been 444 BC.

3   Pierre De Miroschedji, "Susa." *ABD* 6:242-245.

4. After the palace of Darius I burned down, Artaxerxes moved to Persepolis. See Yamauchi, "Archaeological Backgrounds of the Exilic and Postexilic Era, part 4: The Archaeological Background of Nehemiah," 291.

twice, suggesting that Hanani was in fact Nehemiah's real brother, and not just a compatriot.[5] Nehemiah's inquiry about those who survived the exile showed his concern for his people, even though he had a cushy, well-respected job at the royal court of Artaxerxes. Caring for people is one of the most attractive and needed features of Christian leaders today. John Maxwell is credited with the following observation, "People don't care how much you know until they know how much you care."[6]

The Jews who survived the seventy-year captivity were now experiencing trouble and shame in Judah. The word "trouble" referred not only to the physical state of Jerusalem, but also to the demeanor of the people. Jerusalem was described as being economically exploited and culturally deteriorated. However, the word "shame" pointed directly to the condition of the people, who were experiencing shame[7] because of persecution from surrounding nations.

The walls of a city represent its first line of defense, and Jerusalem's walls had not been rebuilt since their destruction in 587 BC, indicating that the city had been without effective or caring Jewish leadership for approximately fifty-years. The Babylonians had no reason to rebuild Jerusalem, and until now, the Jews did not have empowered leaders or resources to rebuild their capital city. During Ezra's leadership the wall had been started (Ezra 4:12), but a full reconstruction was still unaccomplished. This deplorable state did not stop Hanani from telling the truth to someone who was in a position to help. He didn't hide any details or pretend the situation didn't exist. Our churches need people like Hanani who do not ignore the problem, deny the problem, or minimize the problem. We need people who will identify problems, not to criticize or accuse, but to edify and help rebuild. Hanani cared enough to report the problem, and Nehemiah cared enough to take Hanani's

---

5. The word "brother" can mean brother, relative, fellow countryman, or friend.
6. John Maxwell, *The Power of Attitude* (Colorado Springs: Cook, 2001), 70.
7. The word translated "shame" can also mean reproach and it appears more than twenty times in the Old Testament.

report to heart. The type of leader Nehemiah was is seen by what he did next.

II. The man of God feels the bad news (1:4)

> 1:4 As soon as I heard these words I sat down
> and wept and mourned for days, and I continued
> fasting and praying before the God of heaven.

We live in a world that considers weeping a sign of weakness. The Bible, however, shows that weeping can signal care and concern. Jeremiah (Jer. 9:1), Jesus (Luke 19:41), and Paul (Acts 20:19) wept because they cared for and loved the people and were deeply concerned for their fallen condition. We see through a window into Nehemiah's soul when we see him weeping after he heard the bad news. A godly leader is strong enough to weep.

Nehemiah combined his weeping with praying because a godly leader is a man of prayer. The book of Nehemiah records only twelve of his prayers, but we feel that his life was bathed in prayer.[8] Many of today's leaders rely on humanistic, business-oriented approaches rather than turning to the great power of prayer. R.A. Torrey wrote,

> It was a master-stroke of the devil to get the church and the ministry to lay aside the mighty weapon of prayer. He does not mind at all if the church expands her organizations and her deftly contrived machinery for the conquest of the world for Christ, if she will only give up praying. He laughs softly, as he looks at the church of today, and says under his breath: "you can have your Sunday schools, your social organizations, your grand choirs, and even your revival efforts, as long as you do not bring the power of Almighty God into them by earnest, persistent, and believing prayer."[9]

Nehemiah also combined his weeping with fasting. Fasting is almost nonexistent in the Christian life today, even though all the great men and women of the Bible and throughout church history were men and women of prayer *and* fasting. It is hard to talk about fasting in a time when fast food places

8. Nehemiah's prayers are recorded in 1:5-10; 2:4; 4:4, 9; 5:19; 6:9, 14; 9:5-11; 13:14, 22, 29, 31.
9. R.A. Torrey, *How to Pray* (New York: Revell, 1900), 128-129.

dot every corner. Between 1861 and 1954, no book about
fasting was written in the English language. Some people
see fasting as a practice from the past which is not relevant
for today. John Wesley, the founder of Methodism said,
"Some lifted fasting above the Bible and above reason, while
others have totally ignored it." John Chrysostom, one of the
greatest preachers of the fifth century said, "Fasting is, as
much as lies in us, an imitation of the angels, a condemning
of things present, a school of prayer, a nourishment of the
soul, a bridle of the mouth…it mollifies rage, it appeases
anger, it calms the tempests of nature, it excites reason,
it clears the mind, it disturbs the flesh, it chases away
night-pollutions, it frees from headache. By fasting, a man
gets composed behavior, free utterance of his tongue,
right apprehensions of his mind."[10] Fasting gained a bad
reputation during the Middle Ages when many abused it
by practicing it just to be seen by others. Others have viewed
fasting as belonging just to the Jewish religion and having
no correlation to Christianity.[11] Nevertheless, Jesus himself
stands as an example for us, His followers. At the beginning
of his earthly ministry, the Gospels tell of Jesus' forty-day
and forty- night fast (Matt. 4:1-11). In His teaching to the
disciples, Jesus affirmed that fasting will be part of their
lives after Jesus' exodus (Luke 5:35).

III. The man of God shares the bad news (1:5-11)

> 1:5-11 And I said, "O Lord God of heaven, the
> great and awesome God who keeps covenant and
> steadfast love with those who love him and keep his
> commandments, ⁶let your ear be attentive and your
> eyes open, to hear the prayer of your servant that I
> now pray before you day and night for the people
> of Israel your servants, confessing the sins of the
> people of Israel, which we have sinned against you.
> Even I and my father's house have sinned. ⁷We have
> acted very corruptly against you and have not kept

10. John Piper, *A Hunger for God* (Wheaton, IL: Good News, 1997), 125.
11. Richard Foster, *The Celebration of Discipline* (New York: Harper & Row, 1978), 41-42.

the commandments, the statutes, and the rules that you commanded your servant Moses. [8]Remember the word that you commanded your servant Moses, saying, 'If you are unfaithful, I will scatter you among the peoples, [9]but if you return to me and keep my commandments and do them, though your dispersed be under the farthest skies, I will gather them from there and bring them to the place that I have chosen, to make my name dwell there.' [10]They are your servants and your people, whom you have redeemed by your great power and by your strong hand. [11]O Lord, let your ear be attentive to the prayer of your servant, and to the prayer of your servants who delight to fear your name, and give success to your servant today, and grant him mercy in the sight of this man." Now I was cupbearer to the king.

Nehemiah was a man of prayer, and when confronted with a problem, he first shared it with God. Nehemiah didn't say, "There is a need, now let's get to work." Nehemiah didn't say, "There is a need, so let's gather the elders of the church." No, he knew that his work had to start on his knees in prayer. He shared the need with God in a prayer which revealed in part his relationship with God. In prayer he exalted God (1:5) and the fact that God's greatness has been established from the time of Moses (Deut. 7:21). In prayer he confessed sin, both private and corporate (1:6-7) and affirmed that God hears the prayer of His people (1:6, 11; 2:4) and forgives their sin (1:7). This points to Nehemiah's humility. He acknowledged that God gives laws and instruction (1:7-8). Although He is loving and merciful, God is holy, righteous, and just; therefore, He must judge and punish those who do not keep His laws and commandments (1:8b). Nehemiah affirmed that God restores and redeems His people (1:9-10).[12] By this time Nehemiah had set his mind to the work of rebuilding Jerusalem, so he concluded his prayer by appealing for God's mercy and compassion

---

12. K. Baltzer sees a clear parallel between Neh. 1:8-9 and the book of Deuteronomy. See David Shepherd, "Prophetaphobia: Fear and False Prophecy in Nehemiah VI," in *VT* 55/2 (2005): 232-250.

as he prepared for an audience with the king. According to Ezra 4:21, Artaxerxes had ordered the work in Jerusalem to cease, so Nehemiah knew that, humanly speaking, his chances were faint. In appealing for God's mercy and compassion, Nehemiah recounted Yahweh's compassion to the patriarchs (2 Kings 13:23) and to His people after He liberated them from Egypt (Exod. 33:19). Nehemiah demonstrated that if you want to be great and achieve great things for the work of the kingdom of God, you must be a man/a woman of prayer. Nehemiah's humility is also evidenced in the "servant" language. He does not introduce himself as the king's cupbearer, but rather as God's servant (1:6, 11).

Verse 11 reveals that Nehemiah had a well-paying, well-respected job as cupbearer to the king at the Persian royal court. "Nehemiah would have been a man of great influence as one with the closest access to the king, and one who could well determine who got to see the king. Above all, Nehemiah would have enjoyed the unreserved confidence of the king." And yet, Nehemiah was willing to give up his privileges in order to do the work of reconstruction because God had called him to the work (2:12).

Nehemiah's attitude and action reminds us of Jesus Christ, who saw our need for a Savior, left the glory of heaven, and met our deepest need by dying on a Roman cross to give us forgiveness for sin and eternal life. Nehemiah then can serve as a foreshadowing of Jesus, a finger pointing forward to Christ's work of salvation on behalf of humankind.

Nehemiah 2

Outline

I. The man of God has a sensitive heart (2:1-3)

2:1-3 In the month of Nisan, in the twentieth year of King Artaxerxes, when wine was before him, I took up the wine and gave it to the king. Now I had not been sad in his presence. [2]And the king said to me, "Why is your face sad, seeing you are not sick? This is nothing but sadness of the heart." Then I was very much afraid. [3]I said to the king, "Let the king live forever! Why should not my face be sad, when the city, the place of my fathers' graves, lies in ruins, and its gates have been destroyed by fire?"

It is likely that Nehemiah wasn't the king's only cupbearer,[1] so even though Nehemiah was despondent as he contemplated the tragic state of Israel's religious center for four long months, the king didn't see Nehemiah's sad face every day. Since court etiquette dictated that the king's servants have a pleasant demeanor, Nehemiah probably tried to conceal the pain residing in his heart. Eventually, however, his sad

---

1. J.J. Modi, "Wine Among the Ancient Persians," *Asiatic Papers* (Bombay: Royal Asiatic Society, 1905-29: 3), 231-46.

face allowed the king to get a glimpse into Nehemiah's soul, and Artaxerxes recognized that Nehemiah was dealing with "sadness of the heart." Nehemiah was gripped with fear because the king's servants were required to always keep a cheerful countenance before his royal highness, especially since it seems that Nehemiah was serving the king during some festival. Fensham correctly points out that "Persian kings were famous for their drinking parties (cf. Esth. 1:3ff), which were a custom in the Ancient Near East."[2]

Nehemiah's, "Let the king live forever!" was a common form of address to kings (1 Kings 1:31; Dan. 2:4; 3:9; 6:6). It is assumed that the king knew Nehemiah's Jewish ancestry; therefore, Nehemiah appealed to the king's sympathy not by mentioning Jerusalem or the temple, but by mentioning his "fathers' graves," and by painting a tragic picture of Jerusalem lying in ruins with its gates destroyed by fire. Some years earlier Jerusalem had been described as a rebellious city making waves in the sea of ancient empires (Ezra 4:19), but there was none of that in Nehemiah's description of the city which once boasted the great temple built by the great Solomon. Williamson states that "respect for ancestral tombs was universal in the Ancient Near East, and especially among the nobility and royalty."[3] However, Persian customs and Ancient Near Eastern traditions aside, the heart of the king was moved by God. As the wise King Solomon wrote, "The king's heart is a stream of water in the hand of the LORD; he turns it wherever he will" (Prov. 21:1).

II. "The king's heart is a stream of water" (2:4-8)

2:4-6 Then the king said to me, "What are you requesting?" So I prayed to the God of heaven. [5]And I said to the king, "If it pleases the king, and if your servant has found favor in your sight, that you send me to Judah, to the city of my fathers' graves, that I may rebuild it." [6]And the king said to me (the queen sitting beside him), "How long will you be gone, and when will you return?" So it pleased the king to send me when I had given him a time.

---

2. Fensham, *Ezra and Nehemiah*, 158.
3. Williamson, *Ezra, Nehemiah*, 179.

God caused the king to discern that behind Nehemiah's sad heart was an unfulfilled yearning. Before answering the king's direct question, "What are you requesting?" Nehemiah prayed. Indeed, Nehemiah stands as an example for all the godly leaders who want to do great things for God. Nehemiah only answered after he had bathed his heart and life in prayer. Nehemiah's request was simple and with purpose: "Send me...that I may rebuild." We learn from Nehemiah's example that piety is no substitute for preparation, but neither is preparation a substitute for piety. It seems that we, like Nehemiah, need both prayer and planning.

The king's question regarding the length of Nehemiah's absence was probably grounded in his fondness for this cupbearer, and he was pleased to learn that Nehemiah's intended absence was temporary in nature. It is not clear why Damaspia,[4] Artaxerxes' wife, was brought into the narrative, but it could indicate that Nehemiah's conversation with the king and queen was held privately, and not during a more public occasion.

> 2:7-8 And I said to the king, "If it pleases the king, let letters be given me to the governors of the province Beyond the River, that they may let me pass through until I come to Judah, [8]and a letter to Asaph, the keeper of the king's forest, that he may give me timber to make beams for the gates of the fortress of the temple, and for the wall of the city, and for the house that I shall occupy." And the king granted me what I asked, for the good hand of my God was upon me.

Nehemiah took advantage of the king's generosity by requesting official letters that would open both borders and banks. The expression 'Beyond the River' occurs twenty-two times in the Old Testament,[5] eighteen of those times in Ezra–Nehemiah, and it refers to the area between

---

4. Pierre Briant, *From Cyrus to Alexander: A History of the Persian Empire* (Winona Lake, Ind.,: Eisenbrauns, 2002), 571.
5. Josh. 24:3, 14, 15; Ezra 4:10, 11, 16, 17, 20; 5:3, 6; 6:6, 8, 13; 7:21, 25; Neh. 2:7, 9; 3:7; Isa. 7:20.

the Euphrates and the Mediterranean Sea.[6] Asaph is a
Jewish name, suggesting that, like Nehemiah, others who
were employed in the king's service had achieved some
status despite their Jewish ancestry. The timber was going
to be used specifically for the gates of the fortress, the wall
of the city, and Nehemiah's own residence.[7] The fact that
wood was used for the city wall may seem strange to a
present-day audience, but "wood was used extensively in
walls in the Ancient Near East as is shown by the study
done by architect Rudolf Naumann in connection with
Hittite buildings."[8] Nehemiah recognized that Artaxerxes
granted his request not because his words were eloquent or
his desire was noble, but because, in his words, "the good
hand of my God was upon me." Artaxerxes was only the
channel through which God poured out His blessing upon
Nehemiah and God's people. The king's heart was a stream
of water in the hand of the Creator God who is sovereign
over both creation and history.

III. The man of God challenges others (2:9-20)

> 2:9-10 Then I came to the governors of the province
> Beyond the River and gave them the king's letters.
> Now the king had sent with me officers of the
> army and horsemen. [10]But when Sanballat the
> Horonite and Tobiah, the Ammonite servant, heard
> this, it displeased them greatly that someone had
> come to seek the welfare of the people of Israel.

The text does not mention how much time elapsed between
the king's consent and Nehemiah's departure, although the
Jewish historian Josephus suggests five years.[9] Nehemiah's
journey was made safe because of God's protection through
the king's letters and the royal escort made up of cavalry
soldiers and officers of the army. Verse 10 introduces us to
Sanballat and Tobiah, two key opponents of Nehemiah and

---

6   This region is also called Trans-Euphrates.
7   This residence could have been a brand new building or a renovated one. The
    text does not indicate which is the case, so to speculate would be improper.
8   Fensham, *Ezra and Nehemiah*, 163.
9   *Ant.* xi.5

his efforts. According to the Elephantine papyri, Sanballat the Horonite was the governor of Samaria.[10] The term Horonite refers to the town of Sanballat's provenance, Horonaim of Moab (Isa. 15:5; Jer. 48:3). Thus, Sanballat was a Moabite. Tobiah the Ammonite is probably an official in Samaria. The mention of both Sanballat's and Tobiah's ancestry was meant to remind the reader that Moabite–Jewish and Ammonite–Jewish relationships had been less than amicable over the years.[11] Both the Moabites and the Ammonites were prohibited from entering the assembly of the LORD (Deut. 23:3). Sanballat and Tobiah were not pleased that "someone had come to seek the welfare of the people of Israel" (v. 10). These enemies were unaware of what was transpiring at the royal court in Susa. While King Artaxerxes himself favored Israel's reconstruction, Sanballat and Tobiah did not. We are reminded that God's work is sometimes done in the midst of opposition. In this case, the opposition came from the outside.

> 2:11-16 So I went to Jerusalem and was there three days. [12]Then I arose in the night, I and a few men with me. And I told no one what my God had put into my heart to do for Jerusalem. There was no animal with me but the one on which I rode. [13]I went out by night by the Valley Gate to the Dragon Spring and to the Dung Gate, and I inspected the walls of Jerusalem that were broken down and its gates that had been destroyed by fire. [14]Then I went on to the Fountain Gate and to the King's Pool, but there was no room for the animal that was under me to pass. [15]Then I went up in the night by the valley and inspected the wall, and I turned back and entered by the Valley

---

10. Edwin Yamauchi, "Archaeological Background of the Exilic and Postexilic Era, part 4: The Archaeological Background of Nehemiah," 291.

11 Ammon and Moab were Lot's sons, the product of the incestuous relationship between Lot and his daughters (Gen. 19:36-38). The Israelites encountered the Ammonites on their way from Egypt to Canaan (Num. 21; Deut. 2:16-37). During the period of the Judges both the Ammonites and the Moabites fought against God's people (Judg. 3; 10). During the monarchy, Israel's second king David waged war against the Moabites (2 Sam. 8) and the Ammonites. David conquered the Ammonite capital Rabbath-Ammon (2 Sam. 10–12).

Gate, and so returned. [16]And the officials did not
know where I had gone or what I was doing, and
I had not yet told the Jews, the priests, the nobles,
the officials, and the rest who were to do the work.

Nehemiah inspected the situation of Jerusalem at night,
accompanied by only a few anonymous men. This mission
was secretive for obvious security reasons, especially in
light of Sanballat's and Tobiah's vigorous opposition to
Nehemiah's plan. But Nehemiah also had a secret that God
had put in his heart. Thus, Nehemiah's plan was not his own,
but God's; and Nehemiah was carefully following the God
who had called him to do the work. What Nehemiah saw
was exactly what Hanani told him, namely, that the wall of
Jerusalem was broken down and that the gates were burned
(Neh. 1:3). Nehemiah's tour started at the southwestern part
of Jerusalem at the Valley Gate. He continued eastward to
the Fountain Gate and made his way to the King's Pool (the
pool of Siloam) before reentering through the Valley Gate.[12]
Nehemiah had a plan, but he had not yet shared that plan
with either the Persian officials or the Jewish leaders. His plan
obviously had to do with reconstruction because verse 16
says that Nehemiah had not yet shared the plan with those
"who were to do the work."

> 2:17-20 Then I said to them, "You see the trouble
> we are in, how Jerusalem lies in ruins with its gates
> burned. Come, let us build the wall of Jerusalem,
> that we may no longer suffer derision." [18]And I told
> them of the hand of my God that had been upon
> me for good, and also of the words that the king
> had spoken to me. And they said, "Let us rise up
> and build." So they strengthened their hands for
> the good work. [19]But when Sanballat the Horonite
> and Tobiah the Ammonite servant and Geshem the
> Arab heard of it, they jeered at us and despised us
> and said, "What is this thing that you are doing?
> Are you rebelling against the king?" [20]Then I replied
> to them, "The God of heaven will make us prosper,

---

12. Kathleen Kenyon, *Jerusalem: Excavating 3000 Years of History* (New York:
    McGraw-Hill, 1967), 107.

and we his servants will arise and build, but you
have no portion or right or claim in Jerusalem."

The man of God made the right assessment: the people were
in trouble and the city of Jerusalem was not a city to be envied,
but a sight to be mocked. Nehemiah's assessment was consistent with Hanani's report (1:3). But Nehemiah didn't just
weep over the state of Jerusalem (1:4), he moved to action,
challenging those around him to rebuild Jerusalem. His
imperative, "Come, let us build" showed that Nehemiah
would lead by example. He had the vision for rebuilding
Jerusalem, and he was a willing participant in the reconstruction. Nehemiah's motivation was clear, "That we may
no longer suffer derision." The derision Nehemiah referred
to was not only the physical deterioration of Jerusalem, but
also the spiritual disdain that accompanied it.[13] Nehemiah's
call to work was backed by his testimony. The fact that God's
hand was upon him for good could be seen in the king's
support of Nehemiah. Like all good leaders, Nehemiah
inspired confidence. His call and testimony were so effective that the people responded positively, "Let us rise up
and build."

Sometimes opposition is a sign that you're doing something wrong, but in this case, opposition was a sign that
Nehemiah was doing something right. Sanballat and Tobiah
were introduced in verse 10, and by verse 19 there was a
third person who opposed Nehemiah's work. Joining the
opposition was Geshem the Arab.[14] We learn that while
good people can encourage each other to do a good work,
evil people also can poison each other to oppose a good
work. The opposition became more intense as the numbers

---

13. The word translated here "derision" is the Hebrew הַחֶרְפָּה which can be
translated "derision," "shame," or "disgrace." In Nehemiah, the word
appears for the first time in 1:3, it is translated "shame" and it used to
describe Hanani's portrayal of the remnant. The word is used thirty-six
times; once in Genesis, twice in 1 Samuel, twice in Nehemiah, once in
Job, ten times in the Psalms, once in Proverbs, once in Isaiah, ten times
in Jeremiah, once in Lamentations, three times in Ezekiel, once in Daniel,
twice in Joel, and once in Zephaniah.
14. It is possible that Geshem the Arab is the same person identified in
extrabiblical sources as "king of Kedar." See William F. Albright, *The
Archaeology of Palestine* (Baltimore: Penguin, 1960), 145.

increased. In verse 10 we were told only that those opposing the work were greatly displeased that someone came to seek the welfare of the people of Israel. Verse 19 shows us that hatred could no longer be confined to the heart, but sought to express itself through mocking words. The enemies questioned the Jew's motives; "Are you rebelling against the king?" The question was meant to be an indictment. It was one thing to work to rebuild one's temple, but it was another thing to build an edifice that could point to an anti-government stance. Although not true, the accusation had the potential to damage the morale of the people.

Nehemiah, the man of God, showed his superior leadership qualities by not answering the charges directly. While the enemies expressed the hatred of their hearts, Nehemiah expressed his faith in God. Nehemiah humbly declared that he was only a servant, and he humbly proclaimed that the outcome would be God's doing, not man's accomplishment. Despite human opposition, the work would succeed because it was God's work and it was God who had called Nehemiah and inspired him to do the work of reconstruction. His declaration that the enemy would "have no portion or right or claim in Jerusalem," was a statement of fact. Nehemiah's language was legal in nature. The word translated "portion" is a legal term ḥēleq, which can be translated "legal share", and it "refers to a share in the constellation of the Jewish nation. If somebody said that they had no share in a certain nation, it was a declaration of revolt (cf. 2 Sam. 20:1; 1 Kings 12:16)."[15] Raymond Brown affirms that "Nehemiah's testimony captured two vital elements in any rich doctrine of God: transcendence and immanence. He acknowledges His transcendence as he worships 'the God of heaven' (4, 20), but his God is not remote and distant."[16]

Verses 17-20 are especially practical for anyone who is in the ministry. Like Nehemiah, leaders must identify the need and develop the vision for the future, but they must also inspire their workers to stand firm and work faithfully in the midst of opposition.

---

15 Fensham, *Ezra and Nehemiah*, 169.
16 Raymond Brown, *The Message of Nehemiah*, 58.

Nehemiah 3

Outline

3:1-32 The rebuilding of the wall is accomplished through teamwork

The rebuilding of the wall is accomplished through teamwork (3:1-32)

> 3:1-2 Then Eliashib the high priest rose up with his brothers the priests, and they built the Sheep Gate. They consecrated it and set its doors. They consecrated it as far as the Tower of the Hundred, as far as the Tower of Hananel. [2]And next to him the men of Jericho built. And next to them Zaccur[1] the son of Imri built.

Chapter 3 is the blueprint of how the work was accomplished through teamwork.[2] As high priest, Eliashib led by example. He didn't come with the attitude of "I don't do construction; I only do sacrifices at the temple." Eliashib demonstrated humility, a characteristic which is essential in a man of God. History tells the story of Charlemagne, the king of the Franks

---

1   Zaccur is an abbreviation of of Zechariah which means "Yahweh has remembered."

2   Nicholas Bailey notes that the description in Chapter 3 is not accidental, but rather follows "a basic internal logic…and displays external cohesion with the rest of the book of Nehemiah." See Nicholas Bailey, "Nehemiah 3:1-32: An Intersection of the Text and the Topography," *JOTT* 5 (1:1992): 5.

and the only king was who able to unite Western Europe for the first time since the Romans. It is said that when the funeral cortege of Charlemagne came to the cathedral, they were shocked to find the gate barred by the bishop.

"Who comes?" shouted the bishop.

The heralds answered, "Charlemagne, Lord and King of the Holy Roman Empire!"

Answering for God, the bishop replied, "Him I know not! Who comes?"

The heralds, a bit shaken, answered, "Charles the Great, a good and honest man of the earth!" Again the bishop answered, "Him I know not. Who comes?"

Now completely crushed, the heralds said, "Charles, a lowly sinner, who begs the gift of Christ." "Him I know," the bishop replied. "Enter!"

Because Eliashib humbled himself to do the work, his brothers the priests readily followed his example. Together, they worked to rebuild the Sheep Gate, which was on the northeast side of the wall. This gate seems to have suffered extensive damage since the workers had to build it, not just repair it. Its close proximity to the temple was strategic since animals intended for sacrifice were brought through this gate. Beginning reconstruction at the Sheep Gate was no accident. Rather, "the Sheep Gate serves as both a starting point, being analogous to Jerusalem's 'front door' (in contrast to the Dung Gate, its 'back door,' at the opposite end) and as the central reference point, or more exactly, the extension of the Temple as the central reference point."[3]

---

3. *Ibid.*, 6.

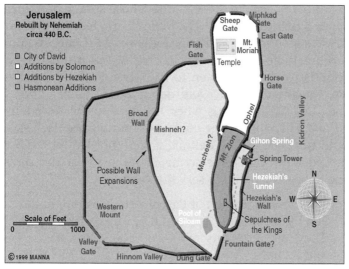

Jerusalem during the time of Nehemiah

3:3-5 The sons of Hassenaah built the Fish Gate. They laid its beams and set its doors, its bolts, and its bars. [4]And next to them Meremoth the son of Uriah, son of Hakkoz repaired. And next to them Meshullam the son of Berechiah, son of Meshezabel[4] repaired. And next to them Zadok the son of Baana repaired. [5]And next to them the Tekoites repaired, but their nobles would not stoop to serve their Lord.

The Fish Gate was probably connected with a fish market located in close proximity. The people working at the Sheep and Fish Gate were the only ones who are said to build or rebuild suggesting that the north wall was probably completely demolished. From that point on, the builders only repaired or reinforced the walls or the gates. In contrast with those who built, we are told that the Tekoite's nobles "would not stoop to serve their Lord." Blenkinsopp suggests that "the refusal of the Tekoan nobles to accept Nehemiah's leadership, may, given the location of Tekoa, be explained by

---

4.   Meshezabel is a participial sentence and means "God is the one who delivers."

proximity to Geshem the Kedarite whose sphere of influence extended to those parts."[5] The Bible clearly teaches that pride is always an obstacle in doing God's work. "I have too much education to do such a menial job," is the unfortunate cry that resounds in churches even today. Though these dissenters from Nehemiah's time were described as nobles, they are in fact low class citizens when it comes to the Kingdom of God and His work. They could not humble themselves and would not serve. They definitely were not led by the Spirit who spoke through Jesus saying, "For the Son of Man did not come to be served, but to serve" (Mark 10:45).

> 3:6-7 Joiada the son of Paseah and Meshullam the son of Besodeiah[6] repaired the Gate of Yeshanah. They laid its beams and set its doors, its bolts, and its bars. [7]And next to them repaired Melatiah the Gibeonite and Jadon the Meronothite, the men of Gibeon and of Mizpah, the seat of the governor of the province Beyond the River.

The Gate of Yeshanah was named as such because it pointed to the town of Yeshanah.[7] Thus, the location of the gate was on the west side of the city.

> 3:8-10 Next to them Uzziel the son of Harhaiah, goldsmiths, repaired. Next to him Hananiah, one of the perfumers, repaired, and they restored Jerusalem as far as the Broad Wall. [9]Next to them Rephaiah the son of Hur, ruler of half the district of Jerusalem, repaired. [10]Next to them Jedaiah the son of Harumaph[8] repaired opposite his house. And next to him Hattush the son of Hashabneiah repaired.

These verses introduce us to the workers who were identified not by their location, but by their profession. Goldsmiths and perfumers would not be someone's first choice for

---

5. Blenkinsopp, *Ezra–Nehemiah*, 234.
6. Besodeiah means "In the counsel/friendship of Yahweh."
7. Some translate this as "The gate of the old city," or "The gate of the new quarter." But since Yeshanah was a town name it seems to make sense that the gate was named after the city, just as the today's Jaffa Gate opens in the direction of Jaffa.
8. Harumaph means "pig," and it may have been a nickname.

(re)construction work, but again we see how God accomplished His work in teams. These men could have said
that they were too skilled for such a task, but they didn't.
A further example of humility was Rephaiah the son of Hur,
who was ruler of half the district of Jerusalem. Good, effective leaders indeed lead by example.

> 3:11-14 Malchijah the son of Harim and Hasshub the
> son of Pahath-moab repaired another section and the
> Tower of the Ovens. [12]Next to him Shallum the son
> of Hallohesh, ruler of half the district of Jerusalem,
> repaired, he and his daughters. [13]Hanun and the
> inhabitants of Zanoah repaired the Valley Gate. They
> rebuilt it and set its doors, its bolts, and its bars, and
> repaired a thousand cubits of the wall, as far as the
> Dung Gate. [14]Malchijah the son of Rechab, ruler of the
> district of Beth-haccherem, repaired the Dung Gate.
> He rebuilt it and set its doors, its bolts, and its bars.

The Tower of the Ovens[9] appears only one other time, in
Chapter 12:38, and it was close to the Valley Gate. The ovens
were probably used for baking. The mention of daughters
for the first and only time in this chapter suggests the pos-
sibility that Shallum didn't have any sons, so it was natural
that his daughters would help with the repair since they
would inherit both his name and his property. The distance
between the Valley Gate and the Dung Gate was approximately 500 yards, and is probably mentioned because this
part of the wall was unusually long,

> 3:15-21 And Shallum the son of Col-hozeh, ruler of
> the district of Mizpah, repaired the Fountain Gate.
> He rebuilt it and covered it and set its doors, its bolts,
> and its bars. And he built the wall of the Pool of
> Shelah of the king's garden, as far as the stairs that go
> down from the City of David. [16]After him Nehemiah
> the son of Azbuk, ruler of half the district of Beth-
> zur, repaired to a point opposite the tombs of David,
> as far as the artificial pool, and as far as the house
> of the mighty men. [17]After him the Levites repaired:

---

9. Some suggest that this is the same as the David Tower near the Jaffa Gate.

Rehum the son of Bani. Next to him Hashabiah, ruler
of half the district of Keilah, repaired for his district.
[18]After him their brothers repaired: Bavvai the son of
Henadad, ruler of half the district of Keilah. [19]Next to
him Ezer the son of Jeshua, ruler of Mizpah, repaired
another section opposite the ascent to the armory at
the buttress. [20]After him Baruch the son of Zabbai
repaired another section from the buttress to the
door of the house of Eliashib the high priest. [21]After
him Meremoth the son of Uriah, son of Hakkoz
repaired another section from the door of the house
of Eliashib to the end of the house of Eliashib.

The Fountain Gate most likely led to a spring of water,
possibly the Pool of Siloam at the end of Hezekiah's tunnel.
The tombs of David were located in the southeastern part
of the City of David and were uncovered by the French
Jewish archaeologist Raymond Weill in a 1913-1914 dig.[10]
The "mighty men" in verse 16 is a reference to the time of
David (2 Sam. 23:8-39), and suggests that these mighty men
probably formed an unparalleled military class in subsequent reigns. Verse 20 begins the description of a part of the
wall which was traced by referencing private homes.

3:22-27 After him the priests, the men of the
surrounding area, repaired. [23]After them Benjamin
and Hasshub repaired opposite their house. After
them Azariah the son of Maaseiah, son of Ananiah
repaired beside his own house. [24]After him Binnui the
son of Henadad repaired another section, from the
house of Azariah to the buttress [25]and to the corner.
Palal the son of Uzai repaired opposite the buttress
and the tower projecting from the upper house of
the king at the court of the guard. After him Pedaiah
the son of Parosh [26]and the temple servants living on
Ophel repaired to a point opposite the Water Gate
on the east and the projecting tower. [27]After him
the Tekoites repaired another section opposite the
great projecting tower as far as the wall of Ophel.

---

10. See *The City of David: Revisiting Early Excavations*, edited by Hershel
Shanks (Washington D.C.: BAS, 2004).

This is the first mention of temple servants joining in the work of reconstruction. Some worked on the king's palace while others worked "opposite the Water Gate." This gate "must refer to a gate in the pre-exilic wall immediately above the Gihon spring and used for access to it. This, of course was not rebuilt by Nehemiah."[11] Ellison explains that "the Water Gate was not one of the city gates, but that it (will have) connected the royal precincts with the Temple area in pre-exilic Jerusalem."

> 3:28-32 Above the Horse Gate the priests repaired, each one opposite his own house. [29]After them Zadok the son of Immer repaired opposite his own house. After him Shemaiah the son of Shecaniah, the keeper of the East Gate, repaired. [30]After him Hananiah the son of Shelemiah and Hanun the sixth son of Zalaph repaired another section. After him Meshullam the son of Berechiah repaired opposite his chamber. [31]After him Malchijah, one of the goldsmiths, repaired as far as the house of the temple servants and of the merchants, opposite the Muster Gate, and to the upper chamber of the corner. [32]And between the upper chamber of the corner and the Sheep Gate the goldsmiths and the merchants repaired.

The location of the Horse Gate is uncertain. During the monarchy period, the gate was said to be somewhere between the palace and the temple (2 Kings 11:16; 2 Chron. 13:15), while Jeremiah referred to it as a city gate (Jer. 31:40). In our context, it seems that the Horse Gate is an actual city gate located on the eastern side of the wall and fairly close to the temple. The location of the Muster Gate is uncertain, as is the meaning of the word translated "muster." The word is derived from the Hebrew root *pqd*, which can be translated "to appoint, attend, visit, muster." The location of the Sheep Gate is widely accepted as being in the northeastern part of the wall and in close proximity to the temple. The location was strategic since sheep meant for temple sacrifice were ushered through this gate. The mention of the Sheep Gate

---

11. Williamson, *Ezra, Nehemiah,* 209.

in verses 1 and 32 forms an indirect inclusio, pointing to the completion of the project that started and ended at the very important Sheep Gate. It shows the right priorities of the workers, beginning and ending with the gate most closely associated with temple worship. "God is our number one priority," the workers say without using words.

Chapter three displays and emphasizes unity in diversity. Even though the workers come from different locations, different levels of education and different professions, they were united under the leadership of Nehemiah to accomplish the work of reconstruction.

Nehemiah 4

Outline

I. Prayer and planning amid opposition (4:1-11)

4:1-3 Now when Sanballat heard that we were building the wall, he was angry and greatly enraged, and he jeered at the Jews. ²And he said in the presence of his brothers and of the army of Samaria, "What are these feeble Jews doing? Will they restore it for themselves? Will they sacrifice? Will they finish up in a day? Will they revive the stones out of the heaps of rubbish, and burned ones at that?" ³Tobiah the Ammonite was beside him, and he said, "Yes, what they are building—if a fox goes up on it he will break down their stone wall!"

Chapter 4 is one of contrasts. The faithless ridicule while the faithful pray. The faithless demean while the faithful plan. The faithless threaten while the faithful are encouraged by their godly leaders. Just as the Pharisees were angered when Jesus did a good deed, so Sanballat and Tobiah derided God's people for rebuilding Jerusalem. The rage of Sanballat's heart was exteriorized in words of ridicule, comprised of four rhetorical questions: "Will they restore…? Will they sacrifice…? Will they finish up…? Will they revive…?" These questions were intended to conjure up a "nothing" or "no" answer. The prospect of the Jews restoring the walls by sacrificing for the LORD was unfathomable to Sanballat. His faithless heart and corrupt mind saw only heaps of burned rubbish, while Nehemiah's faithful heart and visionary mind saw a rebuilt city long before it was a fact. Even when much of the reconstruction was completed, Tobiah ridiculed the finished product and suggested that a solitary fox could bring down their stone wall. One might be tempted to retaliate through harsh words and actions, but Nehemiah appealed to his God, the One who hears and answers prayer.

> 4:4-6 Hear, O our God, for we are despised. Turn back their taunt on their own heads and give them up to be plundered in a land where they are captives. ⁵Do not cover their guilt, and let not their sin be blotted out from your sight, for they have provoked you to anger in the presence of the builders. ⁶So we built the wall. And all the wall was joined together to half its height, for the people had a mind to work.

In prayer Nehemiah asked God to fight the battle for him. He did not deny his feelings, but admitted that he felt despised. Nehemiah's prayer was imprecatory in nature and resembled many of the imprecatory Psalms.[1] Nehemiah correctly judged that the enemy's sin was not against him but against God; therefore, he made the appeal that since they provoked God to anger, God should not provide atonement and forgiveness for their sin. It is important to remember that Nehemiah's prayer was descriptive, not prescriptive. As followers of Christ, we are not permitted to pray these types of prayers because of Jesus' teachings, which instruct us to love our enemies and to pray for those who persecute us (Matt. 5:44-45). Following Nehemiah's prayer, the work advanced due to the workers' renewed calm and unity. Prayer is fundamental in doing God's work, as well as planning, but there comes a time when we must get up from our knees and start working. Under Nehemiah's leadership

---

1. Psalms 35, 55, 59, 69, 79, 109, and 137 can be classified as imprecatory psalms. In these psalms the psalmist prays that evil would befall his and/ or the people's persecutors.

the people united to do God's work and they completed half of the wall's height in spite of the enemy's ridicule and taunts.

> 4:7-8 But when Sanballat and Tobiah and the
> Arabs and the Ammonites and the Ashdodites
> heard that the repairing of the walls of Jerusalem
> was going forward and that the breaches were
> beginning to be closed, they were very angry.
> [8]And they all plotted together to come and fight
> against Jerusalem and to cause confusion in it.

As the faithful united for good, the faithless united for evil. In Chapter 2:10 the opposition consisted of Sanballat and Tobiah; then in Chapter 2:19 they were joined by Geshem the Arab. Now, in Chapter 4:7 the opposition has grown to include Arabs, Ammonites, and Ashdodites. This verse focuses on the fact that opposition came from all sides. Sanballat was from the north, the Arabs were from the south, the Ammonites were from the east, and the Ashdodites were from the west. The anger in their hearts was directly proportional to what their eyes saw, namely the repairing of the walls and the closing of the breaches. This was not the first or the last time in history when the faithless became angered by something good. The religious leaders of the day were upset a number of times when Jesus healed the sick or when people sang His praises (Mark 3:2-6; Luke 19:37-39). While the faithful under the leadership of Nehemiah planned, worked and prayed, the faithless plotted to "fight against Jerusalem and to cause confusion in it." The faithless always do the work of Satan who hates God's people and wants their destruction (1 Chron. 21; Job 1–2; Zech 3; Acts 5; 2 Cor. 11; Rev. 12).

> 4:9-11 And we prayed to our God and set a guard as
> a protection against them day and night. [10]In Judah it
> was said, "The strength of those who bear the burdens
> is failing. There is too much rubble. By ourselves
> we will not be able to rebuild the wall." [11]And our
> enemies said, "They will not know or see till we come
> among them and kill them and stop the work."

Because piety is not a substitute for preparation, Nehemiah combined the heavenly and the earthly. Setting a guard after one prays is a good principle by which to live and lead. Facing opposition, Nehemiah was not paralyzed; rather, he got organized. But now another enemy came to the forefront: discouragement from within. Ridicule and threat from the outside were fought with prayer and planning, but how could they fight the enemy from within? At times this enemy is harder to fight because it is more difficult to identify, but in this case, the words of discouragement were clear: "the strength is failing," "there is too much rubble," "we will not be able to rebuild the wall." To add insult to injury, the enemy continued their tirade of threats. What had begun as anger in the heart of the enemy had become a death threat which was meant to stop the work that would restore the worshipper to his/her place of worship.

II. Words and work in spite of opposition (4:12-23)

4:12-14 At that time the Jews who lived near them came from all directions and said to us ten times, "You must return to us." [13]So in the lowest parts of the space behind the wall, in open places, I stationed the people by their clans, with their swords, their spears, and their bows. [14]And I looked and arose and said to the nobles and to the officials and to the rest of the people, "Do not be afraid of them. Remember the Lord, who is great and awesome, and fight for your brothers, your sons, your daughters, your wives, and your homes."

Nehemiah fought the enemy without by delegating tasks, and he fought the enemy within by encouraging his followers. Swords, spears, and bows were employed to keep the outside enemy at a distance and to protect the work already accomplished. Nehemiah was not into the "Can't we all just get along?" philosophy. Because he realized that the threat from the outside posed a real and present danger, he stationed armed guards. This was followed by an encouraging address in which Nehemiah wisely did not appeal to the human element, but rather he pointed to

God's character and greatness. The imperative, "Do not be afraid of them," was followed by the reason for a fearless attitude, "Remember the LORD, who is great and awesome." The refrain, "Remember the LORD," was used by Moses to encourage the generation that would enter the Promised Land (Deut. 8:18). The same refrain encouraged the exilic community during the time of Jeremiah (Jer. 51:50). "Remember the LORD" now gripped the hearts and minds of the faithful who needed a fearless attitude and trust in God to continue their fight.

> 4:15-18 When our enemies heard that it was known to us and that God had frustrated their plan, we all returned to the wall, each to his work. From that day on, half of my servants worked on construction, and half held the spears, shields, bows, and coats of mail. [16]And the leaders stood behind the whole house of Judah, [17]who were building on the wall. Those who carried burdens were loaded in such a way that each labored on the work with one hand and held his weapon with the other. [18]And each of the builders had his sword strapped at his side while he built. The man who sounded the trumpet was beside me.

The enemy suspected that they were fighting against God and not man, but that didn't stop them. That is clear from Nehemiah's strategy of "Work and Defend." The faithful continued to work with a brick in one hand and a weapon in the other. The trumpeter was close to Nehemiah since the trumpet sounded the alarm or a call to gather.[2]

> 4:19-23 And I said to the nobles and to the officials and to the rest of the people, "The work is great and widely spread, and we are separated on the wall, far from one another. [20]In the place where you hear the sound of the trumpet, rally to us there. Our God will fight for us." [21]So we labored at the work, and half of them held the spears from the break of dawn until the stars came out. [22]I also said to the people at

---

2. Besides warning of imminent danger, the ram's horn (shofar) announced the arrived of the Sabbath, New Moon, or the death of nobility.

that time, "Let every man and his servant pass the
night within Jerusalem, that they may be a guard
for us by night and may labor by day." [23]So neither
I nor my brothers nor my servants nor the men of
the guard who followed me, none of us took off our
clothes; each kept his weapon at his right hand.

The fact that God fought for the Jews does not mean that the
Jews should not fight. This was not a call to pacifism, but
rather a call to unity and a wise work-and-defend strategy.
Another practical emergency measure taken by Nehemiah
was to direct the people from the villages to spend the night
in Jerusalem. There was added danger for those traveling
home at night; thus, staying in Jerusalem protected them
and positioned them to help their brothers in case the enemy
undertook a night attack.

Nehemiah 5

Outline

I. A wrong revealed (5:1-5)

> 5:1-5 Now there arose a great outcry of the people and of their wives against their Jewish brothers. ²For there were those who said, "With our sons and our daughters, we are many. So let us get grain, that we may eat and keep alive." ³There were also those who said, "We are mortgaging our fields, our vineyards, and our houses to get grain because of the famine." ⁴And there were those who said, "We have borrowed money for the king's tax on our fields and our vineyards. ⁵Now our flesh is as the flesh of our brothers, our children are as their children. Yet we are forcing our sons and our daughters to be slaves, and some of our daughters have already been enslaved, but it is not in our power to help it, for other men have our fields and our vineyards."

While Nehemiah was preoccupied with outside opposition, it seems that an internal problem had developed which was was socio-economic in nature and which also revealed wrong dealings and injustice. Four different groups of people made up this situation. First, there were those who did not own land, yet needed food. The second group had difficulty feeding their families even though they owned property. The need was so overwhelming that these had mortgaged their homes and fields to buy food. The third group had borrowed money to pay the royal tax,[1] and were unable to repay because of the exorbitant interest charges. The fourth group was made up of wealthy Jews who were exploiting their Jewish brothers and sisters by "taking their land and children for collateral (Lev. 25:39-40). Jewish parents had been forced to choose between starvation or servitude for their children!"[2] The Jews had disobeyed the spirit of God's Law which always made provision for the poor (Lev. 25), and now the sin of injustice had been revealed and brought to Nehemiah's attention. How would he react?

II. A wrong addressed (5:6-13)

5:6-10 I was very angry when I heard their outcry and these words. [7]I took counsel with myself, and I brought charges against the nobles and the officials. I said to them, "You are exacting interest, each from his brother." And I held a great assembly against them [8]and said to them, "We, as far as we are able, have bought back our Jewish brothers who have been sold to the nations, but you even sell your brothers that they may be sold to us!" They were silent and could not find a word to say. [9]So I said, "The thing that you are doing is not good. Ought you not to walk in the fear of our God to prevent the taunts of the nations our enemies? [10]Moreover, I and my brothers and my servants are lending them money and grain. Let us abandon this exacting of interest.

Twice in the book of Nehemiah we are told that Nehemiah was very angry. The first time is here in the face of the injustice done against his brothers and sisters. (The second occurs in Chapter 13:6-7 when Eliashib allowed Tobiah to

1. It is estimated that Persian kings collected the equivalent of 20 million darics a year in taxes. 1 daric weighed 8.4 grams of gold. See Edwin M. Yamauchi, *Persia and the Bible* (Grand Rapids: Baker, 1996), 274.
2. Warren Wiersbe, *The Bible Exposition Commentary: History*, 655.

live in one of the temple's chambers). Is this relevant for today's Christian? Can the Christian get angry? The answer can be found by looking at Jesus' life. He expressed righteous indignation and anger when dealing with holier-than-thou Pharisees who were oppressing the poor and powerless, and He also got angry when the people transformed the temple into something it was never intended to be (Matt. 21:12-13; Mark 3:1-7). In his anger, Nehemiah accused the nobles and officials of abusing their brothers and of doing the opposite of what Nehemiah has tried to do. The nobles had not acted like brothers, but rather like slave masters. While Nehemiah had been helping his Jewish brothers become secure in their land, these nobles and officials had been selling them. Selling of Jewish slaves to Gentiles was against God's Law under any circumstances (Exod. 21:8). The silence of the nobles and officials was an admission of guilt. Nehemiah took advantage of their silence to emphasize that their lack of fear of God gave the Gentile nations license to taunt the Jews. Nehemiah's solution was clear: "abandon this exacting of interest." For Nehemiah it was not enough to identify the wrong and berate its negative effects. The godly leader took the necessary steps to eradicate the wrong committed. Indeed, before one does the right thing, one must make sure that the evil has been removed so that the good will thrive. The expression "let us abandon this exacting of interest" did not necessarily suggest that Nehemiah was guilty of this offense. Rather, Nehemiah identified himself with the people, just as he has always done (Neh. 1:6).[3]

---

3. One must be careful about applying this text to the contemporary situation. Gary Williams noted that "modern expositors find in Nehemiah 5 teachings on such matters as family planning (5:2), the proper exercise of anger (5:6-7a), thinking before acting (5:7), exemplary living (5:8, 14-18), the church's testimony before a watching world (5:9), promise keeping (5:12-13), sacrificing rights (5:14-18), the fear of God (5:9, 15), nonconformity to the world (5:15), and trust in God's reward (5:19)." However, when one interprets the text in its proper context, "one might expect that the main application of Nehemiah 5 would be that we should help the poor, and the more specific applications would include the sufferings of the poor (based on 5:1-5), condemnation of social injustice (based on 5:1-9), exhortations to get involved in righting social wrongs (based on 5:6-13), advice on how creditors should treat debtors (based on 5:1-12),

5:11-13 Return to them this very day their fields, their
vineyards, their olive orchards, and their houses,
and the percentage of money, grain, wine, and oil
that you have been exacting from them." [12]Then they
said, "We will restore these and require nothing
from them. We will do as you say." And I called
the priests and made them swear to do as they had
promised. [13]I also shook out the fold of my garment
and said, "So may God shake out every man from
his house and from his labor who does not keep this
promise. So may he be shaken out and emptied."
And all the assembly said "Amen" and praised the
LORD. And the people did as they had promised.

Now that the wrong had been identified and addressed,
the wrong had to be made right. Nehemiah's proposal was
simple: return what was taken, even the interest exacted. The
creditors accepted Nehemiah's terms and agreed to right the
wrong. They would restore what has been taken and do what
Nehemiah asked. Nehemiah's requirement of oath-taking by
the priests may have been part of a covenant renewal ceremony
or just a part of social protocol.[4] The shaking of the fold of
the garment was symbolic in nature, a common method used
in that day to reinforce a concept or idea. Nehemiah's act of
shaking the fold his garment was meant to be an object lesson
for those who would renege on their promise: "May God
shake those who don't keep their promise," was the message
of Nehemiah's symbolic act. The "Amen" chorus was more
than the lip service that it sometimes serves in contemporary
services. The "Amen" was "much used as a form of solemn
congregational assent in postexilic times."[5] The "Amen" was
followed by honoring their promise, and they "did as they
had promised." The wrong was identified, addressed, and
subsequently corrected.

---

and suggestions about government's responsibility to the poor (based
on 5:6-18)." See Gary R. Williams, "Contextual Influences in Readings of
Nehemiah 5: A Case Study," in *TB* 53.1 (2002): 58-59.

4.   Dennis J. McCarthy, "Covenant and Law in Chronicles-Nehemiah," in
CBQ 44 (1982): 25-44.

5.   Loring W. Batten, *The Books of Ezra and Nehemiah*, ICC (Edinburgh: T & T
Clark, 1961), 244.

III. A leader leads by example (5:14-19)

5:14-19 Moreover, from the time that I was appointed
to be their governor in the land of Judah, from the
twentieth year to the thirty-second year of Artaxerxes
the king, twelve years, neither I nor my brothers ate
the food allowance of the governor. [15]The former
governors who were before me laid heavy burdens on
the people and took from them for their daily ration
forty shekels of silver. Even their servants lorded it
over the people. But I did not do so, because of the
fear of God. [16]I also persevered in the work on this
wall, and we acquired no land, and all my servants
were gathered there for the work. [17]Moreover,
there were at my table 150 men, Jews and officials,
besides those who came to us from the nations that
were around us. [18]Now what was prepared at my
expense for each day was one ox and six choice sheep
and birds, and every ten days all kinds of wine in
abundance. Yet for all this I did not demand the food
allowance of the governor, because the service was
too heavy on this people. [19]Remember for my good,
O my God, all that I have done for this people.

Nehemiah served two terms as governor[6], the first time for
a twelve-year term, and the second for an undetermined
amount of time (Neh. 13:6).[7] The first time he served from
433 BC until 421 BC during the reign of Artaxerxes I. As a
leader with a sensitive heart and one who identified himself
with the people he served, he did not take advantage of the
legally allowable food allotment for the governor. Verse 15
contrasts Nehemiah with the governors before him who led

---

6. The Hebrew word פֶחָה is a loan word from Persian and is translated
   "governor." The word has a wide range of meanings, and thus, it can
   also be translated "satrap." The term is also used to describe Sheshbazzar
   (Ezra 5:14), Zerubbabel (Hag. 1:1, 14; 2:2), and other Persian officials (Ezra
   5:3, 6; 6:6-7, 13; 8:36; Neh. 2:7, 9; 3:7).
7. Some scholars suggest that Nehemiah's predecessors who were named
   governors, were "special commissioners whose roles were restricted
   to specific and chronologically limited tasks in connection with the
   Jerusalem cult." See H.G.M. Williamson, "The Governors of Judah under
   the Persians," in *TB* 39 (1988): 59-82.

with an iron fist and a hard heart. This verse also affirms that Nehemiah wasn't the first governor appointed by the Persian court, as others have suggested.[8] Based on both biblical and archaeological evidence, the Israeli archaeologist Nahmad Avigad reconstructed the following list of governors of Judah:[9]

Table 6: The Governors of Judah

Name	Source	Date
Sheshbazzar	Ezra 1:8; 5:14	538 BC
Zerubbabel	Haggai 1:1, 14	515 BC
Elnathan	Bula and seal	Late sixth century BC
Yeho'ezer	Jar impression	Early fifth century BC
Ahzai	Jar impression	Early fifth century BC
Nehemiah	Nehemiah 5:14; 12:26	445-432 BC
Bagohi (Bagoas)	Elephantine papyrus	407 BC
Yehezqiyah	Coins	330 BC

The governors who preceded Nehemiah were oppressive and their servants followed their evil example of exploiting the people. The difference between Nehemiah and previous governors was their attitude toward God. While Nehemiah feared God, his predecessors displayed a lack of fear of God, which then led to a lack of love and consideration for their countrymen. Nehemiah led by example and his people followed his example by persevering and uniting to do the work of rebuilding. The number of animals prepared for Nehemiah and those he would daily host was miniscule when compared to King Solomon's slaughtering of 22,000 oxen and 120,000 sheep for a seven-day feast (1 Kings 8:63-65). "Remember for my good, O my God," was the desire of the man who asked God to bless his unselfish leadership and service to the people. Kidner affirms that

8. Sean E. McEvenue, "The Political Structure in Judah from Cyrus to Nehemiah," in *CBQ* 43 (1981): 358.
9. In order to construct this list of governors, Avigad used, among other things, a collection of bullae and seals dating back to the fifth and sixth century BC. See Edwin Yamauchi, "Archaeological Backgrounds of the Exilic and Postexilic Era, part 4: The Archaeological Background of Nehemiah," in *BSac* 137/548 (1980), 298-299.

Nehemiah "exemplified the two great commandments, and anticipated the cheerful disregard of one's entitlements which Paul would expound in 1 Corinthians 9."[10]

---

10. Derek Kidner, *Ezra and Nehemiah,* TOTC (Downers Grove, Il.: IVP, 1979), 98.

Nehemiah 6

Outline

I. The man of God is discerning (6:1-4)

> 6:1-4 Now when Sanballat and Tobiah and Geshem the Arab and the rest of our enemies heard that I had built the wall and that there was no breach left in it (although up to that time I had not set up the doors in the gates), ²Sanballat and Geshem sent to me, saying, "Come and let us meet together at Hakkephirim in the plain of Ono." But they intended to do me harm. ³And I sent messengers to them, saying, "I am doing a great work and I cannot come down. Why should the work stop while I leave it and come down to you?" ⁴And they sent to me four times in this way, and I answered them in the same manner.

God gave Nehemiah discernment to know that the enemy intended to harm him. Although the enemies had multiplied since the beginning of the reconstruction project, God consistently overcame their opposition and the people of God had almost completed the work. The enemies' tactics evolved over time from anger to mocking, and now they desired to physically harm Nehemiah. They proposed a meeting in the plain of Ono. "It may have been proposed as a kind of neutral territory, but Nehemiah recognized the invitation as a trap."[1] Nehemiah's answer did not address their deception, but rather declared that his great work would not be stopped for a committee meeting. Perhaps Nehemiah believed the principle that meetings were places where good ideas got strangled. At any rate, the enemy persisted in their deceptive invitation and Nehemiah persisted in his truthful answer. Nehemiah teaches us that a godly leader must not be distracted with lesser matters when doing the important work of the Kingdom. Many pastors and leaders waste valuable time in frivolous meetings while they should be doing God's work by—among other things—preparing sound sermons, tending to the flock, or making disciples.

II. The man of God fights lies and slander (6:5-9)

> 6:5-9 In the same way Sanballat for the fifth time sent his servant to me with an open letter in his hand. [6]In it was written, "It is reported among the nations, and Geshem also says it, that you and the Jews intend to rebel; that is why you are building the wall. And according to these reports you wish to become their king. [7]And you have also set up prophets to proclaim concerning you in Jerusalem, 'There is a king in Judah.' And now the king will hear of these reports. So now come and let us take counsel together." [8]Then I sent to him, saying, "No such things as you say have been done, for you are inventing them out of your own mind." [9]For they all wanted to frighten us, thinking, "Their hands will drop from the work, and it will not be done." But now, O God, strengthen my hands.

The failure of the enemy to distract Nehemiah prompted Sanballat to change tactics, now resorting to lies and slander. The accusation against Nehemiah was grave. In an open letter he was accused of rebelling against the very office that gave him permission to return and rebuild. Sanballat suggested

---

1. Edwin Yamauchi, *Ezra and Nehemiah*, EBC 4. Edited by Frank E. Gaebelein (Grand Rapids: Zondervan, 1988), 712.

that Nehemiah was preparing not only to bite the hand that feeds him, but also to cut off the hand that allowed him to return to his homeland. According to the accusation, the rebuilt walls were meant to isolate and protect a messianic-like movement. Furthermore, Nehemiah was accused of writing the prophets' sermons in order to enhance his own image. In light of God's plan for the world, this sin would have been much graver than rebelling against the king of Persia since this would have pitted Nehemiah against the God of heaven. Geshem either gave birth to the rumor, or helped spread it. Sanballat's resolution for the problem proposed a meeting with Nehemiah, which the man of God rightly and promptly rejected because he discerned the evil of Sanballat's mind and heart. The enemy tried to weaken the faithful by impregnating their hearts with fear, but the man of God prayed for strength. "Strengthen my hands," is the cry of all the faithful who know that victory is won only when God provides the strength. Nehemiah's cry echoes that of the Psalmist who desires God's strength when his soul is weakened by sorrow (Ps. 119:28).

III. The man of God fights threats and false prophets (6:10-14)

> 6:10-14 Now when I went into the house of Shemaiah the son of Delaiah, son of Mehetabel, who was confined to his home, he said, "Let us meet together in the house of God, within the temple. Let us close the doors of the temple, for they are coming to kill you. They are coming to kill you by night." [11]But I said, "Should such a man as I run away? And what man such as I could go into the temple and live? I will not go in." [12]And I understood and saw that God had not sent him, but he had pronounced the prophecy against me because Tobiah and Sanballat had hired him. [13]For this purpose he was hired, that I should be afraid and act in this way and sin, and so they could give me a bad name in order to taunt me. [14]Remember Tobiah and Sanballat, O my God, according to these things that they did,

> and also the prophetess Noadiah and the rest of
> the prophets who wanted to make me afraid.

Shemaiah the son of Delaiah is a prophet about whom we have no further information. Nehemiah seems to have trusted him enough to go to his house, although we are not told the reason for the visit and speculation would be improper. Once inside the house, Nehemiah was told by Shemaiah that an assassination plot existed against him. Interestingly, Shemaiah knew not only about the plot, but also the time when the shameless act would be carried out. Shemaiah's solution was to have Nehemiah hide in the temple, even though Nehemiah was not a priest and his presence in the temple was against God's Law. As a godly leader, Nehemiah feared God more than man. His question, "Should such a man as I run away?" revealed his character. He was not one to run away in the face of danger, nor one to disobey the Law of God. Indeed, the Law gave the Israelites the ability to assess the authenticity of a prophet, and also the authority to disobey false prophets. "When a prophet speaks in the name of the LORD, if the word does not come to pass or come true, that is a word that the LORD has not spoken; the prophet has spoken it presumptuously. You need not be afraid of him" (Deut. 18:22). Furthermore, Nehemiah's question "what man such as I could go into the temple and live?" pointed to his respect for God, His Law, and His temple. Nehemiah discerned that Shemaiah was nothing but a corrupt prophet who was paid by Tobiah and Sanballat. Like Judas of old, and like many prophets today, Shemaiah sold himself for a price. Instead of speaking the Word of God, Shemaiah spoke the word of man which was intended to scare Nehemiah and to mar his godly reputation. Nehemiah stood firm as a righteous man of God who was not threatened into breaking God's Law. He knew the fate of King Uzziah when he dared to enter the temple, and Nehemiah probably realized that his own fate could be even worse than being struck with leprosy. Kidner correctly points out that had Nehemiah tried "to save himself in such a way, [he] would have lost, possibly, his life, certainly his honor; would have jeopardized the very cause he had at heart."[2]

In addition to Shemaiah, other false prophets were in on this evil plan. Noadiah the prophetess is the only other one mentioned by name, but the abundance of these corrupt prophets indicates that this episode was not unique, but was only one of many instances in which the enemy tried to derail the work of the faithful and to tarnish God's reputation. As in the past, Nehemiah responded to the enemy's attack by praying to the One who reigns over all and who thwarts the enemy's plan.

IV. The man of God succeeds: the wall is finished (6:15-19)

> 6:15-19 So the wall was finished on the twenty-fifth day of the month Elul, in fifty-two days. [16]And when all our enemies heard of it, all the nations around us were afraid and fell greatly in their own esteem, for they perceived that this work had been accomplished with the help of our God. [17]Moreover, in those days the nobles of Judah sent many letters to Tobiah, and Tobiah's letters came to them. [18]For many in Judah were bound by oath to him, because he was the son-in-law of Shecaniah the son of Arah: and his son Jehohanan had taken the daughter of Meshullam the son of Berechiah as his wife. [19]Also they spoke of his good deeds in my presence and reported my words to him. And Tobiah sent letters to make me afraid.

Despite threats, obstacles, and fierce opposition from the enemy, the Jews worked from the third day of Av until the twenty-fifth day of Elul,[3] and they finished the wall in only fifty-two days. Thus, the work that started in the hot summer days concluded in the cooler days of fall. We can safely assume that the Jews greatly rejoiced over this great rebuilding feat. In contrast to them, fear gripped the enemy because they finally and fully perceived God's hand in this momentous accomplishment. While this fear of God should

---

2. Derek Kidner, *Ezra and Nehemiah,* TOTC (Downers Grove, Il.,: IVP, 1979), 100.
3. See The Jewish Calendar chart in Ezra 3.

have prompted the enemy to turn toward Him in repentance, the enemy continued to harden their hearts and to
hone their threatening ways.

Verse 18 points to a sad reality that is present in today's
churches as well. Instead of living their lives according to
biblical principles, some live their lives being led by family
ties. In Nehemiah's day, family ties led some to fight against
the faithful. How many churches today have been damaged
and even destroyed because the leadership of the church
fears their family members instead of fearing God and
trusting His Word?

Even though Nehemiah received some praise, Tobiah
was relentless in his opposition. While the bricks and mortar
provided some defense against the elements and the enemy,
Nehemiah and the faithful needed the protection of the almighty
and powerful hand of God. The last verses of Chapter 6 point
to the ongoing reality that God's work is always accomplished
amid obstacles and opposition. God's work will always be
accomplished with His help, even though He uses the faithful
to carry out His plans.

Nehemiah 7

Outline

I. The humble man of God delegates work (7:1-5)

7:1-5 Now when the wall had been built and I had set up the doors, and the gatekeepers, the singers, and the Levites had been appointed, [2]I gave my brother Hanani and Hananiah the governor of the castle charge over Jerusalem, for he was a more faithful and God-fearing man than many. [3]And I said to them, "Let not the gates of Jerusalem be opened until the sun is hot. And while they are still standing guard, let them shut and bar the doors. Appoint guards from among the inhabitants of Jerusalem, some at their guard posts and some in front of their own homes." [4]The city was wide and large, but the people within it were few, and no houses had been rebuilt. [5]Then my God put it into my heart to assemble the nobles and the officials and the people to be enrolled by genealogy. And I found the book of the genealogy of those who came up at the first, and I found written in it:

Even though the wall had been completed, Nehemiah was careful to appoint gatekeepers as ancient security guards. The singers and Levites probably helped in this role even though guarding the gates was not their primary responsibility. Williamson correctly points out that "these were emergency arrangements only."[1] As a good leader, Nehemiah knew that he could not, and he should not, do the work alone; therefore, he delegated work to Hanani and Hananiah. Hanani was Nehemiah's "brother" who first informed him of the tragic state of exilic Jerusalem (Neh. 1:2).[2] The fact that Nehemiah called him "my brother" twice, suggests that Hanani was in fact Nehemiah's real brother, not just a compatriot.[3] Hananiah served as governor of the castle, thus he was more than qualified to supervise the guarding of the city. But what set Hananiah apart was not his job but his character. His level of faithfulness and fear of God stood above many. As a godly and visionary leader, Nehemiah believed that fear of God and faithfulness were two significant assets for a leader. Indeed, the fear of the LORD is not only the beginning of wisdom, but a necessary element in godly leadership.[4] Nehemiah gave instruction for the people to open the gates later in the day, not at dawn which would have been the normal practice. This strategy shortened the time the guards would have to be posted at the gates.[5]

Even though things had started coming together, the city still needed repopulating and residences needed rebuilding—yet another crisis which Nehemiah faced. How would he deal with it? As in previous dilemmas, Nehemiah waited for God's prompting. In this case God directed him to conduct a census of the population, and in doing so, Nehemiah found "the book of genealogy," which was the list of the returnees from exile.

---

1. Williamson, *Ezra, Nehemiah*, 270.
2. We don't have any more information about Hananiah. Because Hananiah can be an alternate form of Hanani, some scholars suggest that the second name explains the first one.
3. The word "brother" can mean brother, relative, fellow countryman, or friend.
4. Job 28:28; Psalm 19:9; 111:10; Proverbs 1:9; 9:10; Isaiah 11:3; Acts 9:31; 2 Corinthians 5:11.
5. Contra James Barr who argues that "Nehemiah is commanding that the gates should be kept shut during the heat of the day…" See James Barr, "Hebrew עד, Especially at Job I.18 and Nehemiah VII.3," in *JSS* XXVII/2 (1982): 186.

II. The list of returnees (7:6-73)

7:6-73 These were the people of the province who came up out of the captivity of those exiles whom Nebuchadnezzar the king of Babylon had carried into exile. They returned to Jerusalem and Judah, each to his town. [7]They came with Zerubbabel, Jeshua, Nehemiah, Azariah, Raamiah, Nahamani, Mordecai, Bilshan, Mispereth, Bigvai, Nehum, Baanah. The number of the men of the people of Israel: [8]the sons of Parosh, 2,172. [9]The sons of Shephatiah, 372. [10]The sons of Arah, 652. [11]The sons of Pahath-moab, namely the sons of Jeshua and Joab, 2,818. [12]The sons of Elam, 1,254. [13]The sons of Zattu, 845. [14]The sons of Zaccai, 760. [15]The sons of Binnui, 648. [16]The sons of Bebai, 628. [17]The sons of Azgad, 2,322. [18]The sons of Adonikam, 667. [19]The sons of Bigvai, 2,067. [20]The sons of Adin, 655. [21]The sons of Ater, namely of Hezekiah, 98. [22]The sons of Hashum, 328. [23]The sons of Bezai, 324. [24]The sons of Hariph, 112. [25]The sons of Gibeon, 95. [26]The men of Bethlehem and Netophah, 188. [27]The men of Anathoth, 128. [28]The men of Beth-azmaveth, 42. [29]The men of Kiriath-jearim, Chephirah, and Beeroth, 743. [30]The men of Ramah and Geba, 621. [31]The men of Michmas, 122. [32]The men of Bethel and Ai, 123. [33]The men of the other Nebo, 52. [34]The sons of the other Elam, 1,254. [35]The sons of Harim, 320. [36]The sons of Jericho, 345. [37]The sons of Lod, Hadid, and Ono, 721. [38]The sons of Senaah, 3,930. [39]The priests: the sons of Jedaiah, namely the house of Jeshua, 973. [40]The sons of Immer, 1,052. [41]The sons of Pashhur, 1,247. [42]The sons of Harim, 1,017. [43]The Levites: the sons of Jeshua, namely of Kadmiel of the sons of Hodevah, 74. [44]The singers: the sons of Asaph, 148. [45]The gatekeepers: the sons of Shallum, the sons of Ater, the sons of Talmon, the sons of Akkub, the sons of Hatita, the sons of Shobai, 138. [46]The temple servants: the sons of Ziha, the sons of Hasupha, the sons of Tabbaoth, [47]the sons of Keros, the sons of Sia, the sons of Padon, [48]the sons of Lebana, the sons of Hagaba, the sons of Shalmai, [49]the sons of Hanan, the sons of

Giddel, the sons of Gahar, [50]the sons of Reaiah, the sons of Rezin, the sons of Nekoda, [51]the sons of Gazzam, the sons of Uzza, the sons of Paseah, [52]the sons of Besai, the sons of Meunim, the sons of Nephushesim, [53]the sons of Bakbuk, the sons of Hakupha, the sons of Harhur, [54]the sons of Bazlith, the sons of Mehida, the sons of Harsha, [55]the sons of Barkos, the sons of Sisera, the sons of Temah, [56]the sons of Neziah, the sons of Hatipha. [57]The sons of Solomon's servants: the sons of Sotai, the sons of Sophereth, the sons of Perida, [58]the sons of Jaala, the sons of Darkon, the sons of Giddel, [59]the sons of Shephatiah, the sons of Hattil, the sons of Pochereth-hazzebaim, the sons of Amon. [60]All the temple servants and the sons of Solomon's servants were 392. [61]The following were those who came up from Tel-melah, Tel-harsha, Cherub, Addon, and Immer, but they could not prove their fathers' houses nor their descent, whether they belonged to Israel: [62]the sons of Delaiah, the sons of Tobiah, the sons of Nekoda, 642. [63]Also, of the priests: the sons of Hobaiah, the sons of Hakkoz, the sons of Barzillai (who had taken a wife of the daughters of Barzillai the Gileadite and was called by their name). [64]These sought their registration among those enrolled in the genealogies, but it was not found there, so they were excluded from the priesthood as unclean. [65]The governor told them that they were not to partake of the most holy food until a priest with Urim and Thummim should arise. [66]The whole assembly together was 42,360, [67]besides their male and female servants, of whom there were 7,337. And they had 245 singers, male and female. [68]Their horses were 736, their mules 245, [69]their camels 435, and their donkeys 6,720. [70]Now some of the heads of fathers' houses gave to the work. The governor gave to the treasury 1,000 darics of gold, 50 basins, 30 priests' garments and 500 minas of silver. [71]And some of the heads of fathers' houses gave into the treasury of the work 20,000 darics of gold and 2,200 minas of silver. [72]And what the rest of the people gave was 20,000 darics of gold,

2,000 minas of silver, and 67 priests' garments. [73]So
the priests, the Levites, the gatekeepers, the singers,
some of the people, the temple servants, and all Israel,
lived in their towns. And when the seventh month
had come, the people of Israel were in their towns.

The list of names is almost identical to the one in Ezra 2. Some
insignificant divergences in the lists of names are shown
below, which probably occurred in the process of copying.
"By repeating the name list in Ezra 2 and Nehemiah 7, the
author(s) of Ezra–Nehemiah have created a literary inclusio
that unites the three major sections of the book (i.e., Ezra 1-6;
7-10; and Neh. 1-7). Now that the three waves of construction
and renewal were complete, the nation was prepared for the
spiritual revival that followed (Neh. 8-10)."[6]

Table 7: Comparison between the Ezra 2 and Nehemiah 7 lists

Name	Ezra 2	Nehemiah 7
Zerubbabel	x	x
Jeshua	x	x
Nehemiah	x	x
Seraiah[1]	x	-
Raamiah[2]	x	-
Mordecai	x	x
Bilshan	x	x
Mispar	x	x
Bigvai	x	x
Rehum[3]	x	-
Baanah	x	x
Parosh	x	x
Shephatiah	x	x
Arah	x	x
Pahath-moab	x	x
Jeshua	x	x
Joab	x	x
Elam	x	x
Zattu	x	x
Zaccai	x	x

6. Hayyim Angel, "The Literary Significance of the Name List in Ezra–
    Nehemiah," in *JBQ* 35/3 (2007): 148.

Name	Ezra 2	Nehemiah 7
Bani	x	x
Bebai	x	x
Azgad	x	x
Adonikam	x	x
Bigvai	x	x
Adin	x	x
Ater	x	x
Bezai	x	x
Jorah	x	-
Hashum	x	x
Gibeon[4]	x	-
Azmaveth[5]	x	-
Kiriath-arim	x	-
Chephirah	x	x
Beeroth	x	x
Ramah	x	x
Geba	x	x
Michmas	x	x
Nebo	x	x
Magbish	x	-
(the other) Elam	x	x
Harim	x	x
Lod	x	x
Hadid	x	x
Ono	x	x
Jericho	x	x
Senaah[6]	x	x
PRIESTS		
Jedaiah	x	x
Jeshua	x	x
Immer	x	x
Pashhur	x	x
Harim	x	x
LEVITES		
Jeshua	x	x
Kadmiel	x	x
Hodaviah[7]	x	-

Name	Ezra 2	Nehemiah 7
SINGERS		
Asaph	x	x
Shallum	x	x
Ater	x	x
Talmon	x	x
Akkub	x	x
Hatita	x	x
Shobai	x	x
TEMPLE SERVANTS		
Ziha	x	x
Hasupha	x	x
Tabbaoth	x	x
Keros	x	x
Sia[8]	x	-
Padon	x	x
Lebanah	x	-
Hagabah	x	-
Akkub	x	x
Hagab	x	-
Shalmai[9]	x	-
Hanan	x	x
Giddel	x	x
Gahar	x	x
Reaiah	x	x
Rezin	x	x
Nekoda	x	x
Gazzam	x	x
Uzza	x	x
Paseah	x	x
Besai	x	x
Asnah	x	-
Meunim	x	x
Nephushesim[10]	x	-
Bakbuk	x	x
Hakupha	x	x
Harhur	x	x
Bazlith[11]	x	-

Mehida	x	x
Harsha	x	x
Barkos	x	x
Sisera	x	x
Temah	x	x
Neziah	x	x
Hatipha	x	x
THE SONS OF SOLOMON'S SERVANTS		
Sotai	x	x
Hassophereth	x	-
Perida[12]	x	-
Jaalah	x	-
Darkon	x	x
Giddel	x	x
Shephatiah	x	x
Hattil	x	x
Pochereth-hazzebaim	x	x
Amon[13]	x	-
THOSE WITHOUT FAMILY RECORDS		
Delaiah	x	x
Tobiah	x	x
Nekoda	x	x

Table 7 Notes

1. Mentioned in Nehemiah 10:2 as one who signed the covenant.
2. Ezra 2:2 has Reelaiah.
3. Mentioned in Nehemiah 10:25 as one who signed the covenant.
4. Ezra 2:20 has Gibbar where Nehemiah 7:25 has the place-name Gibeon. The text of Ezra is to be preferred because of the "sons of" formula.
5. In Nehemiah 12:29 Azmaveth appears as a geographical location.
6. Mishna Taanith IV 5 (Tosephta Taanith 82) affirms that Senaah was an important clan belonging to the tribe of Benjamin. See, R. Zadok, "A Note on SN'H," in VT 38/4 (1988): 483-486.
7. Listed among the descendants of David and Solomon in 1 Chronicles 3:24 and among the returnees from exile in 1 Chronicles. 9:7.
8. Ezra 2:44 has Siaha.
9. Ezra 2:46 has Shamlai.
10. Ezra 2:50 has Nephisim.
11. Ezra 2:52 has Bazluth. His name means "Onion," and it could be a nickname.
12. Ezra 2:55 has Peruda.
13. Ezra 2:57 has Ami.

Nehemiah 8

Outline

I. The faithful read the Word (8:1-6)

8:1-6 And all the people gathered as one man into the square before the Water Gate. And they told Ezra the scribe to bring the Book of the Law of Moses that the LORD had commanded Israel. ²So Ezra the priest brought the Law before the assembly, both men and women and all who could understand what they heard, on the first day of the seventh month. ³And he read from it facing the square before the Water Gate from early morning until midday, in the presence of the men and the women and those who could understand. And the ears of all the people were attentive to the Book of the Law. ⁴And Ezra the scribe stood on a wooden platform that they had made for the purpose. And beside him stood Mattithiah, Shema, Anaiah, Uriah, Hilkiah, and Maaseiah on his right hand, and Pedaiah, Mishael, Malchijah, Hashum, Hashbaddanah, Zechariah, and Meshullam on his left hand. ⁵And Ezra opened the book in the sight of all the people, for he was above

> all the people, and as he opened it all the people
> stood. ⁶And Ezra blessed the LORD, the great God,
> and all the people answered, "Amen, Amen," lifting
> up their hands. And they bowed their heads and
> worshiped the LORD with their faces to the ground.

The people who assembled together took the initiative of
asking Ezra to read from the Word of God,[1] suggesting a
hunger for the Word which was characteristic of the post-
exilic community. A hunger for the Word of God is a characteristic that the faithful should exhibit daily. These verses
attest to the historicity of the Law of Moses which obviously
existed at this point in written form. Thus, the Law of Moses
could not have been a post-exilic development as some
scholars suggest.[2] The fact that these people willingly spent
many hours listening intently to God's Word emphasizes
their hunger for it. It could very well be that the exile had
deprived them of the opportunity to hear the Law since the
reading of the Law was mainly a temple experience. Besides
their names, we are not told further about the men were
that joined Ezra on the platform, thus to speculate would be
improper. The people stood when the scroll was unfolded,
showing their reverence for God and His Word. In some
cultures, this practice is still alive and well. Many Hispanic,
Asian, African, and European Christian communities stand
out of respect for the reading of God's Word.

---

1. McCarthy compares the law in Nehemiah with the law in Deuteronomy
    and sees differences. "In Deuteronomy the first step is a pledge whose
    object is a personal relationship, the law a guide for living out that rela-
    tionship. In Nehemiah the law itself is the object of the pledge. The com-
    mitment seems to be to the law, not to a person who guides a relationship
    by directives or 'laws.'" See Dennis J. McCarthy, "Covenant and Law in
    Chronicles-Nehemiah," in *CBQ* 44 (1982): 26. I believe that McCarthy is
    mistaken in perceiving a difference between what the Law was supposed
    to accomplish during the time of Moses and during the time of Nehemiah.
    In both cases, God wanted His people to be obedient to the Law, and by
    doing that, show faithfulness to the relationship to the Creator God who
    gave the Law.
2. The JEDP hypothesis advanced but not birthed by the German scholar
    Julius Wellhausen suggests that the Pentateuch was a compilation of
    four sources (J, E, D, and P) that was assembled by a Chronicler around
    the fourth century BC. See John J. Collins, *Introduction to the Hebrew Bible*
    (Minneapolis: Fortress, 2004), 47-65.

Ezra's blessing concluded the reading of the Word and was followed by the people's response, which was marked by three important characteristics: it was vocal, humble, and worshipful. Their vocal Amens were combined with raising their hands which "demonstrated their sense of need and dependence."[3] Their humble worship was seen in their prostrating themselves to the ground. This was a day of worship prompted by the presence and power of God's Word that was delivered by Ezra, the man of God.

II. The faithful explain the Word (8:7-8)

> 8:7-8 Also Jeshua, Bani, Sherebiah, Jamin, Akkub, Shabbethai, Hodiah, Maaseiah, Kelita, Azariah, Jozabad, Hanan, Pelaiah, the Levites, helped the people to understand the Law, while the people remained in their places. [8]They read from the book, from the Law of God, clearly, and they gave the sense, so that the people understood the reading.

The thirteen Levites who helped the people understand what was being read were fulfilling their God-given task as outlined in the Law. Before his death, Moses blessed the Levites and asserted that, "They shall teach Jacob your rules and Israel your law" (Deut. 33:10). During Jehoshaphat's reign some Levites became itinerant teachers and "went around through all the cities of Judah and taught among the people" (2 Chron. 17:7-9). These verses emphasize the importance of the ministry of the Word in a large assembly as well as in a small group. Both are important, necessary and vital to the life of the community of the faithful.

III. The faithful rejoice in the Word (8:9-12)

> 8:9-12 And Nehemiah, who was the governor, and Ezra the priest and scribe, and the Levites who taught the people said to all the people, "This day is holy to the LORD your God; do not mourn or weep." For all the people wept as they heard the words of the Law. [10]Then he said to them, "Go your way. Eat

---

3. Williamson, *Ezra, Nehemiah,* 289.

> the fat and drink sweet wine and send portions to
> anyone who has nothing ready, for this day is holy
> to our Lord. And do not be grieved, for the joy of
> the Lord is your strength." [11]So the Levites calmed
> all the people, saying, "Be quiet, for this day is
> holy; do not be grieved." [12]And all the people went
> their way to eat and drink and to send portions
> and to make great rejoicing, because they had
> understood the words that were declared to them.

For some people the words of the Law probably produced brand new life, while for others it was a reminder of what they had heard in the past. Both groups responded by weeping. The Word cut deep like a living sword into the hearts of the audience (Heb. 4:12), and the tears that were shed led to repentance (2 Cor. 7:10). Their tears were definitely not tears of joy since Ezra and Nehemiah exhorted the people not to be grieved. Ezra and Nehemiah were not getting in the way of the people's repentance, but they taught them that grieving must be followed by rejoicing. After all, the joy of the Lord—not the grieving of the Lord—is the strength of the faithful. Wong affirms "It is Yahweh's joy over his people that is the basis for the hope that they will be saved or protected from his anger." Furthermore, "Yahweh's joy is the basis of their protection from the consequences of their neglect of the law."[4]

The eating and drinking were the outward expressions of an inward state. In the Law the Sabbath was declared to be "holy to the Lord" (Exod. 31:15, 35:2), but Ezra and Nehemiah declared *this* day as "holy to the Lord" because in it the people had acted in accordance to God's Law. The people's obedience caused them to rejoice and feast, and also to share their abundance with those in need. Indeed, the faithful had caught the vision that God's people are to be generous people who care for the less fortunate. Warren Wiersbe summarizes the experience as an important sequence: conviction, cleansing, celebration.[5]

---

4. G.C.I. Wong, "A Note on 'Joy' in Nehemiah VIII 10," in *VT* 45/3 (1995): 384.
5. Warren Wiersbe, *The Bible Exposition Commentary: History* (Colorado Springs, Victor: 2003), 674.

IV. The faithful obey the Word (8:13-18)

8:13-18 On the second day the heads of fathers'
houses of all the people, with the priests and the
Levites, came together to Ezra the scribe in order
to study the words of the Law. ¹⁴And they found it
written in the Law that the Lᴏʀᴅ had commanded
by Moses that the people of Israel should dwell in
booths during the feast of the seventh month, ¹⁵and
that they should proclaim it and publish it in all their
towns and in Jerusalem, "Go out to the hills and
bring branches of olive, wild olive, myrtle, palm, and
other leafy trees to make booths, as it is written." ¹⁶So
the people went out and brought them and made
booths for themselves, each on his roof, and in their
courts and in the courts of the house of God, and
in the square at the Water Gate and in the square at
the Gate of Ephraim. ¹⁷And all the assembly of those
who had returned from the captivity made booths
and lived in the booths, for from the days of Jeshua
the son of Nun to that day the people of Israel had
not done so. And there was very great rejoicing.
¹⁸And day by day, from the first day to the last day,
he read from the Book of the Law of God. They kept
the feast seven days, and on the eighth day there
was a solemn assembly, according to the rule.

The priests, Levites, and heads of households came to Ezra for
an in-depth study of the Word of God as revealed in the Law;
and as they studied, they discovered legislation regarding
the celebration of the Feast of Tabernacles. According to
the Law, the Festival of Booths or Tabernacles began on
Tishri 15 and was primarily a thanksgiving festival, showing
gratitude for God's provision (Exod. 34:22; Lev. 23:33). This
fall harvest festival closed out the agricultural year and also
commemorated the Israelites' wilderness wandering, the
booths being a reminder that the Israelites lived in tents
during the forty-year journey from Egypt to the Promised
Land (Lev. 23:42-43). It was to Succoth the Israelites first came
after leaving Rameses (Exod. 12:7). The Festival of Booths
was observed during the monarchy period (2 Chron. 8:13)

as well as the post-exilic period (Ezra 3:4; Zech 14:16, 18, 19) and during the early church period. This is the only festival which commanded the Israelites to rejoice before the Lord (Lev. 23:40).

The returnees were eager to obey God's Word, which had been ignored since the days of their conquest. The inhabitants of Jerusalem erected the booths next to their houses or on their rooftops, while those from the countryside erected booths in open spaces such as the temple courts, in the squares beside the Water and Ephraim gates. The result of this obedience was great rejoicing. Wiersbe's insight is profound, "God doesn't give us joy instead of sorrow, or joy in spite of sorrow, but joy in the midst of sorrow. It is not substitution but transformation."[6] The people kept the feast promptly and precisely as the Law instructed, with the Book of the Law of God playing the central role. After all, the Israelites were meant to be people of the Book. McCarthy summarizes it well, noting that "the main thing is not general rules but a personal attitude, fidelity and repentant humility, a 'listening heart,' so that the people may enjoy unity with God in worship."[7]

6. Ibid., 676.
7. McCarthy, "Covenant and Law in Chronicles-Nehemiah," 41.

Nehemiah 9[1]

Outline

I. God is great and worthy to be praised

9:1-6 Now on the twenty-fourth day of this month the people of Israel were assembled with fasting and in sackcloth, and with earth on their heads. [2]And the Israelites separated themselves from all foreigners and stood and confessed their sins and the iniquities of their fathers. [3]And they stood up in their place and read from the Book of the Law of the LORD their God for a quarter of the day; for another quarter of it they made confession and worshiped the LORD their God. [4]On the stairs of the Levites stood Jeshua,

---

1   Tollefson and Williamson see three methods used for motivating group change in this chapter:

   • Staging a public demonstration to rally the people (9:1-3)
   • Increasing the magnitude of cultural dissonance to an intolerable level (9:6-35)
   • Rubbing raw public sores of discontent (9:36-37)
   See Kenneth D. Tollefson and H.G.M. Williamson, "Nehemiah as Cultural Revitalization: An Anthropological Perspective," in *JSOT* 56 (1992): 41-68.

Bani, Kadmiel, Shebaniah, Bunni,[2] Sherebiah, Bani,
and Chenani; and they cried with a loud voice to the
LORD their God. [5]Then the Levites, Jeshua, Kadmiel,
Bani, Hashabneiah, Sherebiah, Hodiah, Shebaniah,
and Pethahiah, said, "Stand up and bless the LORD
your God from everlasting to everlasting. Blessed
be your glorious name, which is exalted above all
blessing and praise. [6] "You are the LORD, you alone.
You have made heaven, the heaven of heavens,
with all their host, the earth and all that is on it, the
seas and all that is in them; and you preserve all
of them; and the host of heaven worships you.

Both Ezra and Nehemiah were men of prayer and fasting
(Ezra 9:5; Neh. 1:4). Now the people followed their example.
The days of feasting were followed by fasting. This day
was not linked to any of the festivals prescribed in the
Pentateuch, but was rather an adhoc day of fasting. Wearing
sackcloth and covering themselves with dust was a sign of
mourning quite common in the Ancient Near East. This day
of fasting also included separation from foreigners whose
"participation in the confession of Israelite sins would
have been impossible."[3] The separation from foreigners
was a direct result of the reading of the Law, which was
evidence of the people's intent to return to keeping God's
Law (Lev. 20:26).[4]

Half of the day was spent reading the Law, confessing sins,
and worshipping the LORD. The Levites took the lead by crying
out to the LORD and exhorting the people to do the same. Their
call to worship included some important theological themes.
First, God is eternal. He is "from everlasting to everlasting";
thus, He has no beginning or end. This is a consistent theme
throughout Scripture that is meant to show the contrast
between the man made idols of the nations and the true God

2. Bunni is an abbreviated form of Benaiah, and it means "Yahweh has built."
3. Fensham, *Ezra and Nehemiah*, 223.
4. Mark Boda sees the shared forms and vocabulary with repentance prayers
    found in Ezra 9, Nehemiah 1, Daniel 9, and Psalm 106. The consistent
    themes of covenant, land, and law are also present. See Mark J. Boda,
    "Praying the Tradition: The Origin and Use of Tradition in Nehemiah 9,"
    in *TB* 48/1 (1997): 179-182.

who is the Maker (1 Chron. 16:36, Ps. 90:2, Rev. 1:8). Second, there is no other true God except Himself. "You are the Lord, you alone," is an emphatic affirmation of God's uniqueness. Third, God is the Creator God. The words, "heaven," "earth," and "seas" would have reminded the Jews of Genesis 1 and the six days of creation. Not only is God the Creator God, but He is also the One who sustains the creation. As a result, creation worships God and His glorious name.

II. God chose and cared for Israel[5] (9:7-17)

9:7-17 You are the Lord, the God who chose Abram and brought him out of Ur of the Chaldeans and gave him the name Abraham. [8]You found his heart faithful before you, and made with him the covenant to give to his offspring the land of the Canaanite, the Hittite, the Amorite, the Perizzite, the Jebusite, and the Girgashite. And you have kept your promise, for you are righteous. [9]"And you saw the affliction of our fathers in Egypt and heard their cry at the Red Sea, [10]and performed signs and wonders against Pharaoh and all his servants and all the people of his land, for you knew that they acted arrogantly against our fathers. And you made a name for yourself, as it is to this day. [11]And you divided the sea before them, so that they went through the midst of the sea on dry land, and you cast their pursuers into the depths, as a stone into mighty waters. [12]By a pillar of cloud you led them in the day, and by a pillar of fire in the night to light for them the way in which they should go. [13]You came down on Mount Sinai and spoke with them from heaven and gave them right rules

---

5. The historical events recalled here have reference in the Pentateuch: Exod. 13:21-22; 16:4; 17:6; 19:18-20; 20:22; 32:1-6; Num. 14:14; 30; 20:8; Deut 1:33; 8:4. Bliese sees Nehemiah 9:6-37 as an example of chiasmus, while Boda argues that Bliese's "preoccupation with metre, high-frequency words and a disregard of the cyclical pattern" leads him to present irregular and erroneous chiastic structures. See Loren F. Bliese, "Chiastic Structures, Peaks and Cohesion in Nehemiah 9:6-37," in *BT* 39/2 (1988): 208-215, and Mark J. Boda, "Chiasmus in Ubiquity: Symmetrical Mirages in Nehemiah 9," in *JSOT* 71 (1996): 55-70.

and true laws, good statutes and commandments,
¹⁴and you made known to them your holy Sabbath
and commanded them commandments and statutes
and a law by Moses your servant. ¹⁵You gave them
bread from heaven for their hunger and brought
water for them out of the rock for their thirst, and
you told them to go in to possess the land that you
had sworn to give them. ¹⁶But they and our fathers
acted presumptuously and stiffened their neck and
did not obey your commandments. ¹⁷They refused
to obey and were not mindful of the wonders that
you performed among them, but they stiffened
their neck and appointed a leader to return to their
slavery in Egypt. But you are a God ready to forgive,
gracious and merciful, slow to anger and abounding
in steadfast love, and did not forsake them.

The prayer of the Levites contrasted God's faithfulness
with the Israelites' ingratitude. A better understanding
of God can be achieved by reciting His acts throughout
history; therefore the Levites' prayer recounted God's
actions from the covenant He made with Abraham to the
return from exile. The prayer continued to exalt the God
who not only created the world, but also the God who chose
Abram (exalted father) and changed his name to Abraham
(father of a multitude). Abraham was faithful; therefore, he
received a covenant from the LORD. One of the key covenant
promises was the inheritance of the Promised Land, the
land of Canaan, by Abraham's descendants. God not only
chose Israel by choosing Abraham, but God also showed
His lovingkindness toward them by protecting and caring
for them. The prayer clearly emphasized that God, the
righteous LORD, always keeps His promises.

The focus of the remaining prayer was on God, His faithfulness,
His power, His love, His grace, and mercy. Unlike
the false gods of the neighboring nations that are blind, deaf,
and mute (Ps. 115:4-7), Yahweh is the God who sees the affliction
of His people. God delivered His people from slavery in
Egypt, He led them through the wilderness, and gave them
His laws and commandments, which His people did not

obey. Even so, God continued to love them because He is a forgiving, gracious, merciful, patient, and loving God.

III. God led Israel (9:18-22)

> 9:18-22 Even when they had made for themselves a golden calf and said, 'This is your God who brought you up out of Egypt,' and had committed great blasphemies, [19]you in your great mercies did not forsake them in the wilderness. The pillar of cloud to lead them in the way did not depart from them by day, nor the pillar of fire by night to light for them the way by which they should go. [20]You gave your good Spirit to instruct them and did not withhold your manna from their mouth and gave them water for their thirst. [21]Forty years you sustained them in the wilderness, and they lacked nothing. Their clothes did not wear out and their feet did not swell. [22]"And you gave them kingdoms and peoples and allotted to them every corner. So they took possession of the land of Sihon king of Heshbon and the land of Og king of Bashan.

This portion of the prayer continued to contrast the Israelites' unfaithfulness with God's faithfulness. The Chronicler recounted God's forgiveness of His people and His mercy toward them even though they worshipped a golden calf. God continued to show grace and mercy to them by leading them miraculously through the wilderness by pillars of cloud and fire. The presence of God's Spirit had a didactic purpose—the people could only learn about God through God's Spirit. God provided both spiritual and physical food, and such miracles as "their clothes did not wear out and their feet did not swell." Furthermore, God gave them victory over their enemies. The victories the people experienced from the wilderness to the Promised Land are not attributed to Joshua's military genius, but to God's omnipotence. God gave His people kingdoms and peoples. This prayer reminds us once again that the Bible is a book about God.

IV. God rebuked Israel (9:22-30)

9:22-30 You multiplied their children as the stars of heaven, and you brought them into the land that you had told their fathers to enter and possess. [24]So the descendants went in and possessed the land, and you subdued before them the inhabitants of the land, the Canaanites, and gave them into their hand, with their kings and the peoples of the land, that they might do with them as they would. [25]And they captured fortified cities and a rich land, and took possession of houses full of all good things, cisterns already hewn, vineyards, olive orchards and fruit trees in abundance. So they ate and were filled and became fat and delighted themselves in your great goodness. [26]"Nevertheless, they were disobedient and rebelled against you and cast your law behind their back and killed your prophets, who had warned them in order to turn them back to you, and they committed great blasphemies. [27]Therefore you gave them into the hand of their enemies, who made them suffer. And in the time of their suffering they cried out to you and you heard them from heaven, and according to your great mercies you gave them saviors who saved them from the hand of their enemies. [28]But after they had rest they did evil again before you, and you abandoned them to the hand of their enemies, so that they had dominion over them. Yet when they turned and cried to you, you heard from heaven, and many times you delivered them according to your mercies. [29]And you warned them in order to turn them back to your law. Yet they acted presumptuously and did not obey your commandments, but sinned against your rules, which if a person does them, he shall live by them, and turned a stubborn shoulder and stiffened their neck and would not obey. [30]Many years you bore with them and warned them by your Spirit through your prophets. Yet they would not give ear. Therefore you gave them into the hand of the peoples of the lands.

The prayer continues to show the stark contrast between God's goodness and the people's rebellion. God blessed His children with descendants, with victory over their enemies, and with countless provisions. Instead of answering with dedication, they answered with disobedience. Instead of answering with raw submission, they answered with arrogant rebellion. Instead of getting to know God through the prophets, they killed the prophets of God. The people turned their backs on the good Law instead of turning toward the good LORD who chose them to be His people.

Verses 28-29 recall the days of the Judges when the people of God went through a vicious cycle of sin, oppression by the enemy, crying out to God, and deliverance.[6] Because God's warnings through the Spirit and His prophets were not heeded, God eventually allowed His people to go into exile. Indeed, in 722 BC the Assyrians took over Samaria and took some people of the Northern Kingdom into captivity. Israel's sister Judah did not learn the lessons of Israel, so God sent Nebuchadnezzar to take over Jerusalem. The Babylonian king burned the city with fire, destroyed the temple, and took some into exile. The people's sin was met with God's judgment, but only after God persistently pursued His people, calling them to repent and reform. God's rebuke is always rooted in God's love, and always followed by God's restoration. The message of Israel's sin, followed by God's rebuke and restoration, is central to the message of the pre-exilic, exilic, and post-exilic prophets.

V. God gave Israel grace (9:31-38)

9:31-38 Nevertheless, in your great mercies you did not make an end of them or forsake them, for you are a gracious and merciful God. [32]"Now, therefore,

---

6. Judges 2:11-19 traces this cycle of apostasy that will be repeated seven times throughout the book:
   - Sin of Israel vv. 11-13
   - Servitude to an oppressing neighbor vv. 14-15
   - Supplication by Israel v. 15b
   - Salvation by the judge sent by Yahweh v. 16
   - The cycle repeated v. 17
   - Explanation vv. 18-19

our God, the great, the mighty, and the awesome
God, who keeps covenant and steadfast love, let
not all the hardship seem little to you that has come
upon us, upon our kings, our princes, our priests,
our prophets, our fathers, and all your people, since
the time of the kings of Assyria until this day. [33]Yet
you have been righteous in all that has come upon
us, for you have dealt faithfully and we have acted
wickedly. [34]Our kings, our princes, our priests, and
our fathers have not kept your law or paid attention
to your commandments and your warnings that you
gave them. [35]Even in their own kingdom, enjoying
your great goodness that you gave them, and in
the large and rich land that you set before them,
they did not serve you or turn from their wicked
works. [36]Behold, we are slaves this day; in the land
that you gave to our fathers to enjoy its fruit and
its good gifts, behold, we are slaves. [37]And its rich
yield goes to the kings whom you have set over us
because of our sins. They rule over our bodies and
over our livestock as they please, and we are in
great distress. [38]"Because of all this we make a firm
covenant in writing; on the sealed document are the
names of our princes, our Levites, and our priests."

God is described as merciful[7] and gracious,[8] great,[9] awesome,[10] loyal to the covenant, loving,[11] righteous[12] and just.

---

7. God's mercy (raḥămîm) is the topic of other Old Testament writers and it
    is not unique to Ezra–Nehemiah. The expression "your mercy" or "your
    mercies" also occurs in Nehemiah 9:19, 27-28; Psalm 25:6; 40:12; 51:3;
    69:17; 79:8; 119:77; 119:156; Isaiah 63:15; and Daniel 9:18.
8. God identifies Himself as gracious (ḥannûn) in Exodus 22:6 and He is
    described as such in 2 Chronicles 30:9; Nehemiah. 9:17; Psalm 111:4; 112:4;
    116:5; 145:8; Isaiah 30:19; Joel 2:13; and Jonah 4:2.
9. Other passages where God is declared "great" (gāḏôl) are Nehemiah 1:5;
    9:32; Job 36:26; Psalm 99:2; 135:5; Jeremiah 32:18; Daniel 9:4; and Joel 2:4.
10. The word translated "awesome" (hannôrāʾ) comes from the root "to fear," and
    it has a connotation of being in awe of God's majesty and glory. It is used to
    describe God in Deuteronomy 10:17; 28:58; Nehemiah 1:5; 4:8; and Daniel 9:4.
11. Throughout the Old Testament God is shown as displaying covenant love
    (ḥéseḏ) towards His people (Gen. 39:21; Exod. 34:6; Num. 14:18; Ezra 7:28;
    Ps. 25:10; 33:5; 103:8; 145:8; Jer. 9:24; 31:3; 32:18; Joel 2:13; Jonah 4:2).
12. One of the main characteristics of God is His righteousness. Throughout

God's people are described as wicked, disobedient, rebellious, and unwilling to serve or repent. God's people realized that they became slaves to other nations due to their rebellion and disobedience. They knew that the exile was the vehicle by which they had reaped the fruit of their disobedience and rebellion. The people showed their repentant spirit and redirected their hearts by making a covenant with God.[13]

Table 8: The expressions describing God's greatness, power, love, and grace in the Levitical prayer of Nehemiah 9:6-31.

Text	God's action
9:7	God chose
9:7	God brought out
9:7	God changed Abram's name
9:8	God examines the heart
9:8	God initiates and makes a covenant
9:9	God saw the affliction of His people
9:9	God heard the cry of His people
9:10	God performed signs and wonders
9:11	God divided the sea
9:12	God led them in the wilderness
9:13	God gave His people true laws, good statutes, and commandments
9:14	God informed them about the importance of the Sabbath
9:15	God fed them manna from heaven
9:15	God gave them water from the rock
9:15	God reassured them about the Promised Land
9:17	God forgave
9:17	God was gracious to His people

the Old Testament, God is declared as righteous (ṣaddîq) (2 Chron. 12:6; Ezra 9:15; Ps. 11:7; 119:137; 129:4; 145:17; Isa. 45:21; Jer. 12:1; Lam. 1:18; Dan. 9:14; Zeph. 3:5).

13. The stipulations of the covenant will be detailed in the next chapter.

Text	God's action
9:17	God was patient with His people
9:20	God gave His Spirit to them
9:21	God sustained His people
9:22	God gave His people victory over their enemies
9:23	God made His children fruitful
9:27	God gave His people into the hand of their enemies
9:27	God provided His people with leaders who delivered them
9:29-30	God warned His people when they did evil
9:31	God had grace and mercy for His people

Nehemiah 10

I. The covenant signers (10:1-27)

10:1-27 On the seals are the names of Nehemiah the governor, the son of Hacaliah, Zedekiah, [2]Seraiah, Azariah, Jeremiah, [3]Pashhur, Amariah, Malchijah, [4]Hattush, Shebaniah, Malluch, [5]Harim, Meremoth, Obadiah, [6]Daniel, Ginnethon, Baruch, [7]Meshullam, Abijah, Mijamin, [8]Maaziah, Bilgai, Shemaiah; these are the priests. [9]And the Levites: Jeshua the son of Azaniah, Binnui of the sons of Henadad, Kadmiel; [10]and their brothers, Shebaniah, Hodiah, Kelita, Pelaiah, Hanan, [11]Mica, Rehob, Hashabiah, [12]Zaccur, Sherebiah, Shebaniah, [13]Hodiah, Bani, Beninu. [14]The chiefs of the people: Parosh, Pahath-moab, Elam, Zattu, Bani, [15]Bunni, Azgad, Bebai, [16]Adonijah, Bigvai, Adin, [17]Ater, Hezekiah, Azzur, [18]Hodiah, Hashum, Bezai, [19]Hariph, Anathoth, Nebai, [20]Magpiash, Meshullam, Hezir,[1] [21]Meshezabel, Zadok, Jaddua, [22]Pelatiah, Hanan, Anaiah, [23]Hoshea, Hananiah, Hasshub, [24]Hallohesh,

---

1. Hezir means "Pig," and it may possibly have been a nickname.

Pilha, Shobek, ²⁵Rehum, Hashabnah, Maaseiah,
²⁶Ahiah, Hanan, Anan, ²⁷Malluch, Harim, Baanah.

The names of those who signed the covenant are headed
by Nehemiah who is presented as governor. Indeed, the
title tirshāthāʾ is of Persian origin and it occurs five times
in Ezra–Nehemiah (Ezra 2:63; Neh. 7:65, 69; 8:9; 10:2). The
word identifies the Persian governor in post-exilic Israel.
Zedekiah's duties are unknown, although some suggest he
might have been Nehemiah's secretary.[2] The list includes
twenty-one priests, seventeen Levites, and forty-four lay
leaders.

II. The covenant promises (10:28-29)

10:28-29 The rest of the people, the priests, the Levites,
the gatekeepers, the singers, the temple servants,
and all who have separated themselves from the
peoples of the lands to the Law of God, their wives,
their sons, their daughters, all who have knowledge
and understanding, ²⁹join with their brothers, their
nobles, and enter into a curse and an oath to walk in
God's Law that was given by Moses the servant of
God, and to observe and do all the commandments
of the LORD our Lord and his rules and his statutes.

God's people realigned themselves with God and His Law,
and they covenanted together to walk in God's Law and
to observe His commandments, rules, and statutes. The
idea of "walking" in God's Law is present throughout the
Old Testament. Joshua exhorted the people who entered
the Promised Land to walk in God's Law (Josh. 22:5), and
the Psalmist classified as "blessed" those who do the same
(Ps. 119:1). On the other hand, those who did not walk in
God's Law went on to do evil in the sight of the LORD (2
Kings 10:31), and eventually were carried into exile (Jer. 32:23).
The concept of keeping God's commandments and statues is
also ever-present in the Old Testament, beginning with the
Pentateuch and ending with the Writings (Deut. 4:40, 11:1;
26:17; 1 Kings 2:3; 2 Kings 23:3; 2 Chron. 34:31). The words

2. Myers, *Ezra, Nehemiah,* 236.

"rules" and "statutes" appear together frequently in all three parts of the Old Testament. They appear twenty-seven times in the Pentateuch, twenty-seven times in the Prophets, and ten times in the Writings.

The people's oath was reinforced by a curse. Williamson asserts that "this was probably the ritual acceptance of some form of judgment which they knew would justly fall upon them if they transgressed the terms of their undertaking."[3] This was not an individual spiritual incursion, but rather, the people join with their families to covenant together to follow God and His Law. Indeed, if the people wanted a renewed relationship with God, they had to return to complete and unwavering obedience to His Law.

III. The covenant stipulations[4] (10:30-39)

10:30-39 "We will not give our daughters to the peoples of the land or take their daughters for our sons. [31]And if the peoples of the land bring in goods or any grain on the Sabbath day to sell, we will not buy from them on the Sabbath or on a holy day. And we will forego the crops of the seventh year and the exaction of every debt. [32]"We also take on ourselves the obligation to give yearly a third part of a shekel for the service of the house of our God: [33]for the showbread, the regular grain offering, the regular burnt offering, the Sabbaths, the new moons, the appointed feasts, the holy things, and the sin offerings to make atonement for Israel, and for all the work of the house of our God. [34]We, the priests, the

---

3. Williamson, *Ezra, Nehemiah*, 333.
4. Clines points out that this a not a bilateral covenant (bᵉrît), nor a collection of priestly laws (tôrōt), but "a unilateral pledge by the whole community, priest, Levites, and people." See David J.A. Clines, "Nehemiah 10 as An Example of Early Jewish Biblical Exegesis," *JSOT* 21 (1981): 111. McCarthy sees a dominant structure in the covenant renewal examples in Chronicles-Nehemiah.

    • Parenesis, used here as a general word for various kinds of exhortation
    • Covenant-making
    • Purification of land and people
    • Renewed cult.

    See McCarthy, "Covenant and Law in Chronicles-Nehemiah," 36.

Levites, and the people, have likewise cast lots for the wood offering, to bring it into the house of our God, according to our fathers' houses, at times appointed, year by year, to burn on the altar of the LORD our God, as it is written in the Law. [35]We obligate ourselves to bring the firstfruits of our ground and the firstfruits of all fruit of every tree, year by year, to the house of the LORD; [36]also to bring to the house of our God, to the priests who minister in the house of our God, the firstborn of our sons and of our cattle, as it is written in the Law, and the firstborn of our herds and of our flocks; [37]and to bring the first of our dough, and our contributions, the fruit of every tree, the wine and the oil, to the priests, to the chambers of the house of our God; and to bring to the Levites the tithes from our ground, for it is the Levites who collect the tithes in all our towns where we labor. [38]And the priest, the son of Aaron, shall be with the Levites when the Levites receive the tithes. And the Levites shall bring up the tithe of the tithes to the house of our God, to the chambers of the storehouse. [39]For the people of Israel and the sons of Levi shall bring the contribution of grain, wine, and oil to the chambers, where the vessels of the sanctuary are, as well as the priests who minister, and the gatekeepers and the singers. We will not neglect the house of our God."

The issue of intermarriage was addressed first, and the people pledged to keep themselves holy to the LORD by not allowing their children to intermarry with Gentiles. While the oldest law (Exod. 34:11-16) specifically prohibited marriage to the Amorites, Canaanites, Hittites, Perizzites, Hivites, and Jebusites, Nehemiah expanded this law to include all foreign nations. Clines correctly observes that

"the spirit of the law can be more rigorous than the letter. A more literalistic interpretation of the Pentateuchal law would have allowed marriages with Ashdodites, Ammonites and Moabites—for they are not explicitly mentioned among the prohibited nations. Ezra, Nehemiah, and the scholars of the Nehemian age adopted an interpretation according to the spirit (as we might say), since plainly the intention of the Pentateuchal laws was to forbid marriage with nearby foreigners (Canaanites, Palestinians).[5]

Second, the people vowed to keep the Sabbath and to treat it according to the original intent, namely, to keep it holy. Until now, God's people had ignored His command regarding the sabbatical year. According to the Law, in the seventh year the land was to remain uncultivated (Exod. 23:10-11; Lev. 25:2-7), but the people grossly disobeyed this command and the Chronicler records that this was one of the reasons for the exile. "He took into exile in Babylon those who had escaped from the sword, and they became servants to him and to his sons until the establishment of the kingdom of Persia, to fulfill the word of the Lord by the mouth of Jeremiah, 'until the land had enjoyed its Sabbaths. All the days that it lay desolate it kept Sabbath, to fulfill seventy years'" (2 Chron. 36:20-21). This change also prompted the people to cancel the collection of debts during the sabbatical year, as stipulated in the Pentateuch since the time of Moses (Deut. 15:1-3).

For the temple to function effectively the people were formerly required to contribute half a shekel (Exod. 30:13). The change to a third of a shekel could be explained by the fact that the Persian monetary system was different than the one used in pre-conquest times. This offering ensured that the showbread would be provided for the Holy Place, and that resources would be available for offerings and the celebration of feasts. The casting of lots to decide who would bring the wood necessary for the offerings is not mentioned in Leviticus (1:17; 6:12ff), even though casting lots to decide who was responsible for a certain task was not a foreign concept in the Old Testament (Josh. 18:6-10; 1 Sam. 14:42; 1 Chron. 25:8; Jonah 1:7).

In order for the temple personnel to accomplish their tasks, food had to be provided by the people from their firstfruits. The requirement of firstfruits for these offer-ings was initiated in the time of Moses (Exod. 23:19; 34:26;

---

5. Clines, "Nehemiah 10 as An Example of Early Jewish Biblical Exegesis," 116.

Deut. 26:1-11), thus, what might be perceived as the people's generosity was simply a return to obedience to God's Law. Furthermore, the tithes that were declared holy to the LORD (Lev. 27:30) were intended to benefit the Levites (Lev. 28:30). In Nehemiah's time, the Levites were both the recipients and collectors of the tithes. The promise "we will not neglect the house of our God," could be read as "we will not neglect the house of our God anymore."[6]

---

6. In the book of the prophet Haggai, God rebukes the post-exilic community for caring more about building their own homes, than about rebuilding the temple (Hag. 1:2-8).

Nehemiah 11

Outline

I. The repopulation of Jerusalem (11:1-24)

11:1-2 Now the leaders of the people lived in Jerusalem. And the rest of the people cast lots to bring one out of ten to live in Jerusalem the holy city, while nine out of ten remained in the other towns. [2]And the people blessed all the men who willingly offered to live in Jerusalem.

Chapter 11 focuses on "the fortification of Jerusalem's physical, human, and governmental strength," as well as "the renewed centrality of the holy city."[1] While the leaders already lived in Jerusalem, more people were needed to repopulate Israel's barren capital. Indeed, the returnees needed to engage in an active urbanization project. The practice of redistributing populations, known as *synoikismos*, was also used to establish Greek and Hellenistic cities, and it involved the forcible transfer from rural settlements to urban centers.[2] We are not told how the people reached the decision that 10 percent of the people should reside

---

1. Oded Lipschits, "Literary and Ideological Aspects of Nehemiah 11," in *JBL* 121/3 (2002): 423.
2. Edwin Yamauchi, *Ezra and Nehemiah*, EBC 4 (Grand Rapids: Zondervan, 1988), 744.

in Jerusalem, but there is no evidence of disagreement. Yamauchi suggests that the population of Jerusalem during Nehemiah's time had contracted to 6,000 persons.[3]

Jerusalem is referred to here as "the holy city," an expression used sparingly in the Old Testament, but twice in Nehemiah.[4] Lipschits suggests that "holiness stretched out over the entire city. This was a kind of extension of the holiness that prevailed over the Holy of Holies (compare 1 Kings 8:10; Ezek. 42:13-14; etc.), instead of over the entire sanctuary (compare Isa. 27:13; 56:7; 65:11; Ezek. 20:40; 28:14; 43:12), over the entire city."[5] Thus, "all Jerusalem becomes the house of God."[6]

The practice of casting lots was not foreign to Old Testament Jews,[7] so using it in this case would not have been considered odd. The casting of lots suggests that people preferred not to live in the capital city; therefore, as Fensham points out, "By casting the lot it is no longer Nehemiah who forces them to live in Jerusalem, but it is the will of God."[8] Those who ended up living in Jerusalem because the lots fell on them were contrasted with those who "willingly offered to live in Jerusalem." The ones who volunteered to live in Jerusalem were commended (blessed) by those who would rather live in their native towns and villages. [9]

---

3. Edwin Yamauchi, "Archaeological Backgrounds of the Exilic and Postexilic Era, part 3: The Archaeological Background of Ezra," *BSac*137/547 (1980), 195.

4. Isa. 48:2; 52:1; Dan. 9:24.

5. Lipschits, "Literary and Ideological Aspects of Nehemiah 11," 434.

6. Ibid.

7. Lev. 16:8; Josh. 18:6; 8; 10; 1 Chr. 24:31; 25:8; 26:13f; Neh. 10:34; 11:1; Esth. 3:7; 9:24; Job 6:27; Ps. 22:18; Joel 3:3; Obad. 1:11; Jonah 1:7; Nah. 3:10.

8. Fensham, *Ezra and Nehemiah*, 243.

9. Weinberg's "citizen-temple community" model suggests that the temple "became an autonomous and privileged organization of the ruling upper strata during the second half of the second millennium BCE. By merging with the community, the temple formed an essentially new structure – the citizen-temple community. This citizen-temple community gave to its members an organizational unity and a collective self-administration, and took care of political and economic mutual aid." See Joel Weinberg, *The Citizen-Temple Community*, translated by D.L. Smith-Christopher, JSOTSup., 151 (Sheffield: SAP, 1992), 92-93. Cataldo argues that Weinberg's model is incomplete when it suggests that "the imperially established political institution and the cult eventually merged into one

11:3-9 These are the chiefs of the province who lived
in Jerusalem; but in the towns of Judah everyone
lived on his property in their towns: Israel, the
priests, the Levites, the temple servants, and the
descendants of Solomon's servants. ⁴And in Jerusalem
lived certain of the sons of Judah and of the sons of
Benjamin. Of the sons of Judah: Athaiah the son of
Uzziah, son of Zechariah, son of Amariah, son of
Shephatiah, son of Mahalalel,¹⁰ of the sons of Perez;
⁵and Maaseiah the son of Baruch, son of Col-hozeh,
son of Hazaiah, son of Adaiah, son of Joiarib, son
of Zechariah, son of the Shilonite. ⁶All the sons
of Perez who lived in Jerusalem were 468 valiant
men. ⁷And these are the sons of Benjamin: Sallu
the son of Meshullam, son of Joed, son of Pedaiah,
son of Kolaiah, son of Maaseiah, son of Ithiel, son
of Jeshaiah, ⁸and his brothers, men of valor, 928.
⁹Joel the son of Zichri was their overseer; and Judah
the son of Hassenuah was second over the city.

Verses 3-9 list the leaders of Jerusalem, verses 10-14 list the
priests, verses 15-18 list the Levites, and verses 19-24 list
various other groups.¹¹ The list of leaders is definitely not
comprehensive since only leaders from the tribes of Judah
and Benjamin are given.

11:10-14 Of the priests: Jedaiah the son of Joiarib,
Jachin, ¹¹Seraiah the son of Hilkiah, son of
Meshullam, son of Zadok, son of Meraioth, son

---

governing head with the cultic leaders taking a role of authority over both
the political and theological institutions of Yehud." See Jeremiah Cataldo,
"Persian Policy and the Yehud Community During Nehemiah," in *JSOT*
28/2 (2003): 131-143. Indeed, the biblical text does not seem to support
Weinberg's theory, since Ezra–Nehemiah depicts the rebuilding of both
the political institution and the cult.

10. Mahalalel is a participial sentence and it means "God is one who illumi-
nates."

11. There are similarities between this list and the list in 1 Chronicles 9:2ff,
but there are also differences. While some suggest that one was dependent
on the other, no conclusive evidence exists as to who was dependent on
who, if that was the case. Some scholars prefer the shorter LXX version.
See P.K. McCarter, *Textual Criticism: Recovering the Text of the Hebrew Bible*
(Philadelphia: Fortress, 1986), 93-94.

of Ahitub, ruler of the house of God, [12]and their
brothers who did the work of the house, 822; and
Adaiah the son of Jeroham, son of Pelaliah, son
of Amzi, son of Zechariah, son of Pashhur, son
of Malchijah, [13]and his brothers, heads of fathers'
houses, 242; and Amashsai, the son of Azarel, son
of Ahzai,[12] son of Meshillemoth, son of Immer,
[14]and their brothers, mighty men of valor, 128; their
overseer was Zabdiel[13] the son of Haggedolim.

Five priestly families are mentioned here. The names that appear
elsewhere in Ezra–Nehemiah are Jedaiah (Ezra 2:36), Seraiah
(Ezra 2:2; 7:1; Neh. 10:2; 12:1, 12), and Adaiah (Neh. 11:5).

11:15-18 And of the Levites: Shemaiah the son of
Hasshub, son of Azrikam, son of Hashabiah, son
of Bunni; [16]and Shabbethai and Jozabad, of the
chiefs of the Levites, who were over the outside
work of the house of God; [17]and Mattaniah the
son of Mica, son of Zabdi,[14] son of Asaph, who
was the leader of the praise, who gave thanks, and
Bakbukiah, the second among his brothers; and
Abda the son of Shammua, son of Galal,[15] son of
Jeduthun. [18]All the Levites in the holy city were 284.

The Levites and singers are mentioned together, unlike in
previous lists where they were listed separately (Ezra 7:7).
We are given details as to some of the leaders' responsibilities, something that has been absent in previous lists.
Mattaniah was the leader of the praise. The word translated "praise" comes from the Greek translation, since the
Hebrew text has teshillah, meaning "beginning." This is a
classic example of an intentional scribal error since the
Hebrew word meaning "praise" is tehillah. Mattaniah was
a direct descendant of Asaph. In this case, the expression
"son of" indicates family lineage, not immediate son. The
number of Levites is relatively small when compared to the

---

12. Ahzai is an abbreviated form of Ahaziah, and it means "Yahweh has grasped."
13. Zabdiel means "God has given" or "Gift of God."
14. Zabdi is an abbreviated form of Zabdiel, and it means "God has given" or
    "Gift of God."
15. Galal means "tortoise" or "dung," and it may possibly have been a nickname.

total repatriated population and especially when compared to the number of priests. Batten calculates that "there are slightly more than four priests to each Levite."[16]

> 11:19-24 The gatekeepers, Akkub, Talmon and their brothers, who kept watch at the gates, were 172. [20]And the rest of Israel, and of the priests and the Levites, were in all the towns of Judah, every one in his inheritance. [21]But the temple servants lived on Ophel; and Ziha and Gishpa were over the temple servants. [22]The overseer of the Levites in Jerusalem was Uzzi the son of Bani, son of Hashabiah, son of Mattaniah, son of Mica, of the sons of Asaph, the singers, over the work of the house of God. [23]For there was a command from the king concerning them, and a fixed provision for the singers, as every day required. [24]And Pethahiah the son of Meshezabel, of the sons of Zerah the son of Judah, was at the king's side in all matters concerning the people.

Only two gatekeepers are mentioned here, indicating that this is not a comprehensive list.[17] The temple servants lived on Ophel, "the hill leading up to the Temple at the north end of the city."[18] Verse 24 gives us another glimpse into the Persian monarchy's way of dealing with the Jews. The Persian king appointed a Jewish leader, a Levite, to keep the royal court informed about any needs the people might have. Pethahiah then served as an advisor to the Persian king on behalf of the Jewish people.[19]

II. The villages of Judah and Benjamin[20] (11:25-36)

> 11:25-36 And as for the villages, with their fields, some of the people of Judah lived in Kiriath-arba

---

16. Batten, *The Books of Ezra and Nehemiah*, 271.
17. Akkub and Talmon are listed both on the Ezra 2:42 and Nehemiah 12:25 lists.
18. Kidner, *Ezra and Nehemiah*, 120.
19. Some scholars suggest that this office was previously held by Ezra. While there is no evidence of this, the hypothesis is not without merit.
20. Lipschits suggests that the list of villages is not "an actual reflection of the borders of Judah," but rather "a utopian outlook, based on perceptions of the remote past and on hopes for the future, after the building of the walls of Jerusalem." See Lipschits, "Literary and Ideological Aspects of Nehemiah 11," 430-431.

and its villages, and in Dibon and its villages, and
in Jekabzeel and its villages, [26]and in Jeshua and
in Moladah and Beth-pelet, [27]in Hazar-shual, in
Beersheba and its villages, [28]in Ziklag, in Meconah
and its villages, [29]in En-rimmon, in Zorah, in
Jarmuth, [30]Zanoah, Adullam, and their villages,
Lachish and its fields, and Azekah and its villages.
So they encamped from Beersheba to the valley of
Hinnom. [31]The people of Benjamin also lived from
Geba onward, at Michmash, Aija, Bethel and its
villages, [32]Anathoth, Nob, Ananiah, [33]Hazor, Ramah,
Gittaim, [34]Hadid, Zeboim, Neballat, [35]Lod, and Ono,
the valley of craftsmen. [36]And certain divisions of
the Levites in Judah were assigned to Benjamin.

"From Beersheba to the valley of Hinnom" is a summary
of Judah's borders. Benjamin's territory is summarized by
the mention of both major and minor cities.[21] Some of the
more important cities mentioned were Geba,[22] Anathoth,[23]
and Ramah.[24]

Text	List of settlers	Number of settlers
7:6-71	Those who return from captivity	30,447
11:4-19	Those who settled in Jerusalem	3,044

---

21. Some suggest that these villages "are the settlements that were not
    destroyed by the Babylonians and continued to be settled by Jews,
    although they were subjected to Arab-Edomite influence." See Lipschits,
    "Literary and Ideological Aspects of Nehemiah 11," 430.
22. A city assigned to the Levites (Josh. 21:17) where Saul and Jonathan
    fought the Philistines (1 Sam. 13 and 14).
23. A Levitical city (Josh. 21:18) which was also Jeremiah's hometown (Jer. 1:1).
24. The birthplace of Samuel (1 Sam. 1:19).

Nehemiah 12

Outline

I. Priests and Levites who returned from exile (12:1-26)

12:1-9 These are the priests and the Levites who came up with Zerubbabel the son of Shealtiel, and Jeshua: Seraiah, Jeremiah, Ezra, ²Amariah, Malluch, Hattush, ³Shecaniah, Rehum, Meremoth, ⁴Iddo, Ginnethoi, Abijah, ⁵Mijamin, Maadiah, Bilgah, ⁶Shemaiah, Joiarib, Jedaiah, ⁷Sallu, Amok, Hilkiah, Jedaiah. These were the chiefs of the priests and of their brothers in the days of Jeshua. ⁸And the Levites: Jeshua, Binnui, Kadmiel, Sherebiah, Judah, and Mattaniah, who with his brothers was in charge of the songs of thanksgiving. ⁹And Bakbukiah and Unni and their brothers stood opposite them in the service.

The first nine verses list the family names of priests and Levites who returned under the leadership of Zerubbabel. Kidner identifies three different lists in Nehemiah, chapters 10–12. Nehemiah 12:1-7 contains a list of first-comers, Nehemiah 12:12-21 contains a list of a subsequent generation, while Nehemiah 10:2-8 contains a list of people from Nehemiah's generation.[1]

> 12:10-11 And Jeshua was the father of Joiakim[2], Joiakim the father of Eliashib, Eliashib the father of Joiada, [11]Joiada the father of Jonathan, and Jonathan the father of Jaddua.

Verses 10 and 11 give a list of priests that spans more than 100 years (538-400BC). The list shows the connection between Jeshua, the high priest at the time of the return, and Eliashib, the high priest during the time of Nehemiah, and Jonathan.[3]

> 12:12-21 And in the days of Joiakim were priests, heads of fathers' houses: of Seraiah, Meraiah; of Jeremiah, Hananiah; [13]of Ezra, Meshullam; of Amariah, Jehohanan; [14]of Malluchi, Jonathan; of Shebaniah, Joseph; [15]of Harim, Adna; of Meraioth, Helkai; [16]of Iddo, Zechariah; of Ginnethon, Meshullam; [17]of Abijah, Zichri; of Miniamin, of Moadiah, Piltai; [18]of Bilgah, Shammua; of Shemaiah, Jehonathan; [19]of Joiarib, Mattenai; of Jedaiah, Uzzi; [20]of Sallai, Kallai; of Amok, Eber; [21]of Hilkiah, Hashabiah; of Jedaiah, Nethanel.

Verses 12-21 list the heads of the priestly houses in the time of Joiakim. The twenty-one families listed here have already been named in the first seven verses, and they are repeated here for the purpose of naming the heads of families.[4]

> 12:22-26 In the days of Eliashib, Joiada, Johanan, and Jaddua, the Levites were recorded as heads of fathers' houses; so too were the priests in the

1. Derek Kidner, *Ezra and Nehemiah,* 122.
2. Joiakim means "Yahweh will establish," or "May Yahweh establish."
3. Some suggest that Jonathan is a scribal error for Johanan. If so, Johanan is mentioned in the Elephantine papyri. See L.H. Brockington, *Ezra, Nehemiah and Esther* (Melbourne: Thomas Nelson and Sons, 1969), 199-200, and Fensham, *The Books of Ezra and Nehemiah,* 251.
4. There are some slight differences in spelling between the two lists: Rehum/Harim, Shecaniah/Shebaniah, Meremoth/Meraioth, Ginnethoi/Ginnethon, Mijamin/Miniamin, Maadiah/Moadiah, Sallu/Sallai. The spelling differences may be due to scribal error.

reign of Darius the Persian. [23]As for the sons of
Levi, their heads of fathers' houses were written
in the Book of the Chronicles until the days of
Johanan the son of Eliashib. [24]And the chiefs of the
Levites: Hashabiah, Sherebiah, and Jeshua the son
of Kadmiel, with their brothers who stood opposite
them, to praise and to give thanks, according to
the commandment of David the man of God,
watch by watch. [25]Mattaniah, Bakbukiah, Obadiah,
Meshullam, Talmon, and Akkub were gatekeepers
standing guard at the storehouses of the gates.
[26]These were in the days of Joiakim the son of
Jeshua son of Jozadak, and in the days of Nehemiah
the governor and of Ezra, the priest and scribe.

Verses 22-26 give us a list pertaining to the Levites which is
based on archived material, such as the book of the Chronicles
(v. 23). It is not meant to be an exhaustive list, but we are
given some chronological clues in the mention of Darius the
Persian (v. 22), Joiakim, Ezra, and Nehemiah (v. 26). These
are not mentioned in chronological order, but "mentioned in
their official order of importance."[5]

II. The city wall is dedicated (11:27-43)

12:27-30 And at the dedication of the wall of
Jerusalem they sought the Levites in all their places,
to bring them to Jerusalem to celebrate the dedication
with gladness, with thanksgivings and with singing,
with cymbals, harps, and lyres. [28]And the sons
of the singers gathered together from the district
surrounding Jerusalem and from the villages of the
Netophathites; [29]also from Beth-gilgal and from the
region of Geba and Azmaveth, for the singers had
built for themselves villages around Jerusalem. [30]And
the priests and the Levites purified themselves, and
they purified the people and the gates and the wall.

We are not told how much time elapsed from the completion of the wall until its dedication, but when the time came,

---

5. Fensham, 254.

Nehemiah summoned the Levites who have settled in surrounding rural areas. The celebration involves joy, thanksgiving, and singing.[6] The villages and regions mentioned are from the north of Jerusalem (Netophah, Geba, Azmaveth) and east of Jerusalem (Beth-gilgal). How the priests and Levites purified themselves is not explained, but such purification rituals usually involved the washing of body and clothes, along with the bringing of offerings and abstaining from sexual intercourse (Exod. 19:10; Lev. 16:28; Num. 8:21). How priests and Levites purified the people, gates, and wall is not explained.

> 12:31-37 Then I brought the leaders of Judah up onto the wall and appointed two great choirs that gave thanks. One went to the south on the wall to the Dung Gate. [32]And after them went Hoshaiah and half of the leaders of Judah, [33]and Azariah, Ezra, Meshullam, [34]Judah, Benjamin, Shemaiah, and Jeremiah, [35]and certain of the priests' sons with trumpets: Zechariah the son of Jonathan, son of Shemaiah, son of Mattaniah, son of Micaiah, son of Zaccur, son of Asaph; [36]and his relatives, Shemaiah, Azarel, Milalai, Gilalai, Maai, Nethanel, Judah, and Hanani, with the musical instruments of David the man of God. And Ezra the scribe went before them. [37]At the Fountain Gate they went up straight before them by the stairs of the city of David, at the ascent of the wall, above the house of David, to the Water Gate on the east.

The dedication of the wall included two processionals, one going to the south, and one to the north. Verses 31-37 describe the processional moving to the south towards the Dung Gate, which included a choir (v. 31), trumpeters (v. 35), and an orchestra formed of different musical instruments (v. 36). The procession, then, was a musical celebration led by Ezra (v. 36).[7] This verse provides further evidence that Ezra and

---

6. Mark Boda suggests that the word translated "thanksgiving" could refer to the presentation of sacrifices. See Mark Boda, "The Use of Tôdôt in Nehemiah XII," in *VT* 44/3 (1994): 388.

7. Some suggest that Ezra's name was an editorial insertion meant to show that Ezra and Nehemiah were contemporaries. See Brockington, *Ezra,*

Nehemiah were indeed contemporaries, both being present at the dedication of the wall.

> 12:38-43 The other choir of those who gave thanks went to the north, and I followed them with half of the people, on the wall, above the Tower of the Ovens, to the Broad Wall, [39]and above the Gate of Ephraim, and by the Gate of Yeshanah, and by the Fish Gate and the Tower of Hananel and the Tower of the Hundred, to the Sheep Gate; and they came to a halt at the Gate of the Guard. [40]So both choirs of those who gave thanks stood in the house of God, and I and half of the officials with me; [41]and the priests Eliakim,[8] Maaseiah, Miniamin, Micaiah, Elioenai, Zechariah, and Hananiah, with trumpets; [42]and Maaseiah, Shemaiah, Eleazar, Uzzi, Jehohanan, Malchijah, Elam, and Ezer. And the singers sang with Jezrahiah as their leader. [43]And they offered great sacrifices that day and rejoiced, for God had made them rejoice with great joy; the women and children also rejoiced. And the joy of Jerusalem was heard far away.

The second choir headed to the north and passed by gates and towers already mentioned earlier in Chapter 3. Of notice is the Gate of Ephraim which is not mentioned in Chapter 3, thus, one of the few gates that did not need repair. The celebration reached its highest peak when the choirs met at the temple. The sacrifices offered and the songs sung were an expression of joy, a joy that originated with God, the Giver of joy. The joy of the LORD did not know age or physical boundary. Thus, the songs of joy and the sounds of celebration were heard beyond the walls of the city.[9]

III. Offerings for temple service (11:44-47)

> 12:44-47 On that day men were appointed over the storerooms, the contributions, the firstfruits, and the

---

Nehemiah, and Esther, 205.

8. Eliakim means "God will establish," or "May God establish."

9. Yamauchi points out that archaeological discoveries attest to the fact that the Persians, Greeks, and Romans had similar celebrations. See Edwin Yamauchi, *Ezra and Nehemiah,* 757.

> tithes, to gather into them the portions required by the Law for the priests and for the Levites according to the fields of the towns, for Judah rejoiced over the priests and the Levites who ministered. [45]And they performed the service of their God and the service of purification, as did the singers and the gatekeepers, according to the command of David and his son Solomon. [46]For long ago in the days of David and Asaph there were directors of the singers, and there were songs of praise and thanksgiving to God. [47]And all Israel in the days of Zerubbabel and in the days of Nehemiah gave the daily portions for the singers and the gatekeepers; and they set apart that which was for the Levites; and the Levites set apart that which was for the sons of Aaron.

The people's return to God and His Law continued with provision being made for the tithes, contributions, and other logistical matters that would ensure the proper function of the temple's ministries. The people rejoiced over the priests and Levites whom they considered to be God's provision of leadership and service for them. This stands in stark contrast to some of today's churches which allow their leaders to become targets of people's criticism and ungodly attacks.

The celebration included both music and purification rites (Lev. 11–15), with the music portion going back to the time of David and Solomon. Indeed, 1 Chronicles 23–26 details the organization of the Levites, priests, gatekeepers and musicians. Now, the organization of the temple workers again followed the prescription of David, which was also followed by his son Solomon (2 Chron. 8:14). Everything done in Nehemiah's time was patterned after the past. Just as the patterns of the musicians and gatekeepers were arranged as in the time of David and Solomon, the daily portions were given as in the times of Moses and Aaron.

Nehemiah 13

Outline

I. Reform through exclusion (13:1-3)

13:1-3 On that day they read from the Book of Moses in the hearing of the people. And in it was found written that no Ammonite or Moabite should ever enter the assembly of God, ²for they did not meet the people of Israel with bread and water, but hired Balaam against them to curse them— yet our God turned the curse into a blessing. ³As soon as the people heard the law, they separated from Israel all those of foreign descent.

The restoration of the city's wall was a welcome development for the post-exilic Jews, but the reformation of the people was God's main goal. The reform of exclusion is not a popular topic today, as it probably was not a popular topic during Nehemiah's time, but it was, and still is, a necessary step on the way to godly reformation. The Ammonites and the Moabites had been Israel's enemies for centuries, and here they were used as the representatives of all non-Israelites. The reference to Balaam was to remind the Jews of the historical event when king Balaak of Moab hired the pagan prophet Balaam to curse God's people (Num. 22:4ff), but God, in His sovereignty, made Balaam bless His people instead. In the same way, God will remove the curse of intermarriage with pagans and turn it into blessing, provided His people obey His commands. Intermarriage with non-Israelites had been against God's Law since the time of Moses (Deut. 23:4-7).

II. Reform through expulsion (13:4-9)

> 13:4-9 Now before this, Eliashib the priest, who was appointed over the chambers of the house of our God, and who was related to Tobiah, [5]prepared for Tobiah a large chamber where they had previously put the grain offering, the frankincense, the vessels, and the tithes of grain, wine, and oil, which were given by commandment to the Levites, singers, and gatekeepers, and the contributions for the priests. [6]While this was taking place, I was not in Jerusalem, for in the thirty-second year of Artaxerxes king of Babylon I went to the king. And after some time I asked leave of the king [7]and came to Jerusalem, and I then discovered the evil that Eliashib had done for Tobiah, preparing for him a chamber in the courts of the house of God. [8]And I was very angry, and I threw all the household furniture of Tobiah out of the chamber. [9]Then I gave orders, and they cleansed the chambers, and I brought back there the vessels of the house of God, with the grain offering and the frankincense.

We are not told what prompted Nehemiah's return to the royal palace of King Artaxerxes, but we now learn that while he was in Susa, some inappropriate things transpired in Jerusalem. Eliashib (Neh. 3:1, 20-21; 12:10, 22; 13:28), the high priest, allowed Tobiah, a non-Israelite, to live in a temple chamber that was intended to be a storeroom.[1] Indeed,

---

1 Many scholars suggest that this Eliashib is not the high priest since a high priest's function would not include the overseeing of the temple chambers. See Williamson, *Ezra, Nehemiah,* 386 and Brockington, *Ezra, Nehemiah, and*

Solomon's temple was designed with storerooms to be used for the collection of contributions, tithes and offerings—certainly not to become places of residence (2 Chron. 31:11-13). Nehemiah's reaction was twofold: anger and action. His anger led him to purge and to restore the temple's integrity.[2] Olyan affirms that "Nehemiah's order that the chamber be purified suggests that he viewed it as polluted 'ritually', and the source of the pollution…is the presence of Tobiah the Ammonite, his belongings, and those of his house."[3] The ritually unclean household items of Tobiah were thrown out and replaced by the Temple vessels—probably the same ones taken during Nebuchadnezzar's plunder of Jerusalem, and used by Belshazzar during the feast described in Daniel 5. Replacing the vessels took place only after the chambers were ceremonially cleansed, as required by the Law (Lev. 11–15).

III. Reform through organization (13:10-14)

> 13:10-14 I also found out that the portions of the Levites had not been given to them, so that the Levites and the singers, who did the work, had fled each to his field. [11]So I confronted the officials and said, "Why is the house of God forsaken?" And I gathered them together and set them in their stations. [12]Then all Judah brought the tithe of the grain, wine, and oil into the storehouses. [13]And I appointed as treasurers over the storehouses Shelemiah the priest, Zadok the scribe, and Pedaiah of the Levites, and as their assistant Hanan the son of Zaccur, son of Mattaniah, for they were considered reliable, and their duty was to distribute to their brothers. [14]Remember me, O my God, concerning this, and do not wipe out my good deeds that I have done for the house of my God and for his service.

   Esther, 208.

2. We are reminded of Jesus' righteous anger who cleansed the temple when it became something it was never intended to be (Matt. 21:12ff; Mark 11:15ff; Luke 19:45ff; John 2:14ff).

3. Saul M. Olyan, "Purity Ideology in Ezra–Nehemiah as a Tool to Reconstitute the Community," in *JSJ* 35/1 (2004): 10.

When the temple had ceased to exist, the bringing of the tithes[4] to the temple also ceased. While the temple was in ruins, the Levites had no duties and thus the temple required no dues.[5] The Levites may have been poor, but they were pragmatic. In order to survive, they moved to their appointed rural areas where they could farm the land and provide for their families (Neh. 12:28-29). Nehemiah's question, "Why is the house of God forsaken?" points to the neglect of the proper function of the temple. His question parallels the one God posed to His people through the prophet Haggai, "Is it a time for you yourselves to dwell in your paneled houses, while this house lies in ruins?" (Hag. 1:4). While in Haggai the question focused on the physical aspect of the temple, in Nehemiah, the cultic aspect was brought to the forefront.

Because of the importance of God's Law and a return to it, Nehemiah spelled restoration as "resTORAHtion." Verse 12 represents a turning point in the account where the people acted in obedience to the Law, and they brought in their tithes of grain, wine, and oil once again. Indeed, the Law clearly stated that "Every tithe of the land, whether of the seed of the land or of the fruit of the trees, is the LORD's; it is holy to the LORD" (Lev. 27:30). Their action was also in accordance with the covenant made earlier, where they agreed to bring "the contribution of grain, wine, and oil" (Neh. 10:39). Nehemiah appointed trustworthy men[6] whose duty was to distribute the offerings to "their brothers." Four times in the book of Nehemiah, the leader prays to God, "Remember me" (5:19; 13:14, 22, 31). The figure of speech compares God's memory with a slate on which one's good deeds are recorded.[7] Thus, Nehemiah prays that God will

4. Israel's tithing system was not unique. Yamauchi affirms that "temples in Mesopotamia also levied tithes for the support of their personnel." See Edwin Yamauchi, *Ezra and Nehemiah*, 762.
5. Numbers 18:21 outlines God's command to provide for the Levites through Israel's tithes.
6. These men of integrity represented the priests and Levites; nothing more is known about their identity or background.
7. There are a lot of similarities here with the book of Malachi who discusses similar topics such as intermarriage, tithing, and a book of remembrance (Mal. 2:14; 3:8-10, 16). See also Cyril J. Barber, *Nehemiah and the Dynamics of Effective Leadership* (Neptune, New Jersey: Loizeaux Brothers, 1976), 167-174.

not wipe clean the slate on which Nehemiah's good work for the temple and the cult were recorded. Fensham correctly states that "the temple was regarded as the place where God was present. Care for the temple meant also care for God."[8]

IV. Reform through Sabbath observation (13:15-22)

13:15-22 In those days I saw in Judah people treading winepresses on the Sabbath, and bringing in heaps of grain and loading them on donkeys, and also wine, grapes, figs, and all kinds of loads, which they brought into Jerusalem on the Sabbath day. And I warned them on the day when they sold food. [16]Tyrians also, who lived in the city, brought in fish and all kinds of goods and sold them on the Sabbath to the people of Judah, in Jerusalem itself! [17]Then I confronted the nobles of Judah and said to them, "What is this evil thing that you are doing, profaning the Sabbath day? [18]Did not your fathers act in this way, and did not our God bring all this disaster on us and on this city? Now you are bringing more wrath on Israel by profaning the Sabbath." [19]As soon as it began to grow dark at the gates of Jerusalem before the Sabbath, I commanded that the doors should be shut and gave orders that they should not be opened until after the Sabbath. And I stationed some of my servants at the gates, that no load might be brought in on the Sabbath day. [20]Then the merchants and sellers of all kinds of wares lodged outside Jerusalem once or twice. [21]But I warned them and said to them, "Why do you lodge outside the wall? If you do so again, I will lay hands on you." From that time on they did not come on the Sabbath. [22]Then I commanded the Levites that they should purify themselves and come and guard the gates, to keep the Sabbath day holy. Remember this also in my favor, O my God, and spare me according to the greatness of your steadfast love.

---

8.   Fensham, *The Books of Ezra and Nehemiah*, 262.

In the people's zeal to rebuild through commerce, they ignored God's Law regarding the Sabbath. The pre-exilic prophets were clear that one of the reasons for the exile was precisely the people's failure to obey the fourth commandment (Jer. 17:27; Ezek. 20:16-24). One may expect non-Israelites to engage in business on the Sabbath (13:16), but verse 15 indicated that these lawbreakers were Jews who lived outside Jerusalem. The traffic through the Fish Gate was heavy with Tyrians bringing in fish and other goods. This implies that the Jews both sold and bought on the Sabbath, a practice clearly forbidden in the Law of Moses (Exod. 20:8-10; 31:14-15; 35:2; Lev. 23:3; Deut. 5:14; Jer. 17:22-24). The Sabbath observation was meant to acknowledge God as the Creator and Sustainer (Exod. 20-8:11). By breaking the law for business purposes, the people demeaned both God's greatness and His providence. As a result, Nehemiah first warned the people (13:15) and then he confronted their leaders (13:16). His history lesson reminded the people of the evil of breaking the law, and that it was exactly what had brought destruction and exile upon Israel. The word "destruction" referred to Nebuchadnezzar's destruction of the temple and Jerusalem in 587 BC, as described by both the Chronicler and Jeremiah (2 Chron. 36:15-21; Jer. 52:4-15). His admonition, "Now you are bringing more wrath on Israel (13:18)," suggested theirs was an even greater sin because they had both the testimony of the Law and the witness of history.

As a man of vision and action, Nehemiah took command and things changed. Servants were placed at the gates to prevent the transport of goods during the Sabbath. He also warned that those who set up shop outside the city gates, although keeping the letter of the Law, were guilty of breaking its spirit (13:20-21). He expanded the role of the Levites to include the securing of the temple gates, which was not in the original Law. Nehemiah once again appealed to God's faithful love (Hesed) through an oft-repeated "remember me" plea.

V. Reform through separation from sin (13:23-31)

13:23-25 In those days also I saw the Jews who had married women of Ashdod, Ammon, and Moab.

²⁴And half of their children spoke the language of
Ashdod, and they could not speak the language
of Judah, but the language of each people. ²⁵And I
confronted them and cursed them and beat some
of them and pulled out their hair. And I made
them take oath in the name of God, saying, "You
shall not give your daughters to their sons, or take
their daughters for your sons or for yourselves.

One of the most serious problems was the intermarriage of
Jews with foreign women. This problem did not originate in
Nehemiah's time, since Ezra already took drastic measures
(Ezra 9–10). These marriages were also mentioned in the
covenant renewal which Nehemiah and other leaders
designed (Neh. 10), but it is clear that the problem persisted.
The intermarriage to women from Ashdod, Ammon, and
Moab was aided by the fact that the languages spoken by
these groups were probably similar to Hebrew.[9] Nehemiah's
harsh reaction was descriptive, not prescriptive.[10] Ezra was
a godly man like Nehemiah, but his approach was very
different and much more docile (Ezra 9:3–10:1). This is the
second time in the book that Nehemiah made a group of
people take an oath,[11] and in so doing he sought to prevent
this serious breach of the Law in the future.

13:26-27 Did not Solomon king of Israel sin on
account of such women? Among the many nations
there was no king like him, and he was beloved
by his God, and God made him king over all
Israel. Nevertheless, foreign women made even
him to sin. ²⁷Shall we then listen to you and do

---

9. See Fensham, *The Books of Ezra and Nehemiah,* 266.
10. Today's church leaders cannot take a page from Nehemiah's playbook
    and treat their congregants in the same manner. New Testament ecclesi-
    ology and leadership principles are very much different than the uncon-
    ventional style employed by Nehemiah.
11. The first instance is in chapter 5 when Nehemiah is making the priests
    take an oath sealing their promise to stop taking interest from their Jewish
    brothers and to return the properties of those whom they have wronged
    (Neh. 5:10-12). The address in the second person "You shall not give
    your daughters to their sons…" parallels the second person address in
    Deuteronomy 7:3, "You shall not intermarry with them…"

all this great evil and act treacherously against
our God by marrying foreign women?"

To bolster his point, Nehemiah used perhaps the best-known example from their history. His question is rhetorical since everyone knew that the answer was a resounding, "Yes." Indeed, the Chronicler(s) made it clear that even though Solomon was loved by God (2 Sam. 12:24), and that he was great in fame and wisdom (1 Kings 4:29-34), "his wives turned away his heart after other gods, and his heart was not wholly true to the LORD his God" (1 Kings 11:4). The act of intermarrying with pagan women was described as evil and treacherous. This sin was not against one's ancestors or one's culture, but it was an offense against the Law Giver.

> 13:28 And one of the sons of Jehoiada,
> the son of Eliashib the high priest, was
> the son-in-law of Sanballat the Horonite.
> Therefore I chased him from me.

Although Nehemiah had a working relationship with Eliashib (Neh. 3:1), Eliashib had not only associated himself with Tobiah (Neh. 13:4), but Eliashib's grandson had married a pagan woman. What made the situation worse was that this woman was the daughter of Sanballat the Horonite, one of Nehemiah's worst enemies. The Law forbade the high priest to marry a foreign woman (Lev. 21:14), and because the grandson was in the lineage of Eliashib, he could possibly have become high priest.[12] Kidner notes that "nothing but a marriage to the high priest himself could have been more defiling."[13] Nehemiah expelled this Law-breaking grandson of Eliashib from the Jewish community.

> 13:29-31 Remember them, O my God, because
> they have desecrated the priesthood and the
> covenant of the priesthood and the Levites.
> [30]Thus I cleansed them from everything foreign,

---

12. The first-century Jewish historian, Josephus, reports that "Manaseh, the son of Johanan, brother of the high priest Joiada, had married Sanballat's daughter, that he was expelled by Nehemiah, that he went to Sanballat, and that Sanballat had built a temple for him on Gerizim." See Fensham, 267.
13. Kidner, *Ezra and Nehemiah*, 132.

and I established the duties of the priests and
Levites, each in his work; [31]and I provided for
the wood offering at appointed times, and for the
firstfruits. Remember me, O my God, for good.

Nehemiah contrasts himself with those who "have des-
ecrated the priesthood and the covenant…" While those
from Eliashib's family profaned what is holy, Nehemiah
cleansed the priests and Levites so they could perform their
God-appointed work. Nehemiah further provided what
was necessary for the bringing of offerings. The contrast
can also be seen in Nehemiah's "Remember me" prayers
(Neh. 5:19; 13:14, 22, 31), as opposed to the "remember
them" (Neh. 6:14; 13:29) requests.

The book of Nehemiah begins and ends with prayer, consistent with Nehemiah's view of a powerful God who listens
to the prayer of His people, and indicative of Nehemiah's
humility. Nehemiah understood that apart from God and
a right relationship with Him, nothing lasting could be
accomplished. Fensham concludes,

> A new era of Jewish worship has started; worship according
> to prescribed legal principles. It was only with the coming
> of Christ and the interpretation of His coming by Paul that
> another era was commenced in which the legal burden was
> removed from the shoulders of mankind and the center of
> religion placed in his vicarious suffering on the cross. It is the
> new era of faith and love in Jesus Christ.

Table 9: Nehemiah's "Remember me" pleas

Text	Reason for request	Context
5:19	Nehemiah's good deeds	Nehemiah stopped the lending of money with interest and cancelled debts; he did not lay heavy burdens on the people as had previous governors.
13:14	Nehemiah's appointed temple treasurers	Bringing offerings to the temple stopped during the exile; Nehemiah reinstitued the tithe.

Text	Reason for request	Context
13:22	Nehemiah restores the sanctity of the Sabbath	Nehemiah stopped the people from working and conducting commerce during the Sabbath.
13:31	Nehemiah deals with mixed marriages	The people broke the Law by marrying foreign women. Nehemiah forbade this practice.

As a matter of application, it is important to explain which principles of this text do not apply to today's Christian community. Today's leader is not to follow Nehemiah's example literally. Thus, today's pastor cannot beat up his congregants, pull the hair of those who have sinned, or curse those with whom he disagrees (v. 25). Rather, this chapter outlines some important principles we can follow. First, God desires His people to be set apart and live holy lives. God's people are not to conform to the world, but rather transform it. Second, God's leaders need to make sure that God's Word has the preeminence, and that His Word is the people's standard for both faith and practice.

Appendix A
Authorship Issues in Ezra–Nehemiah

The authorship of the books of Ezra and Nehemiah has been the subject of continuous debate, conjecture, and research. Because both Ezra and Nehemiah write in the first person, some scholars agree with the Talmud that Ezra wrote most of the work, while Nehemiah finished it. Some scholars suggest that an editor/compiler put the book together in its present form. Lately, it's been suggested that the authors of Ezra–Nehemiah were a group of Levites, or at least a pro-Levitical clerical group. In this section I will examine the textual, linguistic, and theological arguments for and/or against these options.

Ezra as the author of Ezra–Nehemiah

Early rabbinic tradition and literature identify Ezra as the author of Ezra–Nehemiah. The fact that the two books were seen as a unity is mentioned both in the Babylonian Talmud (Baba Bathra 15a) and in the writings of the first-century Jewish historian Josephus as well as Eusebius, the third-century Bishop of Caesarea Maritima. In the third-century, Origen divided the books into two separate books as he translated the Old Testament into Greek. When translating the Bible into Latin in the fourth-century, Jerome acknowledged the same division and used it in the Vulgate.[1] W.F. Albright was one of the main proponents of this view. Along with Torrey, he saw Ezra as the author

---

1. Charles Fensham, *Ezra and Nehemiah* (Grand Rapids: Eerdmans, 1982), 1.

of both Chronicles and Ezra–Nehemiah. Albright quotes Torrey, "There is not a garment in all Ezra's wardrobe that does not fit the Chronicler exactly."[2] For Albright, Torrey has demonstrated that nowhere are "the Chronicler's literary peculiarities... more strongly marked, more abundant, more evenly and continuously distributed, and more easily recognizable than in the Hebrew narrative of Ezra 7-10 and Nehemiah 8-10."[3] Torrey believed that Ezra was like the Chronicler, but not the Chronicler. Ezra "was a man precisely like the Chronicler himself: interested very noticeably in the Levites, and especially the class of singers; deeply concerned at all times with the details of the cult and with the ecclesiastical organization in Jerusalem..."[4] In the introduction of his Ezra–Nehemiah commentary, Jacob M. Myers also states that "after further study and the weighing of possibilities at hand, Ezra appears a more and more likely candidate for authorship."[5]

Gleason Archer agrees, placing Ezra's arrival in Jerusalem at 457 BC. Artaxerxes I Longimanus' seventh year (Ezra 7:8). He affirms that "Ezra himself undoubtedly wrote most of the book named after him...but he evidently incorporated into the final edition the personal memoirs of Nehemiah... including even his form of the list of returnees. Using Nehemiah's library facilities, Ezra probably composed Chronicles during this same period."[6]

An unnamed historian/chronicler as the author of Ezra–Nehemiah

The most accepted view today is that a Chronicler with a lot of sources at his disposal was the final author of Ezra–Nehemiah. This view opens the door to a lot of questions. Did the Chronicler alter the sources from which he was

---

2. W.F. Albright, "The Date and Personality of the Chronicler," in *JBL* 40 ¾ (1921), 119.

3. Ibid.

4. Ibid.

5. Jacob M. Myers, *Ezra–Nehemiah*, AB (Garden City, New York: Doubleday, 1965), LXVIII.

6. Gleason L. Archer, *A Survey of Old Testament Introduction* (Chicago: Moody, 1994), 457.

working? Did he work his own ideas? Did he distort "many facts in his zeal to propagate the view of his time?"[7] J.M. Myers and H.H. Grosheide take a positive approach and suggest that the Chronicler used "reliable sources, sometimes reproducing them verbally and other times rendering them in his own words."[8] Fensham concludes that "it still seems best to accept the Chronicler as the author of these two books, especially since 2 Chronicles 36:22-23 presupposes Ezra 1...The Chronicler wrote a pragmatic history, stressing certain religious themes, but this tendency is typical of OT history writing."[9]

Charles C. Torrey suggests that "the Chronicler's great task was to establish the supreme authority of the Jerusalem cultus. Thus, he sees the Chronicler both as an editor and as a narrator. As an editor, he used at least sources: 1) Ezra 4:8-6:18 which he calls the "Aramaic story," and 2) the first six chapters of Nehemiah which he calls "The Words of Nehemiah."[10] Torrey asserts that "it is quite possible that single words, or even phrases, may have been altered or added by him, here and there...but we may be sure that he has contributed nothing of importance to the Aramaic passages just named, and it is quite likely that he has not even changed a single word."[11] As an independent narrator, the Chronicler contributes to about two-thirds of Ezra–Nehemiah. Torrey states that the Chronicler changes the Ezra memoir to the first person "in imitation of the memoir of Nehemiah."[12] The two memoirs were two documents from which the Chronicler worked. However, Torrey calls the Ezra memoir an "Aramaic popular tale of the building of the temple..." dating "unmistakably in the reigns of Artaxerxes I and Darius II."[13] He dates the Nehemiah memoir during the reign of Artaxerxes II (405-359 BC). Torrey concludes that aside from the two memoirs "and

7. Fensham, 3.
8. Ibid.
9. Ibid., 3-4.
10. Charles C. Torrey, *Ezra Studies*, (Chicago, UCP, 1910), 223-224.
11. Torrey, 224.
12. Ibid., 238-239.
13. Ibid., 239.

a few data in the prophets Haggai, Zechariah, and Malachi, the whole Persian period was a blank, which he was free to fill as he saw fit."[14] For Torrey, "the Chronicler became an editor more from necessity than from choice. Whoever the Chronicler was, by taste and gift he was a novelist…with an apologetic purpose."[15]

The common authorship of Chronicles and Ezra–Nehemiah has been accepted by many for a long time. Things started to shift with Sara Japhet's 1968 article in which she investigated the differences between Chronicles and Ezra–Nehemiah. She focused on three categories, namely, 1) linguistic opposition, 2) technical terms, and 3) stylistic peculiarities.[16] In looking at the formation of the imperfect consecutive, Japhet notes that the book of Chronicles the short form of the imperfect consecutive is used while in Ezra–Nehemiah the full form is used.[17] For example, at the dedication of the Temple as described in 2 Chronicles 6:10, Solomon talks about the he has built for the Name of the LORD. The verb form is וָאֶבְנֶה (qal, impf, 1cs, + waw consecutive) = and I have built. In Ezra 1:3, on the other hand, the shortened form וְיִבֶן (qal, jussive, 3ms + waw conjunctive) = let him built, occurs. To bolster her argument that the language in Chronicles and Ezra–Nehemiah is very different, Japhet chooses the first person imperfect forms with the paragogic ה. This form occurs frequently in Ezra–Nehemiah but does not appear at all in Chronicles. As a result Japhet concludes, "the difference between Ezra–Nehemiah and Chronicles is not one of measure but of principle. The main point is not the existence of these forms in Ezra–Nehemiah and their absence in Chronicles but the presence of a normative linguistic principle which is applied in Chronicles in contrast to all the other texts of the same period."[18] Japhet's attack on the single author

14. Ibid.
15. Ibid., 250-251.
16. Mark A. Throntveit, "Linguistic Analysis and the Question of Authorship in Chronicles, Ezra, and Nehemiah," in *VT* 32/2 (1982), 202.
17. Sara Japhet, "The Supposed Common Authorship of Chronicles and Ezra–Nehemiah Investigated Anew," in *VT* 18/3 (1968), 334-337.
18. Japhet, 338.

hypothesis continues with her study of theophoric names. While in Ezra–Nehemiah such names end in the short ending יה, in Chronicles both the short and long endings are used for theophoric names. When it comes to technical terms, Japhet finds that while the book of Chronicles uses כֹּהֵן הָרֹאשׁ as title for the High Priest, the preferred title used in Ezra–Nehemiah is הַכֹּהֵן הַגָּדֹול.[19] Thus, Japhet concludes that "the books could not have been written or compiled by the same author. It seems rather that a certain period of time must separate the two."[20]

Some years later, Williamson himself looked at the alleged similarities between Chronicles and Ezra–Nehemiah. Out of thirty-four entries, he found only six that do not favor diversity of authorship. The six that form the strongest argument for unity of authorship are:[21]

a) אַשְׁמָה = wrongdoing, guiltiness; a word used 7 times in Chronicles and 6 times in Ezra (1 Chron. 21:3; two times in 2 Chron. 24:18; 28:10, 13; 33:23; Ezra 9:7, 13, 15; 10:10, and twice in 10:19).

b) יֹום בְּיֹום = day by day, or from day to day; an expression that occurs 4 times in Chronicles and 3 times in the Hebrew of Ezra–Nehemiah (1 Chron. 12:23; 2 Chron 8:13, 24:11, 30:21; Ezra 3:4, 6:9; Neh 8:18).

c) The use of the definite article ה in place of the relative pronoun.

d) The combination of prepositions עד and ל before a noun. This combination occurs 15 times in Chronicles and 4 times in Ezra.

e) The word מְצִלְתַּיִם = cymbals occurs 11 times in Chronicles, one time in Ezra and one time in Nehemiah.

---

19. I believe Japhet's section on peculiarities of style is subjective and thus I will not use her arguments in this article.
20. Japhet, 371.
21. H.G.M. Williamson, *Israel in the Books of Chronicles* (Cambridge: CUP, 1977), 58-59.

f) The expression שִׂמְחָה גְדוֹלָה = great joy/rejoicing occurs twice
   in Chronicles (1 Chron. 29:9; 2 Chron. 30:26), and three times
   in Nehemiah (8:12, 17; 12:43).[22]

One of the latest scholars to reject the common authorship of
Chronicles and Ezra–Nehemiah is Tamara Cohn Eskenazi.[23]
I will only focus on her examination of the supposed ideo-
logical similarities between Ezra–Nehemiah and Chronicles.
She discusses six such major ideological characteristics:
David and his dynasty, the emphasis on the cult, the gene-
alogies, the concept of retribution, the concept of Israel, and
the Anti-Samaritan polemic.

a) David. It is generally accepted that David is the main focus
   of the Chronicler. He "receives credit for all the important
   aspects of Israel's life, including the building of the
   temple… he is idealized…appearing without the blemishes
   that mark his life in 2 Samuel."[24] Because David is relatively
   insignificant in Ezra–Nehemiah and only plays a peripheral
   role, some scholars conclude that a common authorship
   seems unlikely. Indeed, in Ezra–Nehemiah Zerubbabel is
   not identified as a descendent of David. Moreover, when
   Nehemiah recounts Israel's history in his prayer, he does
   not mention neither David, nor the Temple. Rather, he
   is presented "as a paradigm for sin (Neh. 13:26)."[25] Thus,
   Eskenazi concludes that "a decisive contrast between the
   two books renders common authorship implausible."[26]

b) The emphasis on the cult. Because priests, Levites, musicians, singers, and gate-keepers are very much present in
   both Chronicles and Ezra–Nehemiah, some scholars find
   irresistible the conclusion of common authorship.[27] On
   the other hand, Eskenazi points that "the cultic details in

22. Williamson suggests that the expression occurs 3 times in Ezra, but only
    the word שִׂמְחָה occurs three times in Ezra (3:12, 13; 6:22).
23. Tamara Cohn Eskenazi, *In an Age of Prose: A Literary Approach to Ezra–
    Nehemiah,* SBLMS 36 (Atlanta: Scholars, 1988).
24. Eskenazi, 22.
25. Ibid.
26. Ibid., 23.
27. Eskenazi quotes Curtis and Madsen's work on their Chronicles commen-
    tary, 23.

Ezra–Nehemiah and Chronicles do not always agree, even though the terminology is similar."[28] For example, while the singers and gatekeepers are counted with the Levites in Chronicles (2 Chron. 5:12), they are counted separately in Ezra–Nehemiah (Ezra 7:24).

c) Genealogies. While genealogies and lists are a trademark of the Chronicler, M.Z. Segal shows that such genres appear also in Genesis. "Moreover, it is argued that a close study of these genealogies underscores their differences, not similarities."[29] Robert Wilson points to the fact that genealogies in Chronicles are segmented (1 Chron. 1:5-16), while the ones in Ezra–Nehemiah are linear. He defines a segmented genealogy as a genealogy "that expresses more than one line of descent from a given ancestor." On the other hand, a linear genealogy is one "that expresses only one line of descent from a given ancestor." [30] Marshall D. Johnson argues that while the genealogies in Ezra–Nehemiah are concerned with legitimation, in Chronicles, the author's goal is "to incorporate in his work all the genealogical data contained in Genesis." Johnson argues that "the books of Ezra and Nehemiah as a whole present the idea of genealogical purity more explicitly than any other OT material. The author is concerned lest 'the holy seed' (הַקֹּדֶשׁ זֶרַע) mix itself with the peoples of the lands. So also the genealogical material is here used to safeguard the purity of the nation – a function not explicit in other genealogical sections of the OT." [31]

d) The concept of retribution. The Chronicler posits that each generation's destiny is determined by their obedience or disobedience to God. Reward for obedience and punishment for disobedience is the status quo in Chronicles. Williamson argues that the theology of retribution is absent in Ezra–Nehemiah. "The piety of the leaders and/or the people is not reflected in sudden up-turns of fortune, but on the contrary may entail an increase of opposition (Ezra 4, Neh. 4),

28. Eskenazi, 24.
29. Ibid., 25. See M.Z. Segal, *The Books of Ezra and Nehemiah*, Tarbiz 14, 86-87.
30. Robert R. Wilson, *Genealogy and History in the Biblical World* (New Haven: YUP, 1977), 9.
31. Marshall D. Johnson, *The Purpose of Biblical Genealogies With Special Reference to the Setting of the Genealogies of Jesus* (Cambridge: CUP, 1969), 74.

neither is there any indication that confession of sin leads to restoration (Ezra 9, Neh. 9)."[32] Eskenazi also notes that the role of the prophets which is "so decisive in Chronicles, is almost nil in Ezra–Nehemiah… Haggai and Zechariah, the most prominent prophets in Ezra–Nehemiah, neither warn the people, nor deliver promises; instead, they exhort the people to build."[33]

e) The concept of Israel and her relation to others. While the book of Chronicles acknowledges the division of the kingdom, it still emphasizes "the wholeness of the people throughout its history."[34] Eskenazi quotes Braun who goes further to suggest that Chronicles "reflects a more positive attitude towards the north than earlier generations of scholars supposed:"

> After the division of the kingdom the writer [of Chronicles] is constantly concerned to indicate acceptance of and participation in the Jerusalem cult by people from the north. Immediately after the division of the kingdom priests and Levites from the north take their stand with Rehoboam in Jerusalem, joined by representatives from all the tribes (2 Chron. xi 16). The participation of Yahwists from the north in the covenants of Asa and Hezekiah is explicitly noted (2 Chron. xv 9-15, 31). Prophets of Yahweh, such as Elijah and Oded, continue to function here, and the people of Samaria are said to have responded favorably to their warning and released their Judean captives, who are twice described as their kinsmen (2 Chron. xxviii 8, 11)."[35]

In Ezra–Nehemiah, on the other hand, Von Rad suggests that Judah and Benjamin are now the true Israel.

Anti-Samaritan polemic. In Ezra–Nehemiah it is clear that the Samaritans are part of a clear and active opposition. They are not innocent bystanders but dynamic adversaries. Not only that, but the Jews are not supposed to intermarry with Samaritans. "Consequently, the participation and

---

32. Williamson, *Israel in the Books of Chronicles*, 67-68.
33. Eskenazi, 28.
34. Ibid., 29.
35. Ibid., 29-30.

membership of the Samaritans in the community of Israel are rejected."[36] In Chronicles, the presence of foreigners on the territory of Israel is not acknowledged. Most surprising is the absence of the resettling of Samaria by foreigners under Assyrian leadership, an episode described in detail in 2 Kings 17. Eskenazi concludes, "Nothing is Chronicles can be construed as anti-Samaritanism because there are, in fact, no Samaritans in Chronicles!"[37]

It seems that the one-author hypothesis is fairly weak, and that many have scholars have poked many holes in what appeared to be an impenetrable theory. Thus, we can abandon it and look at other options.

Post-exilic Levites as authors of Ezra–Nehemiah
One of the latest proposals comes from Kyung-Jin Min's revised dissertation at University of Durham under the supervision of Stuart Weeks. In it, Min argues that a clerical class of Levites, or a strongly pro-Levitical body of clerics are responsible for the writing of Ezra–Nehemiah.

Levites in Ezra–Nehemiah. Out of the 65 occurrences of the word לֵוִי in Ezra–Nehemiah, only three seem to have negative connotations. Ezra 9:1 and 10:23 state that Levites took foreign wives, While in Ezra 10:15 we have a Levite who is supporting those who opposed Ezra's reforms. However, this cannot be used to argue for a priestly or pro-priestly authorship since the same criticism is addressed against the priests when it comes to intermarriage with foreign wives (Ezra 9:1, 10:18-22). Min argues that some texts demonstrate a pro-Levitical perspective. Twenty-five times the Levites appear in apposition with the priests, thirty one times they appear together contextually, and nine times the Levites appear without the priests. "Almost all the references to Levites (56 out of 65 occurrences) appear in apposition to, or contextually with, the priests."[38] Indeed, the expression וְהַלְוִיִּם הַכֹּהֲנִים (the priests and the Levites), or a very similar form of

---

36. Ibid., 31.
37. Ibid., 32.
38. Kyun-Jin Min, *The Levitical Authorship of Ezra–Nehemiah*, JSOTSup, 409 (London: T & T Clark, 2004), 74.

it appears 20 times in Ezra–Nehemiah. Thus, it is fairly clear that the Levites are recognized as the social entity and equal partners of the priests. There is "no indication of Levitical subordination to the priests, but rather, show an effort to promote Levitical parity with the priests."[39]

Many texts show the Levites and priests working together. First, they appear together on the lists of social groups, especially "vis-à-vis other cultic personnel (Ezra 2:40, Neh. 3:17; 7:43; 10:10; 11:15-16, 18, 22, 36; 12:8, 22, 24)."[40] Second, in the discussion of the tithe, the Levites are treated favorably (Neh. 10:38-39; 13:5). Not only are they to benefit from the tithe, but they are handle the tithe and transport it from the temple to the storerooms. Thus, in Nehemiah's time, the Levites were both the recipients and collectors of the tithes. Third, "the Levites are described as cooperating with priests in all crucial work."[41] They are seen working together at the rebuilding of the temple in Ezra (3:8ff), and in the reading of the Law in Nehemiah (8).

Min's strongest argument for a pro-Levitical or Levitical authorship of Ezra–Nehemiah comes in his analysis of the texts where the Levites appear without the priests.[42] He notes seven ways in which "the Levites are portrayed favorably.[43]

1. Ezra 8:20 is the only text in the OT that mentions the origin of the נְתִינִים as attendants of the Levites prescribed by David, and thus offers a clue to their promoted status.

2. Ezra 10:15 describes Shabbethai the Levite as cooperating with Ezra's reform, no opposing it. This point is highly debatable since Ezra 10:14-15 reads, Let our officials stand for the whole assembly. Let all in our cities who have taken foreign wives come at appointed times, and with them the elders and judges of every city, until the fierce wrath of our God over this matter is turned away from us." Only Jonathan

---

39. Min, *The Levitical Authorship*, 76.
40. Ibid., 79.
41. Ibid.
42. Ezra 8:20; 10:15; Nehemiah 7:1; 9:4-5; 12:27; twice in 13:10, 22).
43. Min, *The Levitical Authorship*, 80-81. This section is based solely on Min's list.

the son of Asahel and Jahzeiah the son of Tikvah opposed this, and Meshullam and Shabbethai the Levite supported them.

3. In Nehemiah 7:1, the Levites are appointed as custodians of the gates of the rebuilt wall.

4. Nehemiah 9:4-5 depicts the Levites leading the great confession. On the stairs of the Levites stood Jeshua, Bani, Kadmiel, Shebaniah, Bunni, Sherebiah, Bani, and Chenani; and they cried with a loud voice to the Lord their God.[5] Then the Levites, Jeshua, Kadmiel, Bani, Hashabneiah, Sherebiah, Hodiah, Shebaniah, and Pethahiah, said, "Stand up and bless the Lord your God from everlasting to everlasting. Blessed be your glorious name, which is exalted above all blessing and praise.

5. In Nehemiah 12:27, the Levites are not ignored but sought out for participation in the dedication ceremony of the wall. And at the dedication of the wall of Jerusalem they sought the Levites in all their places, to bring them to Jerusalem to celebrate the dedication with gladness, with thanksgivings and with singing, with cymbals, harps, and lyres.

6. Nehemiah 13:10ff describes a rebuke given to those who had neglected to bring the portions owed to the Levites. I also found out that the portions of the Levites had not been given to them, so that the Levites and the singers, who did the work, had fled each to his field. [11] So I confronted the officials and said, "Why is the house of God forsaken?" And I gathered them together and set them in their stations.

7. In Nehemiah 13:22, the Levites are chosen to guard the gates on the Sabbath. "Then I commanded the Levites that they should purify themselves and come and guard the gates, to keep the Sabbath day holy."

Min concludes this section by stating that the Levites are not described as clerus minor or portrayed in a negative light; rather, they are "described favorably, usually as co-workers with the priests."[44]

---

44. Ibid., 81.

Min also points to three additional phrases that he things come from Levitical groups: a) The mouth of Jeremiah, b) Judah and Benjamin, and c) הַכֹּהֲנִים הַלְוִיִּם.

1. Ezra 1:1 states that Cyrus' edict came as a direct fulfillment of God's Word spoken "by the mouth of Jeremiah," יִרְמְיָה מִפִּי. But, what does have to do with the Levites? Jeremiah 1:1 states that Jeremiah is the son of Hilkiah, and a priest from Anathoth in the land of Benjamin. What are priests doing in Anathoth? 1 Kings 2:26-27 describe how Abiathar, the last priest from Eli's family was exiled at Anathoth for taking part in a failed plot to make Adonijah king after David's death. Min connects this episode and Anathoth with the cities of refuge affirming that Anathoth became a "Levitical refuge city."[45] Furthermore, since Jeremiah has strong affinity to the book of Deuteronomy – which also deals extensively with the Levites, and since Jeremiah "was of disenfranchised priestly descent...it is possible that he was associated in some way with the Levitical group."[46]

2. Judah and Benjamin. Whenever the author of Ezra mentions the tribe of Benjamin, it is always "either in apposition to the tribe of Judah (Ezra 1:5; 4:1; 10:9; Neh. 11:4), or contextually with the tribe of Judah (Neh. 11:7, 31; 11:4, 25)."[47] Min writes,

> For example, all areas of Northern Israel as well as Judah (Ezra 2:21-35) are commonly represented simply by the phrase 'Jerusalem and Judah' (2:1) rather than the combination of two tribes, 'Judah and Benjamin.' Thus, this practice means that Judah alone was enough to represent the whole people of Israel. It could be claimed, therefore, that בִּנְיָמִן in the phrase יְהוּדָה וּבִנְיָמִן ('Judah and Benjamin') is not necessarily needed to convey the intended meaning...By putting the word 'Benjamin,' after Judah, the author may have intended that readers treat Benjamin, representing Levitical cities, as the partner tribe of Judah, representing priestly groups.[48]

3. הַכֹּהֲנִים הַלְוִיִּם. The expression הַכֹּהֲנִים הַלְוִיִּם occurs 13 times in the OT, and 5 of those times are in Ezra–Nehemiah (Ezra 10:5;

---

45. Ibid., 83.
46. Ibid.
47. Ibid.
48. Ibid., 85.

Neh. 10:1, 29, 35; 11:20) and it is usually translated "the Levitical priests." What is unusual is the inverted form כֹּהֲנֵינוּ לְוִיֵּנוּ that is generally translated "our Levites and our priests" even though there is no ו conjunction between the nouns. It is interesting to note though that this phrase in this inverted order occurs only one other time in Jeremiah (33:18), which Min sees as pro-Levitical.[49]

With these arguments as foundation, Min goes on to strongly argue for a pro-Levitical or Levitical authorship of Ezra–Nehemiah.

1. Levites as Imperial agents in the Late-Fifth Century BC Is it generally accepted that Ezra–Nehemiah "originated in a pro-Persian group." If this group were the Levites, is there evidence that they enjoyed imperial backing during the time when the book was composed?"[50] After affirming that the Nehemiah Memoir is a reliable historical source, he quotes Noth who suggests "that the official sending of Nehemiah to Yehud should be understood in the context of the empire's interest in restoring stability to that area and its consequent openness to Nehemiah's request, agreement to which he expected to appease the people there."[51] During his second mission is portrayed as valuing the Levites "by equating ill-treatment of them with neglect of the house of God and by ensuring payment of tithes of them (vv. 10-14)."[52] After the Sabbath restoration, Nehemiah nominates the Levites "to guard the gates, to keep the Sabbath day holy," a charge that was initially given to Nehemiah's servants (vv. 15-22). In Nehemiah 13, Nehemiah's prayer "Remember me, O my God, for good," appears four times, and it is important to note that "the Levites are referred to immediately before each remember formula (vv. 13, 22, 29, 30). Min suggests that this is not accidental, but he presumes that "what Nehemiah wanted God to remember is closely connected to the Levites and that the word לִי serves as a linking word for each unit."[53] Min goes on to conclude that the purpose of Nehemiah 13 is to "stress the favor shown to the Levites and

49. Ibid., 86.
50. Ibid., 127.
51. Martin Noth, *The History of Israel* (London, SCM: 1983), 318.
52. Min, *The Levitical Authorship,* 133.
53. Ibid., 132.

the imposition of restraints upon the priests."[54] He goes on to propose that Achaemenid imperial policy was favorable towards a) the priests from 538-520 and 515-458 BC, b) the elders from 520-515 BC, c) various groups including priestly power from 458-453 BC, and d) Levites from 433 BC on. Min then becomes more confident that Ezra–Nehemiah was "composed in the late fifth-century BC, e) and was probably penned by someone with Persian backing," most likely from a Levitical group.[55]

Ezra and Nehemiah as authors of their respective books

This is the view that I have adopted even though it is lacking the backing of many Old Testament scholars. The only renowned scholar that supports this view is R.K. Harrison. He classifies as unwise the view that the Chronicler is "the one who complied and transmitted Ezra and Nehemiah along with his own writings and formulated them into a unified corpus."[56] Harrison notes that the literary styles and historical standpoints diverge widely. Moreover, both authors seemed to have been governed by different theological presuppositions. He affirms that "while the relationship between Ezra–Nehemiah and the work of the Chronicler is still obscure, the least degree of difficulty is encountered when it is supposed that Ezra and Nehemiah were primarily responsible for the writings attributed to them."[57] Harrison draws his conclusions based on the fact that Ezra–Nehemiah "were contemporaries…their writings were in substantially their present form by about 440 and 430 BC, and that the Chronicler compiled his work independently about 400 BC or slightly later."[58]

In a very recent work, Jacob L. Wright disputes both this view and the view that the Nehemiah memoir was written by Nehemiah himself. Wright suggests that the first-person accounts that can be attributed to Nehemiah stop at 6:15. "The rest of the first-person account…represents the work of

54. Ibid., 134.
55. Ibid., 137.
56. R.K. Harrison, *Introduction to the Old Testament* (Peabody, Massachusetts: Prince, 1999), 1149.
57. Ibid., 1150.
58. Ibid.

later editors."[59] Thus, Wright affirms that "the composition of EN culminated in the mid-Hellenistic period – not in the fourth century."[60]

59. Jacob. L. Wright, "A New Model for the Composition of Ezra–Nehemiah," in *Judah and the Judeans in the Fourth Century B.C.E.*, edited by Oded Lipschitz, Gary N. Knoppers, and Rainer Albertz (Winona Lake, Indiana: Eisenbrauns, 2007), 335.
60. Ibid., 347.

Appendix B

Rare Hebrew Verbs (fewer than 50×) in the Ezra Memoir

Hebrew Verb	Times it occurs in the Ezra Memoir	Where it occurs in the Ezra Memoir	Times it occurs in the Hebrew Bible
אבל	1	Ezra 10:6	39
אור	1	Ezra 9:8	44
אנף	1	Ezra 9:14	14
ארב	1	Ezra 8:31	14
בדל	5	Ezra 8:24; 9:1; 10:8, 11, 16	42
זמן	1	Ezra 10:14	3
חשׁך	1	Ezra 9:13	28
חתן	1	Ezra 9:14	11
יחשׂ	2	Ezra 8:1, 3	20
כלם	1	Ezra 9:6	38
כרע	1	Ezra 9:5	36
מעל	2	Ezra 10:2, 10	35
מרט	1	Ezra 9:3	14

Hebrew Verb	Times it occurs in the Ezra Memoir	Where it occurs in the Ezra Memoir	Times it occurs in the Hebrew Bible
נקב	1	Ezra 8:20	19
ערב	1	Ezra 9:2	33
עתר	1	Ezra 8:23	22
פאר	1	Ezra 7:27	14
פרר	1	Ezra 4:5; 9:14	51
פשע	1	Ezra 10:13	41
צהב	1	Ezra 8:27	1 (hapax legomenon)
צום	1	Ezra 8:23	21
קבל	1	Ezra 8:30	13
רעד	1	Ezra 10:9	3
שקד	1	Ezra 8:29	12
שקל	4	Ezra 8:25, 26, 29, 33	22

Appendix C

Rare Hebrew Verbs (fewer than 50×) in the Nehemiah Memoir

Hebrew Verb	Times it occurs in the Nehemiah Memoir	Where it occurs in the Nehemiah Memoir	Times it occurs in the Hebrew Bible
אבל	1	Nehemiah 1:4	36
אצר	1	Nehemiah 13:13	5
בדא	1	Nehemiah 6:8	2
בדל	1	Nehemiah 13:3	42
בזה	1	Nehemiah 2:19	42
ברר	1	Nehemiah 5:18	18
גוף	1	Nehemiah 7:3	1 (hapax legomenon)
הוה	1	Nehemiah 6:6	5
זמן	2	Nehemiah 10:35; 13:31	11
חוס	1	Nehemiah 13:22	24
חמם	1	Nehemiah 7:3	24
חרף	1	Nehemiah 6:13	38

Hebrew Verb	Times it occurs in the Nehemiah Memoir	Where it occurs in the Nehemiah Memoir	Times it occurs in the Hebrew Bible
טלל	1	Nehemiah 3:15	1 (hapax legomenon)
יחשׂ	1	Nehemiah 7:5	20
יטב	1	Nehemiah 2:5	44
יעד	2	Nehemiah 6:2, 10	29
יצת	2	Nehemiah 1:3; 2:17	26
כבשׁ	2	Nehemiah 5:5	14
כנס	1	Nehemiah 12:44	11
לוה	1	Nehemiah 5:4	14
לעג	2	Nehemiah 2:19; 3:33	18
מחה	2	Nehemiah 3:34; 13:14	34
מעל	2	Nehemiah 1:8; 13:27	35
מרד	2	Nehemiah 2:19; 6:6	25
מרס	1	Nehemiah 13:25	14
נכר	2	Nehemiah 6:12; 13:24	49
נער	3	Nehemiah 5:13	11
נשׁא	1	Nehemiah 5:7	6
נשׁא	2	Nehemiah 5:10, 11	18
סתם	1	Nehemiah 4:1	13
עאד	2	Nehemiah 13:15, 21	40
עמס	2	Nehemiah 4:11; 13:15	9
עצר	1	Nehemiah 6:10	46
ערב	1	Nehemiah 5:3	17

Hebrew Verb	Times it occurs in the Nehemiah Memoir	Where it occurs in the Nehemiah Memoir	Times it occurs in the Hebrew Bible
פרד	1	Nehemiah 4:13	26
פרץ	4	Nehemiah 1:3; 2:13; 3:35; 4:1	45
פשׁט	1	Nehemiah 4:17	43
צום	1	Nehemiah 1:4	21
צלל	1	Nehemiah 3:19	2
צרף	2	Nehemiah 3:8, 32	33
קדם	1	Nehemiah 13:2	26
קרה	3	Nehemiah 2:8; 3:3, 6	5
קשׁר	2	Nehemiah 3:38; 4:2	44
רכל	3	Nehemiah 3:31, 32; 13:20	17
רפה	2	Nehemiah 6:3, 9	46
שׁבר	2	Nehemiah 2:13, 15	8
שׁכר	3	Nehemiah 6:12, 13; 13:2	20
שׁלט	1	Nehemiah 5:15	8
שׁנה	1	Nehemiah 13:21	9

Table Notes

1. This verb occurs only in Ezra, Nehemiah, and Chronicles.

Bibliography

Albright, William F. *The Archaeology of Palestine*. Baltimore: Penguin, 1960.

_____. "The Date and Personality of the Chronicler," *JBL* 40 3/4 (1921): 104-119

Allen, Leslie. "For He is Good...": Worship in Ezra–Nehemiah." Pages 15-34 in M.P. Graham, R.R. Marrs, and S.L. McKenzie (eds) *Worship and the Hebrew Bible: Essays in Honor of John T. Willis*. Sheffied: SAP, 1999.

Allen, Lindsay. *The Persian Empire*. Chicago: UCP, 2005.

Angel, Hayyim. "The Literary Significance of the Name List in Ezra–Nehemiah." *JBQ* 35/3 (2007): 143-152.

Archer, Gleason L. *A Survey of Old Testament Introduction*. Chicago: Moody, 1994.

Bailey, Nicholas A. "Nehemiah 31:1-32: An Intersection of the Text and the Topography." *JOTT* 5/1 (1992): 1-12.

Barber, Cyril J. Nehemiah and the Dynamics of Effective Leadership. Neptune, New Jersey: Loixeaus Brothers, 1976.

Barr, James. "Hebrew עד, Especially at Job I.18 and Neh. VII.3." *JSS* XXVII/2 (1982): 177-192.

Batten, Loring. *A Critical and Exegetical Commentary on the Books of Ezra and Nehemiah*. ICC. Edinburgh: T & T Clark, 1961.

Berghuis, Kent D. "A Biblical Perspective on Fasting." *BibSac* 158 (Jan-March 2001): 86-103.

Berquist, Jon L. *Judaism in Persian's Shadow.* Minneapolis: Fortress, 1995.

Blenkinsopp, Joseph. *Ezra–Nehemiah: A Commentary.* OTL. Philadelphia: Westminster, 1988.

Bliese, Loren F. "Chiastic Structures, Peaks and Cohesion in Nehemiah 9:6-37." *BT* 39 (1988): 208-215.

Boda, Mark J. "Chiasmus in Ubiquity: Symmetrical Mirages in Nehemiah 9." *JSOT* 71 (1996): 55-70.

_____. "Praying the Tradition: The Origin and Use of Tradition in Nehemiah 9." *TB* 48/1 (1997): 179-182.

_____. "The Use of Tôdôt in Nehemiah XII." *VT* 44/3 (1994): 387-393.

Boyce, Mary. *Zoroastrians.* London: Routledge & Kegan Paul, 1979.

Breneman, Mervin. *Ezra, Nehemiah, Esther.* NAC, 10. Nashville: Broadman and Holman, 1993.

Briant, Pierre. *From Cyrus to Alexander: A History of the Persian Empire.* Winona Lake, Ind.,: Eisenbrauns, 2002.

Brockington, L. H. *Ezra, Nehemiah and Esther.* Melbourne: Thomas Nelson and Sons, 1969.

Brown, A. Philip II. "Chronological Anomalies in the Book of Ezra." *BSac* 162/645 (2005): 33-49.

_____. "The Problem of Mixed Marriages in Ezra–Nehemiah 9-10." *BSac* 162/648 (2005): 437-458.

Brown, Raymond. *The Message of Nehemiah.* BST. Downers Grove: IVP, 1998.

Cataldo, Jeremiah. "Persian Policy and the Yehud Community During Nehemiah." *JSOT* 28/2 (2003): 131-143.

Clines, David J.A. *Ezra, Nehemiah, Esther.* NCB. Grand Rapids: Eerdmans, 1984.

_____. "Nehemiah 10 as An Example of Early Jewish Biblical Exegesis." *JSOT* 21 (1981): 111-117.

Collins, John J. *Introduction to the Hebrew Bible.* Minneapolis: Fortress, 2004.

Cook, John M. *The Persian Empire.* New York: Schocken, 1983.

Corduan, Winfried. *Neighboring Faiths.* Downers Grove: IVP, 1998.

Creed, Brad. "Oaths." *Holman Bible Dictionary.* Nashville: Holman, 1991. de Miroschedji, Pierre. "Susa." *ABD* 6:242-245.

Davis, John J. *Moses and the gods of Egypt."* Winona Lake, Indiana: BMH, 1986.

Dicks, Brian. *The Ancient Persians: How They Lived and Worked.* North Pomfret, Vt.,: David & Charles, 1979.

Eissfeldt,Otto. *The Old Testament: An Introduction.* New York: Harper and Row, 1965.

Ellison, H.L. "The Importance of Ezra." *EvQ* 53:1 (1981): 48-53.

Eskenazi, Tamara C. *In an Age of Pioze: A Literary Approach to Ezra–Nehemiah.* SBLMS 36. Atlanta: Scholars, 1988.

_____. "Out from the Shadows: Biblical Women in the Postexilic Era." *JSOT* 54 (1992): 25-43.

Fensham, F. Charles "Neh 9 and Pss 105, 106, and 136: Post-Exilic Historical Traditions in Poetic Form." *JNSL* 9 (1981): 35-51.

_____. *The Books of Ezra and Nehemiah.* NICOT. Grand Rapids: Eerdmans, 1982.

Foster, Richard. *The Celebration of Discipline.* New York: Harper & Row, 1978.

Frolov, Serge. "The Prophecy of Jeremiah in Esr 1,1." *ZAW* 116 (4/2004): 595-601.

Frye, Richard N. *The Heritage of Persia.* Cleveland/New York: World, 1963.

Goldingay, John. *Old Testament Theology: Israel's Gospel.* Vol 1. Downers Grove, IVP, 2003.

Harrison, Roland K. *Introduction to the Old Testament.* Peabody, Massachusetts: Prince, 1999.

Hayes, Christine. "Intermarriage and Impurity in Ancient Jewish Sources." *HTR* 92/1 (1999): 3-36.

Hoffmeier, James K. *The Archaeology of the Bible.* Oxford: Lion, 2008.

Holmgren, Frederick C. "Faithful Abraham and the 'amānâ Covenant: Nehemiah 9,6-10,1." *ZAW* 104/2 (1992): 249-254.

Janzen, David. "The 'Mission' of Ezra and the Persian-Period Temple Community." *JBL* 119/4 (2000): 619-643.

Japhet, Sara. "The Supposed Common Authorship of Chronicles and Ezra–Nehemiah Investigated Anew." *VT* 18/3 (1968): 330-371.

Jastrow, Morris. "The Tearing of Garments as a Symbol of Mourning with Especial Reference to the Customs of the Ancient Hebrews." *JAOS* 21 (1900): 23-39.

Johnson, Marshall D. *The Purpose of Biblical Genealogies With Special Reference to the Setting of the Genealogies of Jesus.* Cambridge: CHP, 1969.

Kapelrud, Arvid S. *The Question of Authorship in the Ezra–Narrative: A Lexical Investigation.* Oslo: Jacob Dybwad, 1944.

Kenyon, Kathleen. *Jerusalem: Excavating 3000 Years of History.* New York: McGraw-Hill, 1967.

Kidner, Derek. *Ezra and Nehemiah: An Introduction and Commentary.* TOTC. Downers Grove, Ill.,: Inter-Varsity Press, 1979.

Klawans, Jonathan. "Idolatry, Incest, and Impurity: Moral Defilement in Ancient Judaism." *JSJ* 29/4 (1998): 391-415.

Knowles, Melody D. "Pilgrimage Imagery in the Returns in Ezra." *JBL* 123/1 (2004): 57-74.

Kraemer, David C. "On the Relationship of the Books of Ezra and Nehemiah." *JSOT* 59 (1993): 73-92.

Krasovec, Joze. "Merism: Polar Expression in Biblical Hebrew." *Biblica* 64/2 (1983): 231-239.

Kraemer, David. "On the Relationship of the Books of Ezra and Nehemiah." *JSOT* 59 (1993): 73-92.

Liebreich, L.J. "The Impact of Nehemiah 9:5-37 on the Liturgy of the Synagogue." *HUCA* 32 (1961): 227-237.

Lipschits, Obed. "Literary and Ideological Aspects of Nehemiah 11." *JBL* 121/3 (2002): 423-440.

Marcus, David, ed. *Biblia Hebraica Quinta: Ezra and Nehemiah.* Stuttgart: Deutsche Bibelgesellschaft, 2006.

Mathews, Kenneth A. *Genesis 1-11.* NAC. Nashville: Broadman and Holman, 1996.

Matzal, Stefan C. "The Structure of Ezra IV-VI." *VT* 50/4 (2000): 566-568.

Maxwell, John. *The Power of Attitude.* Colorado Springs: Cook, 2001.

McCarter, P.K. *Textual Criticism: Recovering the Text of the Hebrew Bible.* Philadelphia: Fortress, 1986.

McCarthy, Dennis J. "Covenant and Law in Chronicles-Nehemiah." *CBQ* 44 (1982): 25-44.

McConville, J. Gordon. *Ezra, Nehemiah and Esther.* DST. Edinburgh: SAP, 1985.

McEvenue, Sean E. "The Political Structure in Judah from Cyrus to Nehemiah." *CBQ* 43 (1981): 353-364.

Merrill, David. "Whatever Happened to Kneeling." *Christianity Today* 36 (1992): 24-25.

Min, Kyun-Jin. *The Levitical Authority of Ezra and Nehemiah.* JSOTSup 409. London: T & T Clark, 2004.

Modi, J. J. "Wine Among the Ancient Perians." Pages 231-246 in *Asiatic Papers.* Bombay: Royal Asiatic Society, 1905-29: 3.

Myers, Jacob M. *Ezra–Nehemiah*. AB. Garden City, New York: Doubleday, 1965.

Noth, Martin. *The History of Israel*. London: SCM 1983.

Olyan, Saul M. "Purity Ideology in Ezra–Nehemiah as a Tool to Reconstitute the Community." *JSJ* 35/1 (2004): 1-16.

Parker, R.A. and W.H. Dubberstein. *Babylonian Chronology 626 BC – A.D. 75*. Providence, Rhode Island: BUP, 1956.

Piper, John. *A Hunger for God*. Wheaton, IL: Good News, 1997.

Rosenberg, A.J. *Daniel, Ezra, Nehemiah*. New York: Judaica, 2000.

Ross, Allen P. *Creation and Blessing*. Grand Rapids: Baker, 1998.

_____. *Holiness to the Lord: A Guide to the Exposition of the Book of Leviticus*. Grand Rapids: Baker, 2002.

Rudolph, Wilhelm. *Esra und Nehemia*. HAT 20. Tübingen: J.C.B. Mohr, 1949.

Rundgren, F. "Über einen juristichen Terminus bei Esra 6:6," *ZAW* 70 (1958): 209-215.

Schaper, Joachim. "The Temple Treasury Committee in the Times of Nehemiah and Ezra." *VT* 47/2 (1997): 200-206.

Schwantes, Siegfried J. *A Short History of the Ancient Near East*. Grand Rapids: Baker, 1965.

Segal, Michael. "Numerical discrepancies in the list of vessels in Ezra I 9-11." *VT* 52 (2002/1): 122-129.

Segal, M. Z. "The Books of Ezra and Nehemiah" *Taibig* 14 (1943): 81-86

Shanks, Hershel, ed. *The City of David: Revisiting Early Excavations*. Washington D.C.,: BAS, 2004.

Shepherd, David. "Prophetaphobia: Fear and False Prophecy in Nehemiah VI." *VT* 55/2 (2005): 232-250.

Steiner, Richard C. "Why Bishlam (Ezra 4:7) Cannot Rest 'In Peace': On the Aramaic and Hebrew Sound Changes that Conspired to Blot Out the Remembrance of Bel-Shalam the Archivist." *JBL* 126/2 (2007): 392-401.

Thiontveit, Maik A. "Linguistic Analysis and the Question of Authorship in Chronicles, Ezra and Nehemiah." *VI* 32/2 (1982): 201-216

Tollefson, Kenneth D. and H.G.M. Williamson. "Nehemiah as Cultural Revitalization: An Anthropological Perspective." *JSOT* 56 (1992): 41-68.

Torrey, Charles C. *Ezra Studies*. Chicago: UCP, 1910.

Torrey, R.A. *How to Pray*. New York: Revell, 1900.

Van Wyk, W.C., and A.P.B. Breytenbach. "The Nature of Conflict in Ezra–Nehemiah." *Hervormde Teologiese Studies* 57/3-4 (2001): 1254-1263.

Vaux, Roland de. *The Bible and the Ancient Near East*. Garden City, N.Y.: Doubleday, 1971.

Weinberg, Joel. *The Citizen-Temple Community*. Translated by D.L. Smith-Christopher. JSOTSup., 151. Sheffield: SAP, 1992.

Wiersbe, Warren W. *The Bible Exposition Commentary: History*. Colorado Springs: Victor, 2003.

Williams, Gary R. "Contextual Influences in Readings of Nehemiah 5: A Case Study." *TB* 53.1 (2002): 57-74.

Williamson, H.G.M. *Ezra, Nehemiah*. WBC 16. Waco, Texas: Word, 1985.

_____. "The Governors of Judah under the Persians." *TB* 39 (1988): 59-82.

_____. *Israel in the Books of Chronicles*. Cambridge: CUP, 1977.

Willis, John T., Matt Patrick Graham, Rick R. Marrs, and Steven L. McKenzie. *Worship and the Hebrew Bible: Essays in Honour of John T. Willis*. JSOT 284. Sheffield: SAP, 1999.

Wilson, Robert R. *Genealogy and History in the Biblical World*. New Haven: TUP, 1977.

Wong, G.C.I. "A Note on 'Joy' in Nehemiah VIII 10." *VT* 45/3 (1995): 383-386.

Wright, Jacob L. "A New Model for the Composition of Ezra–Nehemiah." Pages 333-348 in *Judah and the Judeans in the Fourth Century B.C.E.* Edited by Oded Lipschits, Gary N. Knoppens, and Rainer Alberts. Winona Lake, Indiana: Eisenbiauns, 2007.

Yamauchi, Edwin. "Archaeological Backgrounds of the Exilic and Postexilic Era, part 3: The Archaeology Background of Ezra." *BSac* 137/547 (1980): 195-211.

_____. "Archaeological Backgrounds of the Exilic and Postexilic Era, part 4: The Archaeological Background of Nehemiah." *BSac* 137/548 (1980): 291-309.

_____. "Ezra–Nehemiah." Pages 284-295 in *Dictionary of the Old Testament Historical Books* Downers Grove, Il.: IVP, 2005.

_____. *Ezra–Nehemiah*. EBC 4. Edited by Frank E. Gaebelein. Grand Rapids: Zondervan, 1992.

_____. *Persia and the Bible*. Grand Rapids: Baker, 1990.

Zadok, R. "A Note on SN'H." *VT* 38/4 (1988): 483-486.

Scripture Index

Subject Index

Kk

OTHER BOOKS OF INTEREST
IN THE
MENTOR IMPRINT

Volume 1
ISBN 978-1-84550-364-2

Volume 2
ISBN 978-1-84550-379-6

Matthew

A Mentor Commentary
Volumes 1 & 2

Knox Chamblin

Matthew's Gospel is the first document in the New Testament – a suitable location considering some scholars' opinions (for example, Theodor Zahn and Ernest Renan) that it is the pre-eminent piece of literature in antiquity.What sort of book is it? Who is its author, and why did he write it? What historical, literary and theological contexts influence it? Matthew's Gospel also tells a story of Jesus, the son of David the son of Abraham – accordingly it gives attention to characters, plot lines, conflicts and resolution – but the extra dimension is that it also has an effect upon its reader to direct them to the Saviour of the world.

'This thoughtful and thorough commentary on the First Gospel comes from a scholar who has obviously spent many years at the feet of Matthew the teacher, and even more importantly, at the feet of the One to whom Matthew bears witness.'

JONATHAN T. PENNINGTON
Assistant Professor of New Testament Interpretation,
The Southern Baptist Theological Seminary, Louisville, Kentucky

'What, you might say, am I to do with 2 volumes and 1,400 pages on Matthew? Well, what should you do if given two million pounds? Spend it, of course – but not all at once. So with Chamblin's Matthew. Preach an Advent series – and use Chamblin on chapters 1–2; then preach from the Old Testament and come back to the Sermon on the Mount – and use Chamblin on chapters 5–7; then map out a series on Matthew's passion narrative – and use Chamblin on chapters 26–28. I'm not a hypocrite – I'm using him on Matthew 13 even as I write this!'

DALE RALPH DAVIS
Well respected author and Bible expositor

Knox Chamblin is Professor Emeritus of New Testament at Reformed Theological Seminary, Jackson, Mississippi.

Galatians

A MENTOR COMMENTARY

David McWilliams

Galatians

A Mentor Commentary

DAVID MCWILLIAMS

'Yet another Galatians commentary? Here is one that makes a most welcome contribution in addressing a wide range of readers – pastors and teachers in the church, as well as many others interested in growing in their understanding of Paul's overall teaching and particularly of this important letter. Having had the opportunity of reading this clear and gracefully written book during its production, I commend it most highly.'

RICHARD GAFFIN,
Professor of Biblical and Systematic Theology, Emeritus,
Westminster Theological Seminary, Philadelphia, Pennsylvania

'...addresses interpretive issues with clarity and cogent discernment, and he engages recent misperceptions of Paul's central concern – which is not merely sociological or ecclesiastical, but soteriological (How may guilty sinners be reconciled to their holy Creator?) – all the while keeping in view the aim of preaching this good news of sovereign grace. I highly recommend this resource to my fellow-preachers of the good news of God's Son.'

DENNIS E. JOHNSON,
Professor of Practical Theology,
Westminster Seminary in California, Escondido, California

'Timely, lucid, and reliable, this is an excellent commentary for preachers, Bible study leaders and others. David McWilliams admirably succeeds in his aim for brevitas and claritas, the two qualities in commentators that Calvin most commended. He distils a great deal of scholarship into uncluttered and readable prose. Paul's message in Galatians has rarely been so urgently needed as today, when justification only by faith is under attack from many sides. McWilliams explains it with judicious care.'

ROBERT LETHAM,
Senior Tutor, Systematic & Historicial Theology,
Wales Evangelical School of Theology, Bridgend, Wales

David McWilliams is the senior pastor of Covenant Presbyterian Church, Lakeland, Florida.

Christian Focus Publications
publishes books for all ages

Our mission statement –
STAYING FAITHFUL
In dependence upon God we seek to impact the world through literature faithful to His infallible Word, the Bible. Our aim is to ensure that the Lord Jesus Christ is presented as the only hope to obtain forgiveness of sin, live a useful life and look forward to heaven with Him.

REACHING OUT
Christ's last command requires us to reach out to our world with His gospel. We seek to help fulfill that by publishing books that point people towards Jesus and help them develop a Christ-like maturity. We aim to equip all levels of readers for life, work, ministry and mission.

Books in our adult range are published in three imprints.

Christian Focus contains popular works including biographies, commentaries, basic doctrine and Christian living. Our children's books are also published in this imprint.

Mentor focuses on books written at a level suitable for Bible College and seminary students, pastors, and other serious readers. The imprint includes commentaries, doctrinal studies, examination of current issues and church history.

Christian Heritage contains classic writings from the past.

Christian Focus Publications, Ltd
Geanies House, Fearn, Ross-shire,
IV20 1TW, Scotland, United Kingdom
info@christianfocus.com
www.christianfocus.com